[5—0]
Young pot plants in greenhouse

[5—0a]
Display of greenhouse plants

[5–1]
Gloxinia

NEW ILLUSTRATED ENCYCLOPEDIA OF GARDENING

UNABRIDGED

EDITED BY T. H. Everett

Assistant Director (Horticulture) and Curator of Education
The New York Botanical Garden

WITH CONTRIBUTIONS FROM

TWENTY HORTICULTURISTS AND AUTHORITIES IN THE UNITED STATES AND CANADA

Growers, Breeders, Exhibitors, Plantsmen, Writers, Lecturers, Professors, Editors and Superintendents of Famous Estates, who are Experts in all Fields of Horticulture, including Pests and Their Control.

VOLUME FIVE—Fuc-Imp

GREYSTONE PRESS • NEW YORK

Copyright © MCMLX By The GREYSTONE PRESS
100 Sixth Avenue
New York 13, New York
Library of Congress Catalog Card Number 60-7000
MANUFACTURED IN THE UNITED STATES OF AMERICA

Fuchsias are tender evergreen shrubs. Many kinds are used on the Pacific Coast as specimen shrubs, hedges or climbers. They thrive best, for the most part, in partial shade.

The soil used for repotting established plants of Fuchsias should be fertile, well-drained and loamy. It should be packed moderately firmly about the roots.

If the Fuchsias are to be grown in pots during the summer, they should be repotted in 6-in. pots; if they are to be planted out of doors for the summer, or are to be set in window boxes,

Hybrid Fuchsias bear graceful flowers that may be had in various color combinations. Two distinct varieties are shown here.

5-in. flowerpots will be large enough. Those to be used for filling flower beds should be planted late in May or early in June.

The Fuchsia is an excellent plant for a hanging basket in the greenhouse or porch; instead of being repotted in 5-in. pots, the plants should be set in the basket, this being lined with moss. Two or three plants should be set near the edge of the basket and another in the middle.

Standard and Pyramid Fuchsias are very handsome plants; they should be grown in large pots or tubs, placed out of doors during summer and kept under glass safe from frost in the winter. The best time to make a start is by taking cuttings in August in the way already explained. In spring and early summer the plants must be repotted as becomes necessary to prevent their growth being checked. The standard plant is allowed to develop unchecked until the desired height of stem is reached; the top is then cut off and side shoots will grow and form the head of branches.

A pyramid-shaped plant is obtained by pinching the shoots from time to time as may be necessary to ensure the required number of branches; care must be taken always to train one shoot upright to form the main stem. In the course of a few years, if repotted annually in spring, the Fuchsias will develop into large handsome specimens.

A standard Fuchsia.

Varieties. Numerous garden varieties of Fuchsias exist in a wide variety of forms and colors and new ones are developed yearly. The best kinds will be found listed and described in the catalogues of specialists.

FUCHSIA, AUSTRALIAN. See Correa.

FUCHSIA, CALIFORNIA. Zauschneria californica, which see.

FUCHSIA, CAPE. See Phygelius.

FULGENS. A Latin term meaning shining and often used in reference to scarlet flowers. For example, Fuchsia fulgens.

FULLER'S TEASEL. The common Teasel, referred to under Dipsacus fullonum.

FUMARIA—*Fumitory* (Fuma'ria). Mostly annual flowering plants of little horticultural value, natives of Europe, and belonging to the Poppy family, Papaveraceae. The stems, which climb by means of their twisted leafstalks, grow about 3 ft. in length, have fernlike leaves and small tubular, red, pink or white flowers. The name Fumaria is derived from *fumus,* smoke, alluding to the gray foliage and shoots.

FUMITORY. Fumaria, which see.

FUMITORY, CLIMBING. See Adlumia.

FUNGI. The fungi comprise one of the lowest groups of plants. They never contain chlorophyll, the green coloring matter of higher plants, and therefore cannot make their own food, always having to rely on other organisms. Some fungi obtain food from living plants or animals and are called parasitic. Others—e.g., Mushrooms, Toadstools and Molds—get it from decaying matter, and are saprophytic.

The vegetative part of a fungus consists only of finely branched threads, which never form roots and leaves as are found in higher plants. These threads penetrate among the tissue of the host and absorb nourishment from it. Fungi reproduce themselves by means of spores, produced in vast numbers, and, in the case of those which attack cultivated plants, remedial measures must be directed to the prevention of these spores from germinating and gaining entrance into the plant tissue.

Some fungi need two hosts to complete their life history, e.g., the Wheat Rust; the spores formed by the fungus when it is living on the first host, wheat, cannot germinate on the same species, but need a different one, in this case the Barberry; the spores produced when the fungus is growing on the latter will only grow on Wheat.

Although many fungi are harmful, many others are directly or indirectly of much value to man. From the Penicillium fungi is derived the modern drug named after them, and these fungi also play an essential part in the manufacture of certain cheeses. Those that live on dead matter by decomposing it, enable the materials there to be used by other plants. The yeasts, which stand apart from other fungi, are necessary for the manufacture of many alcoholic drinks, and Mushrooms, Truffles, etc., are edible.

FUNGICIDE. See Pests and Diseases.

FUNGOUS DISEASES. See Pests and Diseases.

FUNKIA. Hosta, which see.

FUNTUMIA (Funtum'ia). A small group of tropical African trees, one of which, F. elastica, is a minor source of rubber. The name is derived from Funtum, a vernacular name for F. elastica. Funtumia belongs in the Dogbane family, Apocynaceae. These trees may be grown outdoors in humid, warm climates.

FURCRAEA (Furcrae'a). Handsome foliage plants, natives of tropical America and Mexico, and only suitable for cultivation in mild climates and in large greenhouses. They resemble Agaves, and have long evergreen leaves, 3-5 in. wide, which rise from very short and slow-growing stems. The inflorescences are made up of numerous flowers, which are usually greenish or yellowish-white, and they appear from the centers of mature plants, rising in many instances to a height of several feet. Furcraea belongs to the Amaryllis family, Amaryllidaceae, and the name was given in honor of A. F. Fourcroy, a French chemist of the late eighteenth and early nineteenth centuries.

Culture. In severe climates these plants can only be grown successfully in a large and sunny greenhouse where a winter minimum temperature of 50 degrees is maintained. Loamy soil in which sandstone has been incorporated forms a suitable compost. Drainage must be good, for although plenty of water is required during the growing period, the soil must not remain stagnant about the roots. When plants are growing in large flowerpots and the pots are filled with roots, manure water or a fertilizer should be given occasionally. In winter the water supply must be reduced but the soil should not be allowed to become thoroughly dry. Propagation is by suckers detached from the old plants in spring and potted separately.

In mild climates Furcraeas may be grown outdoors in well-drained soil in full sun or light shade.

The Chief Kinds. F. cubensis, which forms a large rosette of long fleshy leaves with spiny margins, is a native of tropical America; there is a variety inermis which differs from the type by having no marginal spines, and another variety, Lindenii, which has variegated leaves. F. gigantea (foetida) is a plant with a large cluster of long, semierect leaves, which usually have spineless margins; the inflorescence is sometimes over 20 ft. high. It is a native of tropical America and is of commercial value for its fiber.

FURZE. See Ulex.

GAGEA—*Yellow Star-of-Bethlehem* (Ga'gea). Hardy bulb plants with yellow, star-shaped flowers. They grow wild in Europe, and belong to the Lily family, Liliaceae. The bulbs, which are about the size of Peas, give rise to one or two narrow-pointed leaves about 6 in. in length, and the flowers are produced in a spreading cluster at the end of a short stalk. Gagea is named after Sir Thomas Gage, a noted British botanist.

Gagea sylvatica (lutea), the common kind, up to 6 in. tall, is not often cultivated. A moist semishaded position in the rockery or in turf suits it: the best soil consists of equal parts of loam and leaf mold. The bulbs are planted 2 in. deep in October and are not disturbed until signs of deterioration are evident, when they are lifted and replanted. Propagation is by offsets in autumn. The plant blooms in April.

GAILLARDIA — *Blanketflower* (Gaillar'dia). Hardy annual and perennial North American plants, 18 in. to 3 ft. high, which bear large, brilliantly colored flowers during the summer, and are invaluable for garden decoration and for cutting. They belong to the Daisy family, Compositae. Gaillardia commemorates M. Gaillard de Marentoneau, a French patron of botany.

The perennial Gaillardias are indispensable for planting in the perennial border where, in July and August, the golden-yellow and crimson, long-stemmed blooms make an attractive display, and they are valuable for cutting. They should be planted in spring. Unfortunately, on clayey soil, they are liable to perish after having flowered, and it is wise to raise a fresh stock of plants to replace those that have perished during the winter. Rooted offsets of named varieties should be potted in autumn and wintered in a cold frame for planting in April. Gaillardias thrive in ordinary soil, but prefer that which is well drained; there they will pass through the winter safely and bloom a second year. They must have a sunny place. Even in well-drained ground, however, the Gaillardia cannot be considered to be a long-lived plant, and should be raised from seed in alternate years.

When to Sow Seeds. Seeds sown in a cold frame in May will provide flowering plants the following year. When large enough the seedlings

Perennial Gaillardia, Yellow Queen.

Annual Gaillardias are useful for garden decoration.

should be planted in a nursery border. If the ground is heavy and very wet in winter, the plants should be potted separately in 3-in. pots and kept in a cold frame from October to April, when they may be planted out of doors.

If seeds are sown in a greenhouse early in February and the seedlings are grown in flowerpots in a compost of loam, two thirds, and leaf mold and sand, one third, they will bloom in August. They should be planted out of doors in April–May.

Showy Perennial Kinds. The original wild type or species, G. aristata, has been superseded by large-flowered varieties of brilliant coloring commonly classed as Gaillardia grandiflora, though some of them have been given separate names, such as Firebrand, crimson, tipped yellow; Ipswich Beauty, crimson and gold; Wirral Flame, flame-red, tipped gold; and Yellow Queen, bright yellow.

Annual Gaillardias. Gaillardia amblyodon, which has red flowers, G. lanceolata, with red and yellow flowers, and G. pulchella, red and yellow, are annuals which should be raised from seeds sown in a warm greenhouse in March, the seedlings being planted out of doors in May, or by sowing directly outdoors in early spring.

The annual Gaillardias are also excellent for flowering in a cool greenhouse in late winter and spring. For this purpose seeds should be sown in September or October in pots or pans of porous soil. When large enough to handle easily, the seedlings are potted individually in 2½-in. pots and are later transferred to larger containers as their growth makes such moves desirable. Pots of 5- or 6-in. diameter are large enough for the final potting. Throughout their growth, exposure to full sun in a greenhouse where the night temperature is 45-50 degrees and the day temperature is 5 or 10 degrees higher, is needed.

GALANTHUS—*Snowdrop, Fair-Maid-of-February* (Galanth'us). Early spring-flowering bulbs which belong to the Amaryllis family, Amaryllidaceae, and are natives of Asia Minor, the Caucasus, and other parts of Europe. Snowdrops are ideal plants for the rock garden, naturalizing in grass, edging beds of spring-flowering plants, for forming clumps in the front of the herbaceous border, or for cultivating in pots in a cold greenhouse or frame. They grow from 6-12 in. in height, have narrow, strap-shaped leaves and white pendulous flowers produced singly on slender stems, January–March. The name Galanthus is derived from *gala,* milk, and *anthos,* a flower, and refers to the flowers.

When to Plant. For naturalizing in the lawn the bulbs are planted in September, 4 in. deep, in clusters of a dozen or more. Once planted they are not disturbed, as, when favorably located, they increase year by year. When growing in the lawn the grass is not mown until the foliage has withered. In the rock garden they are planted in deep light soil in September. They are set 2 in. apart in irregular clusters and the surface is carpeted with dwarf-growing plants. They should not be disturbed until they show signs of deterioration. When this occurs, it is best to lift the clumps when flowering is finished, separate them into small clusters, and replant at once.

Irregular clumps may also be planted in the herbaceous border or in front of shrubberies, and are given the same treatment.

Cultivation in Pots. The bulbs are potted in deep pans or flowerpots in September. They are set 1 in. deep and 1 in. apart in a compost of equal parts of loam and compost or peat moss to which sand has been freely added. They are kept in a frostproof cold frame until the flower

Snowdrop, Galanthus, the earliest spring bulb, often flowers in January or February in the Philadelphia area. For maximum effect the bulbs should be planted in quantity, 4 in. deep, 4 to 6 in. apart, and located where they may be seen from the house.

buds commence to show when they are taken into the greenhouse or house, and the soil is kept moderately moist. After flowering, the plants are gradually dried off and the bulbs are planted out in the garden.

The Common Snowdrop is Galanthus nivalis, 6 in., white, which blooms from January till early March. There are a number of varieties, including Olgae (octobrensis), autumn-flowering, and a double form (flore-plena).

G. Elwesii (The Giant Snowdrop), 9 in., white, is one of the best Snowdrops. G. byzantinus, white and green, very early; and G. plicatus, 12 in., white, are also noteworthy.

GALAX APHYLLA (Ga'lax). A hardy woodland plant, a native of eastern North America.

The ornamental evergreen leaves are heart-shaped, glossy, of thin, tough texture, carried singly on wiry 4-6 in. stems, and often turn red in winter. The white flowers carried in a graceful slender spike well above the foliage in June are very ornamental. Galax belongs to the family Diapensiaceae. The word is from *gala*, milk, and refers to the white flowers.

Galax thrives best in a cool half-shady position, requires leaf mold or soil of a peaty nature, and resents dryness at the root. This very beautiful plant is well worth the little extra trouble it may demand in the way of a cool position and woodland soil. It is propagated by careful division of the roots in September, the plant sending out underground runners, and by seeds sown in a cold frame in early fall. The leaves are valued for winter decorations.

GALEANDRA (Galean'dra). Orchids found wild in tropical America. Most have stemlike pseudobulbs and spikes of large flowers with narrow sepals and petals and a tubular lip with short funnel-like spur. Galeandra is derived from *galea*, a helmet, and *andros*, stamen, and refers to the crested stamen. It belongs to the family Orchidaceae.

Hothouse Orchids. All these Orchids require a warm greenhouse, particularly during the growing season—spring to autumn. As a rule they flower in late summer and autumn, when growth is usually complete. Water must be given less frequently in autumn, and the shading removed so that the bulbs may be thoroughly matured and hardened before winter. The plants should be wintered in a temperature of not less than 60 degrees F. and be watered only occasionally until about March. When signs of growth are apparent, the plants should be repotted in osmunda fiber, cut into small pieces or in Fir bark or in other kind of bark satisfactory for Orchids, and given increased heat. As growth advances water must be given more often.

The Chief Kinds. One of the best-known of these Orchids is G. Devoniana, from Bahia; its stems often reach a height of 4 ft. and the flowers, 4 in. across, are brownish-purple, the lip white flushed and marked with purple. In G. nivalis, also from Brazil, the sepals and petals are green and the lip white with purple blotch.

In G. lacustris (d'Escagnolleana), the sepals and petals are yellowish and the lip is yellowish, marked with purple.

GALEGA—*Goats'-Rue* (Gale'ga). Hardy, vigorous herbaceous plants with pinnate leaves and, in summer, racemes of small, pea-shaped flowers which are white or lilac-lavender. They are natives chiefly of southern and eastern Europe, and belong to the Pea family, Leguminosae.

Galega is from *gala*, milk, and alludes to the old belief that this plant increased the milk supply of animals which browsed upon it.

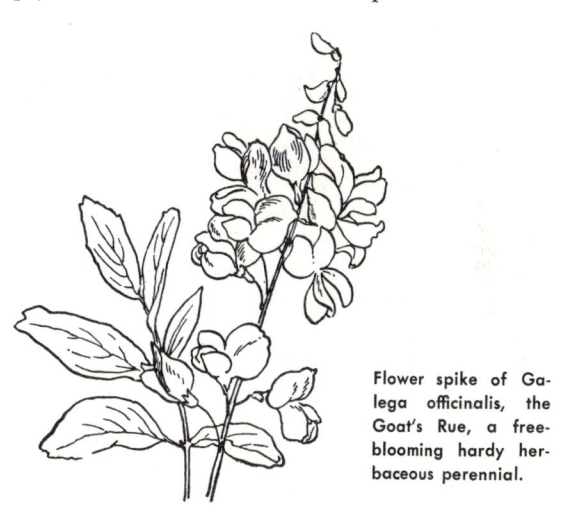

Flower spike of Galega officinalis, the Goat's Rue, a free-blooming hardy herbaceous perennial.

For a Large Flower Border. The Galegas thrive in ordinary well-tilled garden soil if planted in a sunny position. They make vigorous growth and form large, loose bushes 3 ft. or more high, taking up a good deal of room. For this reason they are better suited to a large than a small herbaceous border. Planting may be done in autumn or in spring. When the flowers have faded —the plants bloom in July and early August —the shoots may be cut back partially if they crowd neighboring plants.

If an increased stock is wanted the old plants may be lifted and separated into pieces in spring, though it is better to leave them undisturbed and raise a fresh stock by sowing seeds in sandy soil in a cold frame in April or May. The seedlings are planted in a nursery border in June or July.

The chief kind is G. officinalis, with flowers in shades of lavender blue. There are numerous varieties and color variations, including alba, white; Hartlandii, lilac-blue and white; bicolor, blue and white; carnea, pinkish; and Lady Wilson, rosy-lavender.

GALIUM—*Bedstraw* (Ga'lium). Hardy and tender herbaceous perennials of weak, sprawling growth habit that are of minor importance horticulturally. They belong to the Madder family, Rubiaceae, and are widely distributed geographically. The name is derived from *gala,* milk, and refers to the fact that G. verum has been used to curdle milk.

Bedstraws are of easy culture. They thrive in any ordinary soil in sun or part shade and are increased by seed and by division. G. aristatum, which in gardens is often misnamed G. Mollugo, is one of the plants called Baby's-Breath; it grows 3 ft. tall and has white flowers. G. Mollugo proper is similar and is also called Baby's-Breath. G. verum, Yellow Bedstraw or Lady's Bedstraw, has yellow flowers. All the above are natives of Europe, naturalized in North America. There are also some native kinds.

GALL. A gall is an abnormal growth formed on various portions of plants by insects, fungi, or other organisms. See Pests and Diseases.

GALTONIA CANDICANS—*Cape Hyacinth* (Galto'nia). A bulb from South Africa that is hardy about as far north as Philadelphia; it forms a tuft of large leaves and in August bears a spike, about 3 ft. high, of bell-shaped, white, drooping flowers. It belongs to the Lily family, Liliaceae. Galtonia was named after the scientist, Francis Galton.

This bulb may be left out of doors during the winter except in cold localities or in ill-drained soil; if such conditions prevail the bulbs should be lifted as soon as the leaves have changed color in autumn, and stored safe from frost for the winter. They may be kept in paper bags or in boxes.

The best time to plant is in early spring. The bulbs flourish in sunny positions, in deeply dug, well-drained ordinary soil, enriched with decayed manure, and should be set at such a depth as to be covered with 6 in. of soil. As growth is vigorous, the bulbs should be planted about 15 in. apart. If they are left out of doors for the winter, it is a good plan to cover the soil above them with ashes, salt-marsh hay, or leaves. When the plants show signs of weakening, denoted by less vigorous leaves and smaller flower spikes, the bulbs should be lifted in autumn, stored for the winter and replanted in spring. If an increased stock is needed, the offsets or small bulbs should be saved and planted. Another name for this plant is Hyacinthus candicans.

GAMETE. A botanical term for a sexually reproductive cell.

GAMOLEPIS (Gamo'lepis). Shrubs and herbs from South Africa, belonging to the Daisy family, Compositae. Only one kind is cultivated, Gamolepis Tagetes, an annual, 3 to 10 in. tall, with bright yellow flowers produced very freely. Seeds may be sown under glass in early spring to provide seedlings for planting out later, or the seeds may be sown directly outdoors as soon as the soil can be worked. It makes a colorful edging for summer flower beds. The name Gamolepis is from *gamos,* union, and *lepis,* a scale, and refers to the joined floral bracts.

GARCINIA — *Mangosteen* (Garcin'ia). The chief kind is Garcinia Mangostana, which produces one of the most luscious and highly esteemed tropical fruits, the Mangosteen. The tree is a native of Malaya and is sometimes grown in other tropical countries, though not with such success as many other tropical fruits. Mangosteens are about the size of medium-sized oranges and are exported from Malaya to various not far distant countries. The Mangosteen belongs to the Garcinia family, Guttifeae. The name Garcinia honors Laurent Garcin, a French botanist.

GARDENIA—*Cape Jasmine* (Garde'nia). Tender evergreen flowering shrubs from China, Japan, tropical and South Africa, which belong to the family Rubiaceae. They form bushes or small trees, have ovate, deep green leaves and large, white, single or double, waxy, sweet-scented flowers. Gardenia is named after Dr. Alexander Garden.

Fragrant Hothouse Flowers. The florists' Gardenia, Gardenia jasminoides (Veitchii), requires a minimum winter temperature of 60 degrees, and the best potting compost consists of equal parts of peat, loam, and well-decayed manure with sand added freely, and a small quantity of crushed charcoal. Repotting of old plants is done in February. The long shoots are slightly shortened, the plants being syringed freely to induce new shoots to form, when a little of the old soil is removed and the plants are set in larger pots. When established they are exposed to full sunlight and at all times the atmosphere is kept moist by damping the floor and benches, and the foliage is frequently syringed with plain water.

If the flower buds are removed during the summer, the plants will bloom in autumn and winter. Water is applied freely to the soil in summer and liquid fertilizer is given once a week to established plants. Less water is required in winter but neither the soil nor the atmosphere must be allowed to remain in a dry state for long.

When to Take Cuttings. Two-year-old plants produce more flowers in proportion than older ones, and new plants are therefore raised each year. Cuttings of young shoots 3 in. in length are inserted in sandy peat in March. The cuttings are placed in a propagating case with bottom heat (which see) and must be kept moist until roots are formed. The rooted cuttings are potted separately in 3-in. pots, using a compost of equal parts of loam, peat and leaf mold, freely sprinkled with coarse sand. The plants are returned to the propagating case until established when they are repotted in 5-in. pots and shaded and frequently syringed until the roots have entered the new soil. Later they are transferred to 7-in. pots in which they will flower the following year. Bushy plants are assured by pinching out the tips of the shoots during the summer. Gardenias are also easily propagated by air layering.

As House Plants. Although frequently tried as house plants, Gardenias are seldom really successful when grown under such conditions; this is especially true of the florists' type of Gardenia, the form of G. jasminoides called Gardenia Veitchii, which is mainly winter flowering and is often sold as a pot plant in bloom at Easter. The chief difficulty is lack of sufficient atmospheric humidity, but other factors, including variable temperatures, drafts, insufficient sun and difficulty in keeping the soil at the required acidity, all may play a part.

Air-layering a Gardenia. *(Left)* The branch to be rooted is first girdled by removing a ½-in. ring of bark (here, about one-third down from top); then moist sphagnum is placed around the cut area and polyethylene plastic film is wrapped over the sphagnum and tied at both ends. *(Center)* Roots form at the upper part of the girdled area within two to three weeks; the plastic is then removed. *(Right)* The stem is cut below the new root zone, and the new plant is potted in soil in the standard way.

Gardenia jasminoides Fortuniana is usually more successful; it blooms in summer and, if it is cultivated in large pots or tubs, stood outdoors in summer and kept in winter in a frost-free, cool, light cellar or similar place, it may be grown satisfactorily even in the North.

The chief kind is G. jasminoides, 24 in., white, fragrant, summer. Its variety Belmont (also called Hadley) is very popular. The double variety G. jasminoides Fortuniana (often called Florida) is a comparatively hardy summer-blooming kind that is grown outdoors in the South. Other kinds sometimes cultivated are G. nitida, 3 ft., white; G. radicans floreplena, a low, spreading kind with small, double flowers; and G. Thunbergia, 4 ft., white.

GARDENIA, CITRON-SCENTED. See Mitriostigma.

GARDEN LINE. A garden line consists of a piece of strong, medium-heavy twine or cord. It is used for marking seed drills and rows for planting and for other purposes where it is necessary or desirable to establish straight lines. For the best convenience one end of the line should

A garden line is stretched tightly along the surface of the ground as a guide for making straight seed drills.

be attached to a reel and the other to a stake. Metal reels and stakes, made for the purpose, are sold. A less convenient but frequently used plan is to attach each end of the line to an ordinary wooden stake.

GARLAND FLOWER. See Daphne Cneorum and Hedychium.

GARLIC. A hardy bulbous plant, with narrow leaves; it is 6-12 in. high, is a native of southern Europe, and belongs to the Lily family, Liliaceae. Its botanical name is Allium sativum. All parts of this vegetable have a very strong taste; the bulb is composed of 10-12 cloves enclosed by a thin white or pink skin. Garlic is increased by separating the cloves and planting these separately. It is of great antiquity as a cultivated plant, and the name is said to be derived from the Welsh, *garlteg*.

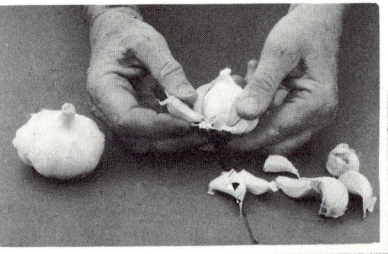

Separating Garlic cloves ready for planting.

Planting Garlic cloves 1 in. deep and 8 in. apart.

When to Plant. In early spring the cloves should be planted in drills, 1 in. deep, setting them 8 in. apart, in rows 12 in. from each other. For an early crop in mild climates planting should be done during October. Subsequent cultivation consists of frequent hoeing and keeping the soil free from weeds. When the leaves turn yellow, the bulbs should be lifted, thoroughly dried in the sun for several days, and then hung in an airy, dry place.

The popular kind is the Common White Garlic; the outer covering of the bulbs is silvery white. The pink variety is earlier than the white. The red Garlic has larger and flatter cloves.

Garlic is much used for flavoring, both in salads and in cookery in southern countries, but it is less commonly used in colder climates.

GARLIC, FALSE. See Nothoscordium.

GARRYA (Gar'rya). Evergreen shrubs or, rarely, small trees, natives of western North America, Mexico and Jamaica. The hardiest kind, G. elliptica, is the one grown most extensively. It is suitable for fairly mild climates only. Male and female flowers are borne in catkins on different plants. Garrya belongs to the family Garryaceae. The name commemorates Nicholas Garry, who was at one time secretary to the Hudson's Bay Company.

Garrya is increased by short cuttings of young shoots taken about July, when they are fairly firm. The cuttings should be inserted in a propagating case in the greenhouse. As plants lifted from the open ground are rather difficult to establish, it is wise to cultivate them in pots until they can be planted in their permanent places. The best results are obtained by setting them out in a sunny position in well-drained loamy soil that is not very rich.

The Most Useful Kind. G. elliptica, a native of California, is the most useful kind, and the male plant is more attractive when in flower than the female. It may grow 12-18 ft. high in favored positions, but becomes stunted in exposed places. As an evergreen it is effective throughout the year, but is most effective in winter when, November to February, it bears greenish catkins which, when fully developed, may be 6-12 in. long, according to the conditions under which the plant is growing.

Other fairly hardy kinds, none of which is as handsome when in flower as G. elliptica, are G. flavescens and G. Fremontii from western North America and G. laurifolia (macrophylla) from Mexico, and G. Thurettii, which is of hybrid origin.

GAS PLANT. Dictamnus albus, which see.

GASTERIA (Gaste'ria). Tender succulent plants, from South Africa, which belong to the Lily family, Liliaceae. They grow from 1-2 ft. in height and form rosettes of long, narrow, fleshy green leaves close to the soil; in some kinds the leaves are covered with small white tubercles. The flowering stem, which rises well above the foliage, is in the form of a spike of small, tubular, pendent red or pink flowers. The name Gasteria is derived from *gaster,* belly, and refers to the enlarged base of the flower.

For a Frostproof Greenhouse. They require a minimum winter temperature of 45 degrees. The best compost consists of two parts loam and equal parts of sand and crushed bricks. Repot-

Gasteria trigona produces its spray of pinkish flowers on long stalks that arise from between the upper leaves.

ting is done in February; the plants are taken out of the pots, the crocks and a little of the old soil are removed, and they are then set in slightly larger pots. Repotting is not necessary every year and should only be done when growth is sluggish. During the summer the soil is kept moist, but throughout the winter, water is only given when the soil is quite dry. No shading is required except a little in high summer to temper the severity of the sun on plants grown in greenhouses.

Propagation is principally by detaching the offsets in spring or summer and setting them in small pots until well rooted. Seeds may also be sown in spring or summer, in pots of finely sifted soil. The pots are covered with a pane of glass until germination has taken place. They are carefully watered, and when two leaves have formed they are pricked out, 1 in. apart, in a seed pan.

The chief kinds are: Gasteria verrucosa, 2 ft., red; G. lingua, 3 ft., scarlet; G. pulchra, 3 ft., scarlet; G. acinacifolia, 2-4 ft., orange-scarlet; and G. trigona, 2-2½ ft., pink.

GAULTHERIA — *Shallon, Wintergreen, Checkerberry* (Gaulthe'ria). Evergreen shrubs of erect or prostrate growth, natives of North America, China, the Himalayas, Australia, New Zealand and Tasmania. G. procumbens, the Wintergreen, is a hardy native of eastern North America but most kinds are suitable for mild climates only. The flowers are often white or pink-tinged, produced in summer, and in some instances are succeeded by attractive fruits. Gaultheria belongs to the Heather family, Ericaceae, and the name was given in honor of a

Gaultheria Forrestii, an evergreen shrub of spreading habit, bears clusters of white flowers in May which are followed by bright blue fruits.

Quebec physician and botanist, Dr. Gaultier.

For Lime-free Soil. The Gaultherias may be increased by means of seeds, cuttings or by division. The commoner kinds are often propagated by division, but the rarer kinds are more frequently raised by seeds sown under glass in sandy peat in spring, or by cuttings of half-ripe shoots inserted in the same kind of soil in a frame in summer. The frame must be kept close. These shrubs succeed in well-drained peat, in sandy peat, and in loam, provided it is free from lime and acid in its reaction. Planting may be carried out in early fall or spring.

The dwarf kinds are suitable for a fairly moist place in the rock garden and for grouping with Heaths and Rhododendrons. One kind, G. Shallon, spreads rapidly by underground stems. It grows $1\frac{1}{2}$-6 ft. high and thrives in sun and shade. For undergrowth in thin woods it is well adapted, and its juicy blue-black fruits are attractive to birds.

Gaultheria cuneata is a dense little bush with leaves $\frac{1}{2}$-$\frac{3}{4}$ in. long and scarcely $\frac{1}{4}$ in. wide, white flowers and small fruits which are first blue then white. It is a native of China, whence it was introduced in 1908. G. Forrestii is a dwarf kind from Yunnan, with ovate leaves 1-$1\frac{1}{2}$ in. long and $\frac{1}{2}$-$\frac{3}{4}$ in. wide, white flowers in short clusters from the axils of the leaves, and small bright blue fruits.

G. nummularioides is a dwarf shrub forming dense tufts 4-6 in. high with slender shoots. The heart-shaped leaves are $\frac{1}{4}$-$\frac{1}{2}$ in. long and the flowers white or pink. It is a native of the Himalayas.

The Wintergreen. G. procumbens, a trailing plant of eastern North America, is known as Wintergreen, Teaberry, and Checkerberry. It forms a spreading mass 2-6 in. high, has dark, glossy-green leaves, small white or pink-flushed flowers and small, bright red fruits. It is hardy and thrives best in moist, peaty soil.

The Salal. G. Shallon, commonly called Salal or Shallon, a native of western North America, may grow 5-6 ft. high but is usually less than half that height, forming a dense mass covered with dark green, leathery leaves up to 4 in. long and $2\frac{1}{2}$ in. wide. The pinkish-white flowers are in conspicuous clusters 3-4 in. long from near the ends of the branches, and they are followed by blue-black or purplish fruits.

G. trichophylla is a very dwarf evergreen suitable for the rock garden, where it will grow 4-6 in. high. It has small leaves, pink flowers and blue fruits, and was introduced from China in 1907. It is of distinct appearance, with very hairy shoots, leathery leaves up to $3\frac{1}{2}$ in. long, dark green with a curiously wrinkled surface. The flowers are white, produced in early summer, and the fruits blue. Some of the New Zealand Gaultherias intercross very readily by natural means.

GAULTHETTYA WISLEYENSIS (Gaulthet'tya). An evergreen shrub raised by crossing Gaultheria Shallon with Pernettya mucronata. It is of dense habit, its stiff shoots clothed with dark green, leathery leaves about 1 in. long and $\frac{1}{2}$ in. wide. The white flowers are in short sprays from the leaf axils and are followed by fleshy, purplish fruits. It requires lime-free soil. Cuttings of short shoots should be inserted in July–August in a firm bed of sandy peat in a close frame and left undisturbed until spring. The plant was raised in 1930 in the Wisley Garden of the Royal Horticultural Society of England and the name is a combination of Gaultheria and Pernettya. It belongs to the Heath family, Ericaceae.

GAURA (Gau'ra). Tender annual and perennial flowering plants of North America, which belong to the Fuchsia family, Onagraceae. The chief species, G. Lindheimeri, grows 3 ft. in height and has a slender branched stem with small, lance-shaped leaves and terminal spikes of rosy-white, tubular flowers with reflexed petals. The name Gaura is derived from *gauros*, superb, and refers to the beauty of the flowers.

For Light, Well-drained Soil. Although some kinds are perennial, the plants are best treated as annuals. The seeds are sown in light soil in a warm greenhouse in March or outdoors when the trees are leafing. The seedlings are pricked out into flats of light, porous compost 2 in. apart. When established they are gradually hardened off and planted out of doors in a sunny position 12 in. apart, in well-drained soil. G. Lindheimeri may be used in summer flower beds.

Cultivated kinds are: Gaura Lindheimeri, 3 ft., rosy-white; G. coccinea, 12 in., scarlet, and G. parviflora, annual, 18 in., yellow.

GAYA (Gay'a). A group of trees, shrubs and herbaceous plants, all natives of South America, except one which is a native of New Zealand. This one, Gaya Lyallii, the Lacebark, is the only kind generally cultivated and is usually known in gardens by the name of Plagianthus Lyallii and sometimes as Hoheria Lyallii. Gaya belongs in the Mallow family, Malvaceae. Its name honors Jacques Etienne Gay, a Swiss botanist.

Gaya Lyallii is a leaf-losing tree that attains a height of about 30 ft. and is adaptable for planting in mild climates such as that of southern California. Its white flowers are borne in early summer in clusters of 3-5 or are sometimes solitary.

This species thrives in any fairly good, well-drained soil in an open situation. It may be propagated by cuttings and layering as well as by seeds.

GAYLUSSACIA—*Huckleberry* (Gaylussac'ia). Although not more than five or six kinds are grown in gardens, about fifty kinds have been described; they are wild in North and South America. Some lose their leaves in autumn, whereas others retain them throughout winter. The fruits of some kinds are used for food. Gaylussacia is closely related to Vaccinium, and belongs to the family Ericaceae (Vacciniaceae). The name was given in honor of a French chemist of the late eighteenth and early nineteenth centuries, Gay-Lussac.

Lime-free Soil Is Necessary. The hardy kinds should be planted under acid-soil conditions such as are required by the hardy Heaths, though they withstand rather more moisture at the roots. Lime soil is fatal to their well-being. Propagation is by seeds sown in sandy peat, or by cuttings in summer inserted in similar soil in a frame kept closed.

The Chief Kinds. Of the several kinds in cultivation G. brachycera, the Box Huckleberry of the eastern United States, grows 9-18 in. high, forming a mass of short shoots bearing small dark, evergreen leaves, white flowers, marked with rose and blue fruits. G. dumosa grows 1-1½ ft. high, spreads widely by underground stems and bears white, bell-shaped flowers freely in May and June, which are followed by round black fruits. Its leaves sometimes color well before falling in autumn.

G. frondosa, the Dangleberry, grows 3-6 ft. high, flowers in summer and bears blue fruits. G. baccata, the Black Huckleberry, 1-3 ft. high, with reddish flowers and black fruits, is a leaf-losing shrub. G. baccata, sometimes called G. resinosa, is regarded as being one of the best Huckleberries in so far as the value of the fruits is concerned.

GAZANIA—*Treasure Flower* (Gaza'nia). Tender perennial plants, from South Africa, which belong to the Daisy family, Compositae. They bear showy orange or yellow flowers in summer, and the chief kind, Gazania splendens, is often used in gardens in California and other warm, dry climates. Gazania commemorates the scholar Theodore of Gaza.

Gazania splendens is a showy tender perennial, with bright orange, black-zoned flowers.

These plants must have a location fully exposed to the sunshine and a well-drained soil, if planted out of doors for the summer; if grown in pots, they must be placed in a compost of sandy loam and peat, in a sunny greenhouse. They should be kept safe from frost in the winter.

A Very Showy Flower. Gazania splendens, probably of hybrid origin, which bears very showy orange-colored flowers, with a ring of black, grows about 12 in. high, and provides a brilliant display of bloom in July and August, even though the flowers do close in the afternoon. It should be propagated from cuttings in August. These are inserted in a cold frame which is kept close for a few weeks until the cuttings are rooted. If they are left in the frame until spring, protection must be given by a covering of mats in cold weather. It is safer, however, to plant the rooted cuttings in flats in a frostproof greenhouse.

If required to bloom in the greenhouse the cuttings should be potted separately in March. Otherwise they may remain in the flats until late May, when they are planted out of doors after having been hardened off in a cold frame. The old plants may be lifted in autumn, potted and kept in a frostproof greenhouse for the winter and planted out for the summer.

Other kinds are G. longiscapa, golden yellow; G. Pavonia, orange-red, and G. rigens, orange. These have been intercrossed to produce a race of very showy hybrids.

GEISSORHIZA (Geissorhiz′a). South African cormous plants that are hardy only in mild climates but that are suitable for growing in pots and pans in cool, sunny greenhouses. They bloom in late winter and spring. They belong to the Iris family, Iridaceae. The name is derived from *geisson,* a tile, and *rhiza,* a root, from the tilelike appearance of the skin covering the corms.

The kind most likely to be grown is G. hirta, 1 ft., tall, flowers red. They require the same care and cultivation as Ixia, which see.

GELSEMIUM SEMPERVIRENS — *Carolina Yellow Jessamine* (Gelse′mium). A climbing shrub, native of the southeastern United States and belonging to the family Loganiaceae. It has twining stems with ovate, shining leaves about 3 in. in length, and bears large, yellow, fragrant flowers in spring. The name Gelsemium is derived from *gelsemino,* the Italian name for Jessamine, and refers to the shape of the flowers.

Outdoors in the South. From Virginia southward this plant is hardy on the coastal plain and is a fine subject for covering porches, and trellises. It thrives in any ordinary soil and stands partial shade.

In the Greenhouse. It requires a minimum winter temperature of 40 degrees F. and the best compost consists of equal parts of loam, leaf mold and well-decayed manure. The plants are set in large pots or tubs, or planted in a prepared bed in the greenhouse and the shoots trained to wires fixed to the greenhouse wall or roof. Pruning consists of shortening the side shoots to one third after flowering.

Propagation is by cuttings of shoots, 3 in. in length, inserted in spring in a greenhouse or frame.

GENIP. Melicocca bijuga, which see.

GENISTA—*Broom* (Genis′ta). Many handsome flowering shrubs are found in this genus. They are of very diverse habit, some growing 18-20 ft. high, while others are scarcely 6 in. high. Most are not very hardy and are best suited for mild climates. G. spinosa, G. sagittalis, G. tinctoria, G. aethnensis and G. silvestris are hardy at New York City and perhaps further north. Leaves are small and sparingly produced, but the stems are in most cases green and function as leaves. In all cases the leaves fall in autumn. Genista belongs to the Pea family, Leguminosae, and the name is said to be taken from the Celtic *gen,* meaning a small bush. Most of the hardier kinds are found wild in Europe.

Propagation and Cultivation. The best method of propagation is by seeds which should be sown as soon as ripe or in early spring. The seeds are sown in pots or pans of light, loamy soil, in a greenhouse or frame. As soon as the seedlings are large enough to handle, they are placed singly in small pots until large enough to plant in a nursery border. They must not be left there for long, for large plants do not transplant very well; as a rule two-year-old plants are old enough to set out in permanent places. They thrive in any good garden soil, that of a light loamy nature being most suitable.

Pruning. The tall kinds should be cut back a few times when young to induce a bushy habit of growth; otherwise no regular pruning is required. When the more vigorous sorts, such as G. aethnensis and G. virgata, are set out in places exposed to wind, the plants should be staked until they have become well established, for the top has often grown out of proportion to the roots and the plants are easily blown down.

Some of the Genistas are not very long-lived, and as soon as signs of deterioration are noticed, a fresh stock should be raised and the old plants replaced.

The Tall Brooms. The following three tall-growing kinds are particularly handsome shrubs. They should be given room to develop without undue crowding and may be used as informal groups, in large beds, or as isolated specimens. G. aethnensis, the Mount Etna Broom, a bush 16-20 ft. high with slender, green rushlike branchlets, forms a plant of graceful outline and is particularly attractive when covered with golden-yellow flowers in July. This beautiful shrub is found wild in Sardinia and Sicily. G. cinerea is an erect bush, 10 ft. or more high and 6 ft. through, with slender, twiggy branches and small leaves; it bears a profusion of golden-yellow flowers in June. In Spain and other parts of southwestern Europe it grows wild. G. virgata is rather like the last-named; a native of Madeira, it grows at least 12 ft. high with a spread of 6-8 ft.; the golden-yellow flowers are borne freely in June. As it tolerates partial shade it is excellent for woodlands.

Genista sagittalis is a low, spreading plant. It bears golden yellow flowers in erect racemes in early summer.

Spanish Broom. Quite distinct from the above are several kinds that have spiny branches. One of the best is G. hispanica, the Spanish Broom. It is a native of southwestern Europe and grows naturally into a dense bush 2-3 ft. high, forming wiry spiny shoots and producing a wealth of

Genista pilosa is a low evergreen shrub with golden yellow flowers.

golden-yellow flowers in May and June. It must be given a sunny position in well-drained ground. G. silvestris variety pungens, the Dalmatian Broom, may be looked upon as a dwarf form of the Spanish Broom; it grows only about 6 in. high but flowers freely. G. horrida is another low-growing, spiny-branched shrub; it is found in the mountains of central Spain and southern France, and the yellow flowers are borne freely in July.

The Needle Furze or Petty Whin, G. anglica, found wild in the British Isles, and the German Broom, G. germanica, are other kinds that have spiny shoots and yellow flowers. They are, however, less generally useful than those previously mentioned. G. radiata, from central and southern Europe, grows into a shapely bush, 2-3 ft. high, and is distinct by reason of its opposite and conspicuously jointed branches; the yellow flowers are borne freely in June.

A very different plant from those previously mentioned is G. sagittalis, the Winged Broom of central and southeastern Europe. It is a low-growing plant with spreading, winged branches, rarely more than 9-12 in. high. The golden-yellow flowers appear in erect racemes in June. This is an excellent border plant by reason of its dwarf, compact habit.

The Dyers' Greenweed, G. tinctoria, so-called from the fact that it was at one time used to furnish a dye, is very variable in character, and may be found from a few inches to 2 ft. in height. Its golden-yellow flowers are produced freely in June–July. Forms that have been singled out for varietal names are apennina, of dwarf habit; virgata, an erect shrub 2-6 ft. high; flore-pleno, with double flowers; humifusa, of dwarf habit, and mantica, with purplish shoots, which flower earlier than the type.

For the Rock Garden. Several of the dwarf species are valuable in the rock garden. The flowers of all are yellow. All the rock garden Genistas are easily grown, only requiring a well-drained position in full sun.

Genista silvestris variety pungens forms a low, rounded bush, 1 ft. or more across, and 6-9 in. high, with heads of golden, gorselike blossoms. Genista pilosa forms a semi-prostrate bush with bright yellow flowers, and is a most useful and beautiful plant.

Other dwarf kinds are G. delphinensis, like a miniature G. sagittalis, from southern France; and G. lydia, of Asia Minor, with spine-tipped flower shoots.

A double-flowered variety of the Dyers' Greenweed, Genista tinctoria, is sometimes grown in rock gardens; it is a pretty dwarf shrub. The plant grown in pots as Genista racemosa (fragrans) is Cytisus fragrans, which see.

GENTIAN. See Gentiana.

GENTIANA or GENTIAN

Aristocratic Plants for Rock Garden and Wild Garden

(Gentian'a). Annual, biennial and perennial plants which grow wild in the temperate, alpine and arctic regions in various parts of the world. They belong to the family Gentianaceae. The name is from *Gentius*, a king of Illyria.

The Gentians comprise some of the most fascinating of all rock garden plants and some are suitable for wild gardens. A few are difficult to manage in the garden, though most respond to reasonably skillful cultivation in favored climates. They range from minute plants less than an inch high to stately perennials three or four feet in height. In color the Gentians are chiefly blue, rarely white, or yellow.

Cultivation. In North America, the Pacific Northwest and other sections where summers are not excessively hot and dry, are the best areas for growing Gentians. Elsewhere only a few kinds can be grown easily. Among the most tolerant are G. Andrewsii, G. asclepiadea, G. cruciata, G. hascombensis, G. Olivieri (dahurica), and G. septemfida and its varieties such as Freyniana, Lagodechiana, and procumbens.

Most Gentians can be grown in loamy soil; a few require scree or moraine treatment; some need a moist, humus-rich soil almost approach-

[5–2]
Blanketflower
(Gaillardia pulchella picta)

[5–2a]
Snowdrops
(Galanthus nivalis)

[5–3]
Carolina Yellow Jessamine
(Gelseminum sempervirens)

[5–3a]
Gordonia alatamaha

ing bog conditions; and all, or nearly all, require sunshine.

Propagation is most satisfactory from seed; some kinds may be divided, and a few may be grown from cuttings. Seed is best sown in autumn, and the pans or flats should be exposed to frost and snow; if placed in a frame or greenhouse in spring, they germinate more readily than when the seeds are kept and sown in spring.

Gentiana acaulis is very attractive but is exacting in the matter of soil; in some it refuses to flower. The question of exactly what is lacking in such soils to prevent flowering has never been satisfactorily explained.

Special Soil Bed for the Spring Garden. Gentiana verna has a reputation for being difficult to grow; when buying Gentiana verna, you should insist upon well-established pot-grown plants. A bed of light, rich gritty soil consisting of fibrous loam, leaf mold, sand and stone grit or crushed bricks in about equal parts, should be made for it on the level, and in full sun.

This compost should be 3 or 4 in. deep, and immediately below it should lie a layer of a richer and more spongy compost, 2 or 3 in. thick. Planted in such a bed, the Gentiana verna roots will work down into the lower, richer material, and the moisture which it retains will encourage strong growth and flowers.

Thorough watering in hot, dry weather and a top-dressing, after flowering, of the same compost as that in the upper layer of the bed, will keep the plants in good health. The flowers should be removed as they fade, as the formation of seeds tends to weaken the plants.

Gentiana Farreri enjoys light, well-drained soil, and is apparently indifferent to the presence or absence of lime.

For Peaty Soil. Gentiana sino-ornata is a lime hater; it prefers a soil in which Rhododendrons and Heathers are happy, one that is fairly acid.

Gentiana Lawrencei, G. bavarica, G. ornata (Veitchiorum), G. hexaphylla and G. pyrenaica require much the same treatment as G. sino-ornata. G. pyrenaica and G. bavarica, especially, need a peaty soil and ample moisture at the roots throughout summer.

Gentiana cruciata, G. hascombensis, G. Olivieri, G. Pneumonanthe, G. Purdomii and G. septemfida variety Lagodechiana and its other varieties are perhaps the easiest Gentians to grow and flower, demanding only loamy soil and sunshine. They are extremely handsome plants with showy flowers. Gentiana ascelepiadea, the Willow Gentian, is another easily grown and very handsome Gentian for ordinary loamy soil in an open position or light shade. The Willow Gentian, although happy in an open position, is almost the only kind which can be grown in shade: it is most beautiful in half-open woodland.

The tallest kind is Gentiana lutea, an erect-growing perennial with handsome leaves and spikes 3 ft. high of light yellow, star-shaped flowers. This is best in the meadow outskirts of the rock garden, as also are the interesting, if rather coarse, G. purpurea and G. pannonica, with heads of brownish-purple flowers, and G. punctata with heads of yellow-spotted flowers.

Of hybrid Gentians the most noteworthy is Gentiana Macaulayi, a brilliant hybrid between G. Farreri and G. sino-ornata: this is easily managed in light, rich loamy soil in a sunny place. Another hybrid is Gentiana hascombensis. Its parents are G. septemfida var. Lagodechiana and var. cordata. The original plant is beautiful, but seedlings from it are variable.

The foregoing are the best of the Gentians. There are many others, some of them worthy plants, others are dowdy weeds not worth garden room.

American Gentians. Several species of Gentian are natives of North America; most of them are very lovely, but many are difficult to grow. Among the latter are the Fringed Gentian, G. crinita, and beautiful G. Porphyrio of the acid pine barrens of eastern North America. The Fringed Gentian is a biennial that favors moist meadows. In wet meadows at high elevations in the Rocky Mountains and the Northwest is found the charming G. calycosa. When attempting to grow native kinds it is well to simulate the conditions under which they grow naturally in so far as is possible. The Closed Gentian or Bottle Gentian, G. Andrewsii, is easy to grow. It thrives in moist or wet loamy soil in sun or light shade and blooms freely, although its flowers remain more or less permanently closed.

Gentiana Macauleyi is a hybrid of G. Farreri and G. sino-ornata, with flowers of deeper color than the former, produced freely in September-October.

The Willow Gentian. Gentiana asclepiadea, the Willow Gentian, forms clumps which increase in strength each year. A good plant will throw up a dozen or more arching wiry stems about 2 ft. tall, leafy below, and carrying in the upper portion a quantity of trumpet flowers of a fine blue. There is a white variety, alba, and a beautiful pale blue form. Seeds provide the best means of increase.

Gentiana acaulis is best represented in the garden by a form known as "Gentianella." Several varieties of G. acaulis are found in the Alps, but none is so satisfactory or so beautiful as the garden form, whose botanical identity is somewhat obscure. It forms mats of leaves of rich glossy green, spreads by means of underground shoots, and produces in May and June large and extremely handsome trumpet-shaped flowers of an intense pure blue. These are carried erect upon short stems, just above the foliage, and the whole height of the flower is 2-3 in.

A variety of G. acaulis having ivory-white flowers with lizard-green markings in the throat is in cultivation, and although it lacks the brilliance of the blue type it is nevertheless beautiful. A variety called coelestina, with pale-blue flowers, has also been reported.

G. bavarica is a dwarf kind, forming small clumps of bright-green, rounded leaves, from which spring erect, star-shaped flowers, only an inch or so high, of deep pure blue. The blue of G. bavarica is perhaps the most intense and pure of all the Gentians. It is possible to grow and flower it, but not easy to do so.

G. brachyphylla is a high alpine form of G. verna, dwarfer, with wedge-shaped leaves, and extremely brilliant, blue, star-shaped flowers. The plant forms compact clumps an inch or two across.

G. Farreri was one of the finest introductions of the late Reginald Farrer from the Orient. It forms clumps of narrow, grasslike leaves, from which come prostrate stems, clothed also with narrow leaves, and each terminates in a large trumpet-shaped flower, rather smaller than G. acaulis; the mouth of the trumpet is a brilliant Cambridge blue, the throat white, and the outside of the tube handsomely striped. It flowers in late summer, August and September. It varies a good deal from seed, many forms of poor washy colors occurring. In its best forms it is one of the most beautiful of all Gentians. Good forms may be increased by careful division of the root, or from cuttings in spring.

G. Freyniana closely resembles G. septemfida. It has semiprostrate stems, 6-9 in. long, carrying heads of fine, blue, bell-shaped flowers in late summer. G. hexaphylla is an attractive low kind with stems 2-3 in. high, clothed with whorls of short, narrow leaves; it bears beautiful pale blue flowers.

The Fringed Gentian, G. crinata, is a lovely native American species that is difficult to establish in gardens.

Gentiana imbricata is a high alpine form of G. bavarica, more dwarf and with deep blue flowers. G. Kurroo forms a rosette of long narrow leaves. The flower stems are prostrate, each carrying two or three large upturned flowers of light periwinkle-blue. It is not easy to manage. G. Lawrencei is like a slightly smaller, frailer G. Farreri, with very lovely pale blue flowers. It is rare and difficult, but worth any pains to grow.

Gentiana lutea is a large handsome plant, too big for most small rock gardens, but admirable in the outskirts or in the background of the rock garden and in the flower border. The broad leaves, 18 in. long, are handsomely ribbed, and the 3 ft. stem carries several tiers of rather star-shaped citron-yellow flowers.

G. ornata is near G. Farreri, and has pale blue flowers.

Gentiana Pneumonanthe is a European wild plant. The erect 6-9 in. stems carry heads of four or five good-sized blue flowers. It is a desirable species, easily raised from seed. Although a bog plant in nature, it grows well in ordinary loam in the garden, and does not need a specially damp position.

Gentiana ornata is related to G. sino-ornata; it is a smaller plant, with smaller flowers, of fine deep Oxford blue. It needs the same treatment, and produces its flowers in branched heads of from three to five or six, at the ends of trailing prostrate stems in late summer. It is a very desirable and beautiful kind.

Gentiana pyrenaica might almost be described as a small edition of G. sino-ornata with violet-colored flowers. It grows in healthy soil and swampy places in the eastern Pyrenees, and in the garden enjoys the same soil as G. sino-ornata, viz., a bed of rich well-rotted leaf mold, and abundant moisture at the roots. The flowers, though much smaller than those of G. sino-ornata, being only about nine inches high and half an inch across, are very like those of sino-ornata in form. They are carried erect on short stems—not trailing as in G. sino-ornata. In color they are deep violet.

This beautiful little Gentian is somewhat exacting. It flowers in May and June.

Gentiana septemfida is an easily grown and handsome plant, forming strong clumps, and throwing up a forest of erect 9- to 12-in. stems, each carrying in June or July a head of large blue, trumpet flowers. It is one of the easiest of all Gentians to manage, thriving in loamy soil and enjoying full sunshine.

G. septemfida variety Lagodechiana is a valuable kind with semiprostrate stems and heads of fine sapphire-blue, trumpet-shaped flowers in June.

Gentiana sino-ornata, a fairly recent introduction from the Orient, is one of the best and finest of all Gentians. It forms dense clumps of narrow leaves, which in winter are scarcely noticeable. In spring a number of trailing stems appear each of which, lengthening during summer, produces in autumn a large brilliant blue flower, handsomely striped on the outside. The color is intensely brilliant, and the blue is as pure as that of G. acaulis, and about the same depth and tone. Each flower is some 3 in. in length, and turns upward at the end of its trailing stem. When suited, the plant rapidly forms a strong clump, and quite small specimens, planted out in spring or summer, will flower well the same autumn. Gentiana sino-ornata flowers later than G. Farreri, and carries on the floral display. Its blooms are delightful for home decoration, lasting well in water.

After flowering, the plant almost disappears; all that is visible is a short, close tuft of next year's shoots, almost hidden in the soil. The plant is easily increased by division of the clumps in spring.

As it is quite easy to grow, in favorable climates, in a prepared bed of decayed leaf mold, and as it flowers right into the dead season of the year, it is a plant that should be grown freely in rock gardens in regions suitable to its growth.

Gentiana verna is a brilliant and typical high alpine. It forms colonies of rosettes of wedge-shaped leaves, from each of which springs an erect, solitary star-shaped flower, half an inch or so across, and an inch or so high, the five petals spread out in a flat star-shaped pattern, and of an intense blue.

Some forms of G. verna are better than others, but none is bad. There are large-flowered, vigorous-growing varieties which are especially desirable. White-flowered varieties occur occasionally and are interesting. There are some pale blue varieties, most are beautiful, and one with violet-colored flowers occurs in the Dolomites.

GENTIANELLA. The popular name of Gentiana acaulis.

GENTIANOIDES. A botanical term meaning gentian-like; for example, Veronica gentianoides.

GENUS. In botanical classification a genus (plural, genera) consists of one or more species of plants so closely related to each other, and sufficiently distinct from all other plant species, as to warrant giving them a distinct generic (group) name. Thus, all Roses are grouped in the genus Rosa, all Oaks in the genus Quercus and all Willows in the genus Salix. The three genera mentioned each include a number of species. For example, Quercus contains the Pin Oak, Quercus palustris; the Red Oak, Quercus coccinea; the Black Oak, Quercus velutina, and many others. Some genera, as for instance Ginkgo and Sanguinaria, consist of a single species. All species included in the same genus are considered to be derived from a common remote ancestor.

The name of a genus (generic name) consists of one word and, when employed as a scientific name, is always written with an initial capital letter. The name of a species (specific name) consists of two words, formed by adding a specific epithet (an additional word) to the generic name. The initial letter of the specific epithet may be capitalized or not, according to the style followed.

Many generic names of plants are also employed as common names. Examples are Rhododendron, Chrysanthemum, Petunia, Verbena, Forsythia, Delphinium and Dahlia.

GEONOMA (Geono'ma). Tropical Palms from Costa Rica, Brazil and Peru, which belong to the Palm family, Palmaceae. These elegant plants grow from 5-15 ft. in height, and have a slender ringed stem surmounted by a tuft of broad leaves which are two-lobed at the ends or, in some cases, pinnate. The name Geonoma is derived from *geonomos,* which means skilled in agriculture, and alludes to its method of producing buds at the apex, which become new trees.

In southern Florida these Palms may be grown outdoors in shaded locations.

Greenhouse Palms. At one time these plants were extensively used for table decoration in their young stage. They require a shady position in a greenhouse having a winter temperature of not less than 50 degrees. Repotting is done in March, and a compost of two parts of loam and one part of leaf mold, with sand freely added, is the most suitable. During the summer, abundance of water is required; but throughout the winter it is only applied when the soil becomes fairly dry.

Propagation is by seeds, sown in spring or summer, in pots of sandy soil. These are plunged in a propagating case; when the seedlings are 2 in. high, they are potted separately in 3-in. pots and subsequently in larger ones.

The chief kinds are Geonoma gracilis, 6 ft., and G. Schottiana, 9 ft.

GEORGIA, GARDENING IN. See Regional Gardening.

GERANIUM—*Crane's-bill* (Gera'nium). Hardy perennial flowering plants, closely allied to Erodium and belonging to the family Geraniaceae. The "Geraniums" which are grown in pots for greenhouse or home decoration and for summer bedding are known botanically as Pelargoniums (which see).

The true Geraniums are mostly hardy, varying in height from 4 in. to 2½ ft., and are natives of most temperate regions, including the United States. They have deeply cut and, in some cases,

Geranium grandiflorum, a showy violet-flowered hardy perennial for the herbaceous border.

The Transvaal Daisy, Gerbera Jamesonii, is excellent for growing in cool greenhouses, either in pots or benches.

fernlike leaves and flowers which vary in color from white to rose, red, blue, purple and almost black. The dwarf kinds are suitable for the rock garden and the taller ones for the herbaceous border or wild garden. The name Geranium is derived from *geranos,* a crane, and alludes to the resemblance of the seed pods to the beak of that bird.

The low-growing kinds are planted in fall or spring in well-drained sunny positions in the rock garden. Ordinary light garden soil is suitable.

The low-growing Geranium sanguineum prostratum is an attractive kind for planting in rock gardens. It has pink flowers.

The taller kinds are planted in the herbaceous border in a sunny position, in ordinary garden soil in October or in spring. Once planted, they need little attention as they do not spread unduly; they may be left undisturbed for years. All are easily increased by division, and the natural species, unlike the improved horticultural varieties, are easily raised from seeds sown in fall or spring.

The very dainty pink or soft lilac-flowered G. Farreri, a species well adapted for growing in rock gardens.

The Chief Kinds. For the rock garden: Geranium argenteum, 6 in., rose-pink, silvery foliage; G. cinereum, 6 in., red-purple; G. Farreri, 4 in., pink; G. Pylzowianum, 3 in., purplish pink; G. sanguineum prostratum, 4 in., rose-crimson, and G. Wallichianum, 6 in., purple-blue, which appreciates partial shade.

For herbaceous borders: G. Endressii, 1 ft., rose; G. grandiflorum, 1 ft., violet; G. grandiflorum variety alpinum (a dwarf form of G. grandiflorum); G. ibericum, 18 in., violet; G. macrorrhizum, 18 in., red-purple; and G. pratense, 2 ft., light blue. All flower in summer.

GERBERA—*Transvaal or Barberton Daisy* (Ger'bera). Tender herbaceous plants from South Africa, which belong to the Daisy family, Compositae. The leaves, which are in the form of a rosette close to the soil, are lance-shaped, deeply lobed, hairy and about 12 in. in length. During the summer the plants produce numerous, long-stalked, daisy-like, orange-scarlet flowers. There are also numerous hybrids which range in color from white to cream, yellow, orange-pink, crimson, purple and violet. Except in mild climates Gerberas are chiefly grown in greenhouses for cut flowers, but in the South they may be cultivated out of doors. The name Gerbera commemorates Traugott Gerber, a German botanist.

For a Cool Greenhouse. Gerbera requires a minimum winter temperature of 40 degrees. Repotting or replanting is done in April. A compost of equal parts of loam, peat or leaf mold with sand freely added, is used. The plants are shaded and lightly syringed after replanting but, when established, no shading is required.

From November until May water is applied to the soil only when it becomes fairly dry, but during the summer the soil is kept moist and occasional applications of weak liquid fertilizer are given.

Propagation is by detaching the basal shoots in April and inserting them as cuttings in sandy soil. The cuttings are kept in a glass-covered box until roots are formed, when they are potted separately in 3-in. pots and subsequently in 5-in. pots, in which flowers are produced. Seeds may also be sown in pots of sandy soil in spring or early summer. The seed pots are covered with a pane of glass and when the seedlings are 1 in. in height they are pricked off into deep pans and, later on, into separate pots.

The chief kind is Gerbera Jamesonii, which grows 12 in. high, and bears orange-scarlet flowers in summer. There are many hybrids having single or double flowers of yellow, orange, salmon and other colors.

GERMAN CAMOMILE OR CHAMOMILE. A name sometimes applied to Matricaria Chamomilla, which see.

GERMAN CATCHFLY. Lychnis Viscaria, which see.

GERMANDER. Teucrium Chamaedrys, which see.

GERMAN IRIS. Iris germanica, which see.

GERMAN IVY. Senecio mikanioides, which see.

GERMINATION. A term used to denote the commencement of growth in a seed.

GESNERIA (Gesner'ia). Tropical herbaceous plants and subshrubs, natives of the West Indies and Central America, belonging in the Gesneria family, Gesneriaceae. The name honors Conrad Gesner, a sixteenth century student of botany and natural history. Very few true Gesnerias are or have been in cultivation. Most plants called by this name by gardeners and horticulturists belong more properly in the genus Rechsteineria, others belong in the genus Naegelia (Smithiantha). True Gesnerias differ from Rechsteineria and Smithiantha in having their leaves in opposite pairs and in being without tubers or rhizomes.

A kind recently introduced to cultivation in America is G. cuneifolia, a native in the West Indies from Cuba to Porto Rico and Hispaniola. It is a low plant with oblanceolate, alternate green leaves which are pale on their undersurfaces and bears bright red, tubular flowers in the leaf axils. It requires the same culture as Alloplectus and Nautilocalyx, which see.

GEUM—*Avens* (Ge'um). Several hardy herbaceous plants are included in this genus; they

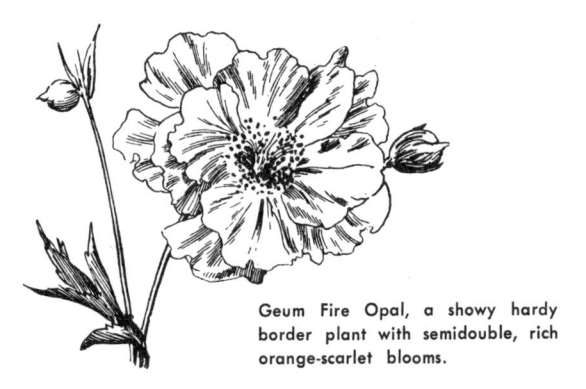

Geum Fire Opal, a showy hardy border plant with semidouble, rich orange-scarlet blooms.

form low tufts of leaves and bear brightly colored, strawberry-like flowers in May and June principally, though some of them bloom during a prolonged period in summer. Several of the Geums are wild in Canada and the United States, but those valued in gardens are natives of South America and the Near East chiefly. Geum belongs to the Rose family, Rosaceae. The derivation of the name is obscure.

Planting and Raising Seedlings. Most Geums are valued for planting in the herbaceous border; a few are suitable for the rock garden. They are easily managed in ordinary garden soil which is well drained; on heavy, clayey land they are apt to perish in winter, but this clayey soil can be made suitable by adding sand and compost. Planting may be done in autumn or spring. Propagation is carried out by sowing seeds in a box of sandy soil in a cold frame in April; when well developed, the seedlings should be planted in a nursery border for the summer and set in their permanent places in October to bloom the following year.

For the Perennial Border. Favorite varieties are Mrs. Bradshaw, scarlet; Lady Stratheden, orange-yellow; Fire Opal, orange-scarlet; Orangeman, orange-yellow, semidouble; Princess Juliana, copper-orange; and Red Wings, deep orange-red. All grow 18 in.-2 ft. tall and bloom from June onwards. These are varieties of the South American G. chiolense.

Geum Borisii, orange scarlet, grows about 12 in. high and is suitable for the rock garden or the front of the herbaceous border. Another kind for the rock garden is G. reptans, of low growth, with yellow flowers. G. Heldreichii grows about 8 in. high, has orange-red flowers and is suitable for rock gardens and flower borders.

The Water Avens, G. rivale, 18 in. tall, likes moist soil and is suitable for planting by the side of a pool or pond in the bog garden; it bears flowers of bronze-rose coloring.

GEVUINA AVELLANA—*Chilean Nut, Chile Hazel* (Gevu'ina). An evergreen tree with large, pinnate, dark-green, glossy leaves and white flowers in long racemes in summer. It is a native of South America and belongs to the Proteaceae. It bears fleshy fruits like Cherries, which are edible. Gevuina is the old Chilean name.

This plant, which reaches a height of 40 ft. is sometimes grown in southern California. Young plants may be raised from seeds sown in pots of sandy soil in a temperature of 60 degrees in spring, or shoots may be inserted as cuttings in a greenhouse.

GHERKIN. This name is usually applied to young cucumbers of a size suitable for pickling; that is too young fruits of Cucumis sativa. Cucumis Anguria, the West India or Burr Gherkin, is a distinct species, the fruits of which are also used for pickling. It is a tender, trailing vine that occurs as a native from the southern United States to Brazil.

GIANT FENNEL. Ferula communis, which see.

GIANT GROUNDSEL. See Ligularia Wilsoniana.

GIANT REED. See Arundo.

GIBBAEUM (Gibbae'um). A group of South African succulent plants formerly included in Mesembryanthemum and requiring the same general culture. (See Mesembryanthemum.) The name is derived from *gibba,* a hump, and refers to the fact that one leaf of each pair is prolonged into a hump.

GILIA (Gil'ia). The chief kinds of Gilia grown in gardens are annuals and one tender biennial. They grow wild in various parts of North America and belong to the Phlox family, Polemoniaceae. The name commemorates a Spanish botanist, named Gil.

The annuals may be raised from seeds sown out of doors in April in a sunny place and well-drained, rather light soil, or the seeds may be sown in a frame or greenhouse in March, the seedlings being planted out of doors late in April or early in May. They grow 15-18 in. high and should be planted towards the front of the mixed flower border, where they provide attractive groups of color in summer. If the seeds are sown out of doors the plants should be thinned to 5 or 6 in. apart.

The chief annual kinds are G. achilleæfolia, 12 in., blue; G. androsacea (Leptosiphon androsaceus), 12-18 in., white, pink or lilac; G. capitata, 12-15 in., lavender-mauve; G. densiflora (Leptosiphon densiflorus), 1-2 ft., lilac or white; G. tricolor, 18 in., pale lavender; there are several forms of this with flowers of various colors, including nivalis, white.

A Very Beautiful Plant. Gilia rubra (coronopifolia) is a tender plant which is grown as a biennial; that is to say, seeds are sown one year to provide plants that will bloom the following year. It produces an upright leafy stem 3 ft. or more high, which bears brilliant rose-scarlet flowers for the greater part of its length. Several varieties with flowers of various charming colors have been raised; seeds of these can be purchased in mixture.

Seeds should be sown in a pan of sifted loam, leaf mold and sand in July; the pan is placed in a shaded frame which is kept close and shaded until the seeds have germinated. When large enough the seedlings are potted singly in small pots and subsequently in those 5 or 6 in. wide, in a compost of loam, two thirds, leaf mold and decayed manure, one third, with a scattering of sand.

During the winter months the plants should be kept in a greenhouse having a minimum temperature of 45-50 degrees. They will bloom in summer. Care must be taken not to overwater them, especially in winter; water should be given only when the soil is moderately dry and the pots should then be filled to the rim. The plants are useless after they have flowered.

Gilia rubra (coronopifolia) may also be grown as an annual by sowing seeds in a greenhouse, temperature 60 degrees, in January; they will bloom in summer. Finer plants, however, are assured by raising the seedlings in the previous year in the way advised.

GILLENIA—*Indian Physic* (Gille'nia). Hardy, herbaceous, flowering plants which grow wild in North America and belong to the Rose family, Rosaceae. These plants are from 2-4 ft. in height, have trifoliate leaves and panicles (loose clusters) of white or pinkish flowers in summer. The name Gillenia commemorates Arnoldus Gillenius, a German botanist.

These plants require a moist shaded bed or border and are planted in fall or spring. After flowering, the stems are cut down. Propagation is by division of the roots at planting time and by sowing seeds in fall or spring.

The chief kinds are Gillenia stipulata, 18 in., white, June, and G. trifoliata, 2-4 ft., pink, June.

GILLIFLOWER. An old name applied originally to the Carnation, but later, in England, to the Stock and Wallflower.

GILL-OVER-THE-GROUND. Nepeta hederacea, which see.

GINGER LILY. See Hedychium.

GINGER PLANT. Zingiber, which see.

GINGER, WILD. See Asarum.

GINKGO—*Maidenhair Tree* (Gink'go). This exceedingly interesting and ornamental, leaf-losing tree is sometimes included among the Conifers, although its botanical characters actually place it between the Conifers and Ferns. It gives its name to the family Ginkgoaceae; Ginkgo is the old Chinese name. The tree is hardy in the North.

Only one kind is known, G. biloba, com-

A very beautiful, hardy, deciduous conifer, the Maidenhair Tree, Ginkgo biloba. Illustration shows the habit of growth, leaves, and bark.

monly called the Maidenhair Tree by reason of its fan-shaped leaves resembling leaflets of a Maidenhair Fern. The native country of this tree is given as China, although there are doubts as to whether it actually exists there in a wild state. The tree is of great antiquity and is represented in fossil beds. It is suggested that the Ginkgo has been preserved from extinction by its being regarded as a sacred tree and one eminently suitable for planting in the vicinity of temples.

The existence of such a tree was originally brought to the notice of European botanists in 1690 by a surgeon named Kaempfer, who was in the employ of the Dutch East India Company, but it was not until 1730 that it was introduced into Europe.

A Beautiful Hardy Tree. In the Orient the tree grows 90-100 ft. high, and may attain a girth of 18-20 ft. It is very suitable for growing in

North America. It cannot be mistaken for any other tree because of its peculiarly shaped leaves, which are bright green in summer but change to gold before falling in autumn. Male and female flowers are borne on different trees.

The fruits resemble small yellow plums when ripe. They are about ½-¾ in. in diameter, rather longer than broad, and a large central seed is enclosed in an outer pulp. As the fruits fall and the pulp begins to decay, a disagreeable odor is given off. The kernels of the seeds are edible and form an article of food for the Chinese and Japanese.

Pistillate (female) trees of the Ginkgo bear plumlike fruit if a staminate (male) tree is growing nearby.

For City and Country Gardens. The Maidenhair Tree gives good results in well-drained, loamy soil, and thrives in city as well as country gardens. In a young state it is inclined to develop with few side branches, but as it advances in age a well-balanced branch system is formed. It is an excellent garden or park tree either for an isolated specimen or for avenues, and can be safely transplanted from nursery rows when quite large. Seeds may be sown singly in small pots in a greenhouse, temperature 55 degrees, but the young plants should be planted out before they become pot-bound.

Several distinct forms have been given varietal names, notably fastigiata, of stiff erect habit; laciniata, of which the margins of the leaves are deeply divided; pendula, with pendent branches; and variegata, with variegated leaves. All are increased by grafting, but none is such a beautiful tree as the typical kind.

GINSENG. See Panax.

GIRASOLE. The Jerusalem Artichoke, Helianthus tuberosus. See Artichoke, Jerusalem.

GITHOPSIS (Githop'sis). A genus consisting of one annual, Githopsis specularioides, up to 10 in. tall, with narrow leaves and blue, bell-shaped flowers, native of California, and similar to Venus's-Looking-Glass (Specularia) in appearance. It is of easy cultivation from seeds sown under glass in March–April, or in the open ground in May.

This plant belongs to the Bellflower family, Campanulaceae. The name is derived from Githago, a genus of plants, and *opsis,* like.

GLABROUS. A botanical term meaning smooth, from the Latin *glaber.* It is often used in describing leaves which are smooth in contradistinction to others which are hairy.

GLACIALIS. A term meaning "of the ice," and used as a specific name for high alpine plants like Dianthus glacialis.

GLACIER PINK. Dianthus glacialis, which see.

GLADIOLUS: FOR GARDEN DISPLAY AND CUTTING
Stately and Richly Colored Flowers for Summer and Autumn

(Gladi'olus; Glad'iolus). Few flowering plants have been so greatly improved in recent years as the Gladiolus; it is now one of the most popular of all for garden decoration and for cutting. The range of coloring in the flowers has been extended considerably and now includes innumerable shades from white, cream, and pink, through yellow, orange, apricot, salmon, red and scarlet, to deep crimson and purple. Gladiolus belongs to the Iris family, Iridaceae. The name is derived from the Latin *gladius,* a sword, and alludes to the sword-shaped leaves.

The original species or wild types are natives of South Africa principally, though some grow

Garden favorites everywhere, Gladioli thrive in almost all sections of the United States. They are unsurpassed for planting in flower borders and for cutting.

wild in southern Europe and the Near East. Few of these are now grown by amateurs. Preference is given to the modern Gladioli which have been raised by crossbreeding and selection throughout many years, originally between species or wild kinds, and later between hybrids raised from them.

Formerly Gladioli were grouped in various sections characterized by flowers which were more or less distinct in form and markings. But those types are no longer distinct and crossbreeding has now bridged the gaps between them.

Classification. For garden and competition purposes present-day Gladioli are classified as follows.

Early-flowering. These include the dwarf nanus (G. Colvillei) varieties, and taller Herald and Tubergenii types, all suitable for cultivation under glass and, in the South, out of doors.

This group blooms in late winter and early spring; included in it are the nanus popular varieties The Bride and Peach Blossom. The Tubergenii varieties bloom about the same time as those of the nanus group but are taller. Varieties of the Herald group of Gladioli also bloom in late winter and spring but have stouter stems and larger flowers than the nanus and Tubergenii varieties.

Summer-flowering. Here belong all the popular hybrid Gladioli that normally bloom in summer and were once classified into such groups as Primulinus Hybrids, Large Flowered, Orchid Flowered, etc. According to modern classification they are grouped as Formal and Informal. The Formal varieties have their flowers arranged regularly on the stems, close together and approximately in opposite pairs; the Informal varieties have their flowers arranged less regularly, in looser spikes and spaced alternately on the stem.

Both the Formal and Informal groups are further divided into groups according to the diameters of the individual flowers. Those with flowers 5½ in. or more in diameter are Giants, those with flowers 4¼ to 5½ in. in diameter are Large, those with flowers measuring 3¼ to 4¼ in. in diameter are Small, those with flowers under 2½ in. in diameter are Miniatures.

Yet a further division of the groups based in size is made according to color of flowers. These are classified as White and Cream; Yellow and Buff; Orange; Salmon and Scarlet; Pink; Red; Rose and Lavender; Purple and Violet; Smoky; and A.O.C. (any other color).

When to Plant. By planting the corms of Gladioli at intervals of ten days or two weeks from the time the trees begin to leaf in spring until

Gladiolus tristis variety concolor has pale cream-colored, fragrant flowers.

about two months before the first killing frost of fall is expected, a long succession of bloom is assured. These plants thrive in ordinary cultivated garden ground without any special preparation, but it is worth while taking pains to make the

Small-flowered Gladioli are excellent cut flowers.

The corms (bulbs) of Gladioli should be planted so that their tops are 3-5 in. beneath the surface. A trowel is a handy tool here.

soil as suitable as possible for their needs. If it is heavy and clayey, compost, thoroughly decayed manure and sand should be mixed in. Light land can be made suitable by adding compost and thoroughly decayed manure.

How Deep to Plant. The corms of the primulinus or small-flowered Gladioli should be set 6 in. apart and at such a depth that they are covered with 3 in. of soil on light land and with 2 in. on heavy land. The corms of large-flowered Gladioli should be planted about 2 in. deeper and 8 in. apart.

When planting Gladioli in groups in the perennial border it is wise to dig out a hole of the required depth and width and to set the corms at the correct distance apart. They may, however, be planted in separate holes made with a trowel; it is unwise to plant in holes made with a dibber. These Gladioli look most attractive when grouped among the dwarf and medium-height plants in the herbaceous border, and they are grand for planting among summer bedding plants.

Summer Management. During the summer, Gladioli need the minimum of attention; there is, in fact, little that can be done for them; thus it is all the more important that the ground be prepared correctly before they are planted. The soil should be hoed frequently to destroy weeds and to promote the growth of the plants, and the large-flowered varieties will need to be supported by canes, to keep them upright in windy weather. The primulinus varieties do not, as a rule, need staking.

The size of the blooms is improved by the application of liquid fertilizer every ten days or so from the time the buds are seen until the flowers begin to open, and a top-dressing of wood ashes is beneficial.

Lifting and Storing the Corms. After killing frost the plants should then be lifted. If placed under cover for a week or so, it will be a simple matter to remove the soil and stems preparatory to storing the corms for the winter. The stems should be cut off ½ in. or so above the corms.

If necessary, the small corms or "spawn," which will be found at the base of many of the old ones, may be saved, stored separately for the winter, and planted in flats of soil in spring; they will bloom in two years. Gladioli, however, are so cheap that amateurs will find this method of increasing their stock to be scarcely worth while.

When all soil has been removed and the stems cut down, the corms are stored in boxes or paper bags in a cool, dry, frostproof place for the winter; there they will keep perfectly until planting time comes round again.

When grown for use as cut flowers, Gladioli may be planted in shallow trenches.

In the trenches, the corms (bulbs) may be set in single or double rows, spaced a few inches apart, and at such a depth that they are covered with 3-5 in. of soil.

Before replanting the corms in spring it is a good plan to grade them into sizes, choosing only the largest and best for the show borders; the smaller ones may be planted in a nursery border, where they will furnish small blooms for cutting.

Before the foliage grows too tall, support may be afforded by means of stakes and string. These rows of Gladioli are being grown for cutting.

It is worth while planting a few rows of Gladioli in the vegetable garden, or in a spare sunny border, solely for the purpose of providing a supply of flowers for cutting. When grown in rows it is an easy matter to support the plants by fixing a post at each end of the row, stretching a wire from one post to the other, and tying the plants loosely to the wire.

Raising Gladioli from Seeds. There is no difficulty in growing Gladioli from seeds. Most of the seedlings will bloom in the following year. Sowing may be done in February or March in a greenhouse, temperature 50 degrees, or in a cold frame in April. A box, 8 or 10 in. deep, should be drained by boring a few holes in the bottom and filled with a compost of two thirds loam, and one third leaf mold or peat moss, with a good scattering of sand.

The seeds are sown 1 in. apart and covered with about $\frac{1}{4}$ in. of the compost. If the soil is kept moderately moist, the seedlings may be expected to show through in a few weeks. During the summer months the box of seedlings is placed out of doors in a fairly sunny place. The seedlings are not disturbed until the autumn after the leaves have died down. The small corms are then taken out, stored for the winter in a frostproof place and planted in a reserve border, in March, about 3 in. apart.

Early Gladioli for the Greenhouse. Gladiolus Colvillei and its varieties are commonly grown under glass where they bloom in late winter and spring. This type of Gladiolus is less vigorous than others, and comes naturally into flower earlier. The blooms are smaller. The corms are potted in September–October, several being set in a 6-in. flowerpot.

They should be kept in a frostproof frame for 5-6 weeks, and then placed in a greenhouse. A minimum temperature of 50 degrees is suitable. The soil must not be overwatered, especially during the few weeks following potting, but when the plants are in full growth care must be taken that the soil does not become dry. Gladiolus Colvillei bears flowers of crimson-purple shade; the varieties The Bride, white, and Peach Blossom, pink, are more attractive. In mild climates G. Colvillei and its varieties, if planted out of doors in autumn, bloom in spring.

After frost has killed the foliage, Gladioli should be carefully dug from the ground.

After the tops have dried, they are removed from the corms; corms are then cleaned and stored for the winter.

Good Modern Varieties. Each year sees the introduction of many magnificent varieties, for the Gladiolus enjoys great popularity with the plant raisers, especially in the United States, Canada, Holland, and Australia. Consult dealers' catalogues for descriptions of the best up-to-date varieties.

Of the true species or wild types, there is G. tristis, which bears pale primrose-yellow flowers in spring, and, like G. Colvillei, may be planted out of doors in autumn in the South and cultivated in greenhouses for early blooms indoors. The flowers of G. tristis and those of its excellent variety concolor are deliciously fragrant.

Gladiolus byzantinus, which bears reddish-purple blooms, is hardy enough to be left out of doors during the winter months as far north as Philadelphia provided it is given some winter protection; it is useful for grouping in informal parts of the garden. G. segetum, with purplish flowers thrives under similar treatment.

Spawn or baby corms, which are produced around the bases of mature corms, can be saved and used for propagation purposes.

GLADWIN. Iris foetidissima, which see.

GLANDULOSUS. Bearing glands, as, for instance, Aquilegia glandulosa.

GLASSHOUSE. A greenhouse or conservatory.

GLASTONBURY THORN. The name given to a Hawthorn, Crataegus Oxyacantha bicolor, that flowers out of season. Where winters are not excessively severe, it often bears flowers from November onwards throughout winter, its best time being January, when the weather is mild. Its extraordinary habit of flowering at such an abnormal time, coupled with the fact that long ago an old tree grew at Glastonbury, England, led to the legend that when St. Joseph of Arimathea came to England to convert the inhabitants to Christianity, he arrived with his companions at the spot where the ruins of Glastonbury Abbey are now to be found. Being wearied, they sat down to rest, and St. Joseph stuck his Hawthorn staff in the ground; it immediately took root and grew, and opened its flowers on Christmas Day. This was regarded as a good omen, and led to the foundation of a religious house. The Glastonbury Thorn is perpetuated by grafting or budding upon English Hawthorn stocks.

GLAUCESCENS. A botanical term meaning bluish or sea green.

GLAUCIDIUM PALMATUM (Glaucid'ium). A perennial herbaceous plant, native of Japan, belonging to the Buttercup family, Ranunculaceae. This is a beautiful plant for a cool, semishady position in open woodland or elsewhere, where it will thrive in leafy or peaty soil. From short, fleshy rhizomes it produces stems up to 15 in. tall, carrying two or three large palmate leaves and a large terminal flower of which the four pale-mauve sepals are the showy part. It is a rare plant, increased by division of the rhizomes, but best left undisturbed once it has become established. The origin of the name is unknown.

GLAUCIUM — *Sea Poppy, Horned Poppy* (Glau'cium). Hardy annual, biennial and perennial flowering plants, natives of Europe and naturalized in eastern North America. They belong to the Poppy family, Papaveraceae, and grow about 2 ft. tall. The leaves are glaucous (blue-gray), and the poppy-like flowers are red, crimson, or yellow. The name Glaucium is derived from *glaukos,* glaucous, and refers to the grayish-green color of the leaves.

Suitable for Sandy Soils. The Sea Poppies should be planted in autumn or spring in an open sunny position, and flourish in ordinary soil which is light and well drained.

The chief kind is G. flavum, 18 in., yellow; this is the Horned Poppy, so named because of its long hornlike seed pods. It is best treated as a biennial. A supply of plants is obtained by sowing seeds annually, ½ in. deep, in sandy soil out of doors in May. The seedlings are afterwards pricked out, 6 in. apart, into a nursery bed, and are finally transplanted to their permanent positions in fall or spring.

Glaucium corniculatum is an annual, 9 in., crimson and black.

GLAUCOUS. A botanical term describing plants or parts of plants that are gray, blue-gray or greenish gray because they are covered with a thin layer of fine, usually waxy, particles.

GLECHOMA. Nepeta hederacea, which see.

GLEDITSIA — *Honey Locust* (Gledits'ia). A small group of mostly hardy leaf-losing trees; the stems are usually armed with formidable spines and the deeply cut leaves are very graceful and attractive; the small, greenish blossoms have no floral beauty, but they are followed by long beanlike pods which usually remain on the trees during the winter. They are good decorative and shade trees.

About twelve species have been described. They are natives of North America, central and eastern Asia, tropical Africa and South America. The name commemorates Gottlieb Gleditsch, Director of the Botanic Garden at Berlin, who died in 1780. Gleditsia belongs to the Pea family, Leguminosae.

Planting and Pruning. These trees thrive best in an open sunny position and in deep, well-drained, but fairly moist loamy ground. Planting should be done in early fall or spring.

The only pruning necessary is to thin out crowded branches, shorten long branches which are likely to spoil the shape of the tree, and maintain a straight leading shoot, when the trees are young, to form the trunk.

Propagation. Gleditsia is propagated by seeds sown in sandy soil in a greenhouse or cold frame as soon as possible after they are ripe. If the seeds have been kept for any length of time they should be soaked in warm water for twelve hours before sowing. Failing a supply of seeds, the rare and uncommon kinds may be grafted on the common kind, G. triacanthos, in spring out of doors or under glass.

The Best Kinds. The best known and most useful of the Honey Locusts are G. triacanthos

The Moraine Locust grows fast. This is a five-year-old specimen. Note its lacy foliage and vigorous habit of growth.

and its varieties. This hardy native of the eastern States is sometimes called Sweet Locust or Black Locust. At maturity it attains a height of 125 ft. or even more. In its typical form its trunk and branches are furnished with long, formidable, branched thorns but these are absent or nearly so in the variety named inermis. In recent years the Moraine Locust, a variety of G. triacanthos which is thornless and which does not produce seed, has been widely recommended as a substitute for the American Elm as a shade tree but, although it is very promising, it is perhaps yet too early to pass final judgment on its value for this purpose.

Following the introduction of the Moraine Locust, in 1949, other clones of G. triacanthos have been segregated and named but, once again, it is yet too soon to fully evaluate them for horticultural purposes. Among these newcomers are Brownii, Imperial, Majestic, Shademaster, Skyline and Sunburst. The last named is thornless and has golden yellow young foliage.

In addition to these recently named clones there is G. triacanthos columnaris, of columnar outline, and G. triacanthos nana, a narrow, upright, slow-growing kind.

Gleditsia aquatica, the Water Locust or Swamp Locust, is somewhat less hardy than G. triacanthos. It is native from South Carolina to Florida and Texas and attains an eventual height of about 60 ft. G. japonica, which grows to 75 ft. tall, is also less hardy than G. triacanthos. It is a native of China and Japan; a good shade tree.

GLEICHENIA—*Umbrella Fern* (Gleiche'nia). Tender evergreen ferns, from Australia and New Zealand. They grow from 3-6 ft. in height, have forked, feathery fronds and wiry, creeping rhizomes or rootstocks. Gleichenia belongs to the family Gleicheniaceae, and is named after W. F. Gleichen, a German botanist.

Greenhouse Ferns. The cool greenhouse kinds require a minimum winter temperature of 45 degrees and the hothouse kinds, one of 55 degrees. The best compost consists of two parts fibrous peat, one part turfy loam, and a scattering of sand; a few pieces of crushed charcoal should also be added. Repotting is done in February or March, when a little of the old compost is removed and the plants are set in slightly larger, well-drained pots. They are carefully watered until established, and during the remainder of the summer the soil is kept moist. Very little water is required in winter, its application only being necessary when the compost becomes quite dry. A shaded position is required, but the fronds should not be syringed; a moist atmosphere is maintained by moistening the pots and benches.

Propagation is by division of the roots in spring, a difficult operation, and by spores.

The principal kinds are: For the cool greenhouse: G. cryptocarpa, 3 ft.; G. circinata, 6 ft.; G. dicarpa, 6 ft.; and G. rupestris, 5 ft. For the hothouse: G. laevigata, G. pectinata, G. linearis.

GLOBE AMARANTH. See Gomphrena.
GLOBE ARTICHOKE. See Artichoke.
GLOBE DAISY. See Globularia.
GLOBE FLOWER. See Trollius.
GLOBE MALLOW. See Sphaeralcea.
GLOBE THISTLE. See Echinops.
GLOBE TULIP. See Calochortus.

GLOBOSE. A term sometimes used in botanical descriptions. It means nearly spherical.

GLOBULARIA — *Blue Daisy, Globe Daisy* (Globula'ria). A small group of hardy and tender perennial plants and shrubs which grow wild

Globularia cordifolia has heads of lavender-blue flowers and is a most attractive rock-garden plant.

chiefly in southern Europe. They belong to the family Globulariaceae. The name Globularia is derived from *globulus,* a small round head, and alludes to the spherical shape of the flower heads. Most kinds have dark green leaves of leathery texture, and the button-shaped flower heads are of an attractive lavender blue.

For the Rock Garden. The Globularias are suitable for the rock garden and the cool greenhouse; they thrive in ordinary, well-drained, loamy soil in full sun or in partial shade, and are propagated by means of seeds sown in a frame in May, by cuttings in July, or by careful division in September.

Favorite Kinds. Globularia trichosantha forms clumps of rosettes of spoon-shaped leaves, 3 or 4 in. long; the flower heads are carried singly upon erect, slightly leafy stems, 6-9 in. tall. Globularia nudicaulis bears a strong general resemblance to G. trichosantha, but is without leaves on the flower stems. Both are attractive and easily grown rock plants. G. incanescens grows 3 in. high and has pale blue flowers in June.

Globularia cordifolia is a prostrate, subshrubby kind which creeps over the ground and the rocks; its wiry stems are clothed with small, heart-shaped, dark green leaves, and throw up countless lavender blue, button-shaped flower heads on stems only ½ in. high. Globularia repens is a small, neater form of G. cordifolia, with blue flower heads on even shorter stems.

Globularia major censis is an interesting and rare plant, resembling a giant form of G. trichosantha, with a branched woody base, forming clumps up to 2 or 3 ft. across; the handsome lavender-blue flower heads are on 12 in. stems. Globularia Alypum is a very beautiful shrubby kind; it is an erect wiry bush up to 2 ft. tall, with numerous pale blue flower heads.

GLOBULARIS. A Latin term meaning globular.

GLORIOSA — *Glory Lily* (Glorio'sa). Tender climbing plants, with showy flowers, from Asia and Africa, belonging to the Lily family, Liliaceae. The long, slender stems grow about 6 ft. in length, bear lance-shaped sessile (without stalks) leaves and axillary (in the axils of the leaves) orange and red, or yellow and red flowers. The blooms, which are borne singly on long stalks, have six reflexed perianth segments (petals) with wavy edges. The stamens are conspicuously displayed on long filaments (stalks). The name Gloriosa is Latin for glorious, and refers to the showy flowers.

A Greenhouse Climbing Plant. Gloriosa, which climbs by means of tendrils at the ends of the leaves, is suitable for a greenhouse with a minimum temperature of 55 degrees. It requires a compost of equal parts of peat, loam, leaf mold, and well-decayed manure. The plants are grown from bulbs which are potted in February. They are set 2 in. deep; one in a 6-in. pot or several in larger pots. Water is carefully applied until the shoots appear, when it is given freely. As the shoots develop they are tied to canes, or wires are fixed below the roof to which the hook-like tendrils can cling. After the flowers have faded, less water is given, and when the foliage has died down the soil is kept dry until February; the bulbs are then removed from the old soil and repotted.

Outdoor Cultivation. In the far South, Gloriosas may be grown out of doors in rich soil. In the North, plants grown from tubers started early indoors may be set out in early June to produce flowers in summer and early fall. They will grow in light shade or full sun. The flowers produce their finest color in sun.

Propagation is by offsets, removed very carefully as growth is commencing in spring. Seeds are sown in pots of finely sifted soil in March. They are set singly ½ in. apart and ¼ in. deep. When the seedlings are 2 in. high they are potted separately in 3-in. pots and subsequently into larger ones.

Most popular kinds are: Gloriosa superba, yellow and scarlet; and G. Rothschildiana, crimson and yellow. Both flower in summer. Other kinds grown in American gardens are: G. lutea, buff yellow; G. Rothschildiana variety citrina, citron yellow and claret color; G. Carsonii, red and yellow; G. virescens (simplex), orange and yellow; G. virescens variety grandiflora, with yellow flowers larger than those of G. virescens; G. virescens variety Plantii, reddish-yellow flowers; and G. Verschuuri (perhaps a variety of G. Rothschildiana), red and yellow. In addition, a number of hybrid Gloriosas have been raised in recent years.

GLORY BOWER. Clerodendrum, which see.
GLORY BUSH. Tibouchina, which see.
GLORY LILY. Gloriosa, which see.
GLORY-OF-THE-SNOW. See Chionodoxa.
GLORY-OF-THE-SUN. See Leucocoryne.
GLORY PEA. See Clianthus.
GLOTTIPHYLLUM (Glottiphyl'lum). Dwarf succulent plants, previously included in the genus Mesembryanthemum and belonging to the family Aizoaceae. The short, branching stems are furnished with thick, fleshy leaves arranged in 2 rows and united at the base. The large, yellow flowers are produced from July onwards and set seeds freely, from which plants are easily raised. Cuttings and division are other methods of increasing these plants, the cultivation of which is the same as for Mesembryanthemums, which see. The name, derived from *glottis,* tongue, and *phyllon,* leaf, refers to the shape of the leaves.

The chief kinds, all natives of South Africa, and yellow-flowered, are G. depressum, G. fragrans, which has scented blooms 4 in. across; G. latum, G. linguiforme, and G. propinquum.

GLOXINERA (Gloxin'era). Bigeneric hybrids between species of Rechsteineria and species of Sinningia. They require the same culture as their parents.

The kind most commonly cultivated is G. rosea (S. eumorpha x R. cyclophylla), a free-flowering plant with clusters of pink, tubular flowers. One clone of this cross is known as G. Rosebells.

GLOXINIA (Gloxin'ia). The true Gloxinia of the botanist comprises a small group of tropical herbaceous flowering plants, natives of South America, that are suitable for growing in warm, moist greenhouses. They differ from the plants commonly grown by florists under the name Gloxinia (which are discussed under Gloxinia below) in that they have no true tubers, and in other botanical details. The florists' Gloxinias belong in the botanical genus Sinningia.

Gloxinia perennis, the true Gloxinia of botanists, is a tall leafy plant that differs markedly in appearance from the Sinningia, which florists and gardeners call Gloxinia.

Gloxinia was named in honor of Benjamin Peter Gloxin, a botanical writer of the sixteenth century, and belongs in the Gesneriaceae, the Gesneria family.

Gloxinia perennis (G. maculata) is the only kind cultivated. It attains a height of 2-4 ft., has erect, branched, succulent stems that are purple on their older parts, and green, marked with purple streaks, on their upper portions. It is a leafy plant, the leaves being broadly heart shaped and up to 6-7 inches across.

The flowers are borne freely in terminal racemes in late summer and fall. Each is about 1 in. long, about 2 in. across, and resembles a florists' Gloxinia in shape. The outside of each flower is covered with a dense growth of white hairs. The flowers are a beautiful clear lavender color with a deep purple blotch inside the throat.

Gloxinia perennis is easily propagated by cuttings of young shoots taken in spring. Culture is generally the same as for the florists' Gloxinia (Sinningia), which see below. Single plants may be grown to such a size that they need to be accommodated in 9-in. pots. After blooming, the plants are dried off and kept without water until the following late winter or spring, when they are repotted, watered and started into growth.

GLOXINIA (Gloxin'ia). This name is commonly applied to a group of popular, tuberous-rooted, flowering plants which have been developed from the Brazilian plant named Sinningia, which see. For the botanical genus Gloxinia, see Gloxinia above. The florists' Gloxinias (Sinningia) are invaluable for providing a display in the greenhouse and window garden during the summer. From an underground tuber, rosettes of roundish, hairy leaves are formed; these are deep green or flushed with red. The handsome funnel-shaped flowers are on stout stems 6 in. or more in length, and include a glorious range of colors from white to rose, crimson and purple. Some are self-colored, others are edged, or spotted, with harmonizing or contrasting colors. Those having nodding flowers are called Slipper Gloxinias. Varieties having double flowers are grown.

Potting the Tubers. Although the best flowers are produced by 2-year-old plants, raised from seed or cuttings, old tubers may be grown for several years. They require a minimum winter temperature of 50 degrees and the best compost consists of equal parts of peat and good soil, with a little well-decayed manure and coarse sand. The tubers are shaken free of old soil in February or March and placed in peat moss and sand

Leaf cuttings of Gloxinia (Sinningia) are made by cutting the bases of the leaves into wedge-shaped pieces.

The leaf cuttings are planted about 1 in. deep in a mixture of sand and peat moss and are kept in a warm, humid, shaded place to root.

This is a plant which gardeners call Gloxinia but botanists call Sinningia.

in a shallow box. They should not be covered.

The tubers, when set in a minimum temperature of 65 degrees and a humid atmosphere, quickly form roots and when the shoots are 1 in. in length the tubers are potted separately. Well-drained 5-in. or 6-in. pots are used, and the tubers are set with their tops level with the surface of the soil, which should be ¾ in. below the rims of the pots to allow space for watering. No further potting is required. Water is carefully applied until the plants are well rooted: the soil must then be kept moist, but a waterlogged condition should be avoided.

The leaves should not be syringed and they must be sheltered from the strong rays of the sun, as they are easily damaged. A moist, warm atmosphere is essential. When the flower buds are forming, liquid fertilizer is applied twice a week. As soon as the flowers open, feeding is discontinued, and the plants are set in a cooler atmosphere to prolong the display.

After the blooms have faded, water is gradually withheld and when the leaves have died, the pots are stored on their sides under the benches for the winter.

Raising Gloxinias from Seeds. Propagation is effected by seeds, cuttings of shoots and leaves, and by division of the old tubers. Seed sowing is the most popular method except when it is desired to increase especially fine varieties, when propagation by cuttings or division is practiced. Packets of mixed seeds or separate colors can be obtained. The seeds are sown in February in shallow seed pans, which are well drained and filled with finely sifted compost of equal parts peat, leaf mold and sand. The soil is moistened by immersing it in a pail of tepid water, and after the surplus water has been allowed to drain away, the seeds are sown thinly on the surface. A little fine sand is sprinkled over them, and a pane of glass is placed over the flower pan. They are not covered with paper or kept dark by any other means as the seeds germinate more freely when exposed to the light, but not strong sunshine.

As soon as the seedlings have germinated the glass is removed and when the second leaves have developed the plants are potted separately in 2½-in. pots. Many will produce a few blooms in late summer, but all are gradually dried off in the autumn and are stored and treated as advised for the older ones.

Propagation by Leaves. Mature leaves are detached from the plants in summer and notches are cut just below the junction of the main veins on the undersides. They are then laid on peat moss and sand or leaf mold, anchored with pebbles, and the young plants which eventually

After Gloxinias (Sinningias) have finished flowering, they are gradually dried off and are stored dry during their dormant period.

form at the cuts are potted in small pots. An alternative method is to cut the leaves into wedge-shaped pieces (with the stem of the leaf forming the point of the wedge) and plant these nearly vertically and about 1 in. deep in a mixture of peat moss and sand.

Cuttings are obtained from the tubers in spring. When the new shoots are 1 in. in length they are removed with a sharp knife, inserted around the edges of pots filled with sandy soil, and kept in a close, warm propagating case until roots are formed. The old tubers may also be divided in spring, as soon as they are starting into growth. They are cut with a sharp knife, each portion having a shoot or shoots, and are potted separately in small pots.

GLOXINIA, HARDY. See Incarvillea Delavayi.

GLYCINE—*Soybean* (Glyci'ne). A group of mostly twining plants belonging to the Bean family, the Leguminosae, and natives of warm climates in Asia, Africa and Australia. The name is derived from *glykys,* sweet, and refers to the fact that the leaves and roots of some species taste sweet. Only one species, G. Max, of the Soybean, a native of China and Japan, is of horticultural importance; it is represented in cultivation by many varieties. The Soybean is used as a cover crop, green manure and vegetable. For its cultivation see Beans: the Principal Types.

GLYCOSMIS (Glycos'mis). Evergreen shrubs and trees from the Philippines, India, Malaya, and Australia, one of which is sometimes planted in the far South and which may be cultivated in tropical greenhouses. The name is derived from the Greek words for sweet and smell, and refers to the fragrant flowers. It belongs in the Rue Family, Rutaceae.

Glycosmis pentaphylla is an attractive shrub; its pink translucent berry-like fruits are very decorative. It is easily raised from cuttings and thrives in any fairly good soil.

GLYCYRRIZA—*Licorice, Wild Licorice* (Glycyrrhi'za). A group of subshrubs and herbaceous (nonwoody) perennials, natives of the Mediterranean region, tropical Asia, North America and South America, that belong to the Pea family, the Leguminosae. The name is derived from *glykys,* sweet, and *rhiza,* root, and refers to the fact that the roots of at least some species have a sweet flavor.

The most important kind is G. glabra, the source of the common licorice of commerce. This species grows 3-4 ft. high and has lavender-colored flowers; it has seed pods that are smooth or nearly so. It is propagated by seeds, root cuttings and division, and for its satisfactory growth needs a rich, moist soil and a sunny location. It is a native of the Mediterranean region and central Europe and is much cultivated as a crop plant in southern Europe. G. uralensis, a native of Siberia, Turkestan and Mongolia, is grown as a crop plant in China and is said to be an ingredient of soy sauce.

The Wild Licorice of North America is G. lepidota, a native of moist prairies from Minnesota to Alberta and Washington and southward to Arkansas, Texas and California; it is now common in waste places in the Middle West and more rarely in the East. This kind grows 3-4 ft. high and has pale yellow flowers followed by small brown pods covered with hooked prickles. Although not possessed of medicinal qualities, its roots have an agreeable sweet flavor and were a favorite food of the Indians. The roots were favored for chewing by white people also.

GLYPTOSTROBUS PENSILIS (Glyptostro'bus; Glyptos'trobus). A rare leaf-losing Conifer from China, closely allied to the Bald Cypress of the southeastern United States (Taxodium), but differing in the structure of cones and seeds. It is planted in the warmer parts of the United States. The leaves are small, bright green in summer, but turn brilliant gold and bronze before they fall. In the province of Canton, in southern China, it is usually found on the banks of streams and in other damp places. It belongs to the Pine family, Pinaceae, and the name is derived from *glyptus,* carved, and *strobus,* cone.

GNAPHALIUM—*Cudweed* (Gnapha'lium). A large group of annual, perennial, and shrubby plants found wild in most temperate countries, including the United States and Canada. They belong to the Daisy family, Compositae. The name Gnaphalium is derived from *gnaphalon,* soft down, and refers to the woolly covering of the plants.

Very few of these plants have any particular garden value, although G. trinerve, from New Zealand, a prostrate shrub with white inflorescences in summer, is useful for sunny positions in the rock garden.

GOATSBEARD. Aruncus, which see. Tragopogon is also called Goatsbeard.

GOAT'S-RUE. See Galega.

GODETIA (Gode'tia). Beautiful hardy annuals, named in honor of the Swiss botanist, C. H. Godet. The genus belongs to the Evening Primrose family, Oenotheraceae.

Few of the original wild types or species are now cultivated; they have been superseded by the numerous richly colored varieties now available, these having been bred chiefly from the North American G. amoena, which has given rise to the taller strains, and G. grandiflora, from which most of the more dwarf garden varieties have been derived.

Godetias provide a delightful show of bloom in the garden in spring and summer and are useful for cutting for decorative purposes indoors.

The cultivation of Godetias is simple. They thrive where summers are not excessively hot and humid and at those times of the year when temperatures are not excessive. In general they may be grown under conditions that suit garden

Godetia, a showy tall-growing variety with rose-edged carmine flowers.

Peas and Sweet Peas. In the Northeast the seeds are sown out of doors towards the end of March or in April where the plants are to bloom. The seedlings must not be transplanted; in any event, unless the work is done very carefully and when the soil is moist, the roots will be damaged and the seedlings will be checked so severely as to spoil all chances of a successful blossoming.

Godetias develop into splendid plants if they are allowed enough room; if crowded, as so often they are, they do not branch freely, the flowers are comparatively few and the blossoming season is short. The tall varieties ought to be 8-10 in. apart when the work of thinning out is completed, and the dwarf varieties should be 5-6 in. from each other. If grown in groups to-

A dwarf single variety of Godetia.

wards the front of the border, Godetias add considerably to the charm of the display and in cool climates they last in bloom for many weeks if the plants are well grown.

No elaborate ground preparation is required but the soil should be dug and pulverized before the seeds are sown. The seeds need only a slight covering; after sowing it is sufficient to rake the soil over lightly. As the seeds usually germinate freely it is necessary to sow them thinly.

The dwarf varieties (9-12 in. tall), need no staking, but it is usually advisable to support the taller (2-2½ ft.) kinds by means of twiggy pea sticks; these will be hidden when the plants are fully developed. It is worth while sowing a row or two of Godetias to supply flowers for cutting; tall varieties should be chosen for this purpose.

Godetias are admirable annuals for cultivation in pots to provide a display of bloom in spring. They are suitable for a cool greenhouse. The greenhouse must be sunny; in a shady greenhouse the growth of the plants will be weak and the show of bloom a poor one.

Seeds should be sown in September in pots or pans of fine soil compost, the seeds being just covered with a sprinkling of sand or sifted soil. If kept moist by syringing or watering with a fine spray, placed in a cold frame and shaded, the seeds soon germinate. When the seedlings are an inch or so high they should be placed in the pots in which they are to bloom under glass. They may be set singly in 5-in. pots or several in 6-in. or 7-in. pots. If the plants do not branch freely naturally the tops should be pinched off.

Beautiful Strains and Varieties. Of the tall types, the double-flowered strains in distinct colors are most attractive, especially Cherry Red, Shell Pink, Rosy Morn, Rose, Carmine, Rich Pink and Mauve. Notable more dwarf (intermediate) varieties, 12-18 in. tall, include Crimson Beauty, Charming, satiny rose; Firelight, crimson; Kelvedon Glory, deep salmon-orange; Pelargonium, carmine, edged blush-pink; Pink Pearl, rich pink; and Sybil Sherwood, salmon pink, shaded orange, with white margin.

Especially good strains 12 in. tall are Sutton's Blue, Flamingo, crimson scarlet; Glow, crimson scarlet with white base; and Lady Satin Rose. Really dwarf strains, 6-8 in., are also available in lavender, mauve and salmon, and make colorful edgings.

The double azalea-flowered or Whitneyi type of Godetia is very handsome; the plants reach a height of 12 in. and bear large double blooms of rich shades of color, chiefly in pink, salmon and pale lilac.

Native Wild Kinds. Although not commonly cultivated, several species of Godetia that are natives of the western United States and western Canada are worth growing in wild gardens and rock gardens where climatic conditions are suitable; this generally means in the West. Among the best of the wild types are: G. amoena, Fare-

A modern semidouble variety of Godetia.

well-to-Spring, which grows from British Columbia to California, is up to 3 ft. high and has flowers varying from white through pink to red; G. grandiflora (G. Whitneyi), a native of California, 1 ft. high, with flowers varying from red to white, and G. viminea, native from California to Oregon, to 3 ft. high, with purple or crimson flowers that have dark centers.

Godetias are good beeflowers. Seeds of Godetia may be sown out of doors in August to provide flowers in late spring and early summer where winters are mild.

GOETHEA (Goe'thea). Tropical evergreen flowering shrubs from Brazil, which belong to the Mallow family, Malvaceae. They grow 2 ft. or more tall, have ovate green leaves and clusters of yellowish, white or pink flowers and conspicuous red or crimson bracts. The name Goethea commemorates Goethe, the great German poet and botanist. They may be grown outdoors in southern Florida.

For a Warm Greenhouse. They require a minimum winter temperature of 55 degrees, and the best compost consists of two parts loam, and one part of peat, with sand added freely. Repotting is done in March; the plants are removed from the pots, a little of the old compost is pricked off with a pointed stick and they are set in slightly larger pots. They require a shady position and the atmosphere must be kept moist. During summer the soil is kept moist, but throughout the winter dry atmospheric and soil conditions are maintained.

Propagation is by inserting cuttings of young shoots 2 in. in length in pots of sandy soil in summer. They are plunged in a close case in the greenhouse until roots are formed, when they are potted in 3-in. pots and subsequently in 5-in. pots.

The chief kinds are G. Mackoyana, 2 ft., crimson bracts, and G. strictiflora, yellowish, red-tinted bracts. Two hybrids, G. floribunda and G. kermesia, which have pink bracts, are more attractive.

GOLD-DUST. Alyssum saxatile, which see.

GOLD-DUST TREE. Aucuba japonica variety variegata, which see.

GOLDEN APPLE. See Spondias.

GOLDEN ASTER. See Chrysopsis.

GOLDEN BAMBOO. Phyllostachys aurea.

GOLDEN BELL. Forsythia, which see.

GOLDEN BELLS. Emmenanthe penduliflora, which see.

GOLDEN CHAIN. Laburnum, which see.

GOLDEN CHESTNUT. See Castanopsis.

GOLDEN CLUB. Orontium aquaticum, which see.

GOLDEN DROP. Onosma, which see.

GOLDEN EARDROPS. Dicentra chrysantha, which see.

GOLDEN ELDER. See Sambucus.

GOLDEN ELM. See Ulmus.

GOLDEN FEATHER. See Chrysanthemum Parthenium aureum.

GOLDEN GARLIC. Allium Moly, which see.

GOLDEN GLOW. Rudbeckia laciniata hortensia, which see.

GOLDEN HEATH. See Cassinia fulvida.

GOLDEN LARCH. Pseudolarix amabilis, which see.

GOLDEN PRIVET. See Ligustrum.

GOLDEN-RAIN TREE. Koelreuteria, which see.

Goethea strictiflora is an attractive tropical shrub for growing in greenhouses, and outdoors in the far South.

GOLDENROD. See Solidago.

GOLDENSEAL. Hydrastis, which see.

GOLDEN SHOWER. Cassia Fistula, which see.

GOLDEN STAR. Chrysogonum virginicum, which see.

GOLDEN STARS. Bloomeria crocea, which see.

GOLDEN TUFT. Alyssum saxatile, which see.

GOLDEN WILLOW. See Salix alba vitellina.

GOLDEN YEW. See Taxus.

GOLD FERN. See Pityrogramma chrysophylla.

GOLD-FIELDS. See Baeria.

GOLDILOCKS. See Linosyris vulgaris.

GOLDTHREAD. See Coptis.

GOMPHRENA—*Globe Amaranth* (Gomphre′na). Annual flowering plants, which grow wild in tropical countries and belong to the Amaranth family, Amaranthaceae. The flowers may be cut and dried for winter decoration. The plants grow about 18 in. tall, have ovate leaves about 4 in. long and 1½ in. wide, and bear large, pink, yellow, white or purple flowers with conspicuous bracts, in summer. The name Gomphrena is derived from the Latin, *gromphaena,* a kind of Amaranth.

Everlasting Flowers. These plants are grown in the garden in summer and for filling vases in the winter. The blooms are cut just before they are fully open and hung upside down, in bunches, in a cool, airy place until dry.

The plants are propagated by sowing seeds indoors in March. When the seedlings are 1 in. high they are pricked out, 2 in. apart, in seed flats; later, when the weather is warm and settled, they are planted in the garden. Good results may be also had by sowing the seeds directly outdoors in spring. Water is only applied to the soil when it becomes dry; the plants soon suffer if overwatered. The plants must be exposed to full sun. The chief kind is G. globosa.

As a Greenhouse Plant. Gomphrena globosa makes an attractive plant for cultivating in pots in greenhouses. It is easy to grow and remains in bloom over a very long period. Seeds sown in January to March provide plants for blooming through the summer and fall. The young plants are first transplanted to flats as advised above and, when they begin to crowd each other in the flats, are potted singly in 3-in. pots. Later they are transferred to 5-in. pots, in which they bloom.

When grown in pots, these plants need good drainage and a rich, porous soil. In their early stages care must be taken to keep the soil moist but not wet. When the pots are well filled with

The Globe Amaranth, Gomphrena globosa, is an annual with brightly colored heads of flower.

roots and the plants have made substantial growth, they need more water, although at no time must they be overwatered to the extent that the soil stagnates. Healthy, well-rooted specimens benefit from weekly or semiweekly applications of dilute liquid fertilizer. At all stages of growth these plants need full sun or, at most, very slight shade from the strongest summer sun.

GONGORA—*Punch-and-Judy Orchid* (Gongo′ra). The popular name of these Orchids is due to the curious structure of the flowers, in which the sepals, lip and column are so shaped that if a single flower be held in profile a resemblance to Punch and Judy can be traced. The name was given in honor of D. Antonio Cabellero of Gongora. They belong to the family Orchidaceae.

All are epiphytal, with evergreen leaves and pseudobulbs 2-4 in. high, strongly ribbed or furrowed. The flowers are on long drooping scapes produced at various times but usually in spring and summer; the floral segments are often very narrow.

Orchid baskets or pans are preferable to pots for these plants; they should be suspended near the glass throughout the year. The atmosphere of the greenhouse must be kept moist and the temperature should be tropical in summer and not fall below 60 degrees in the winter. When the plants are in full growth, abundance of water may be given, but in winter the compost should be allowed to get quite dry before water is applied. A potting mixture of cut osmunda fiber or of Fir bark is satisfactory. Annual repotting is not usually necessary, but when required it should be done in early spring.

Gongora atropurpurea, from British Guiana, has dark purplish-brown flowers about 2 in. across; G. quinquenervis (maculata), from Guatemala, has similarly shaped flowers but they are yellow marked and spotted with red; G. Sanderiana, from Peru, has yellowish, red-spotted flowers; G. armeniaca, from Nicaragua, has fragrant yellow-spotted-red flowers.

GONIOPHLEBIUM. Polypodium, which see.

GOOD-KING-HENRY. See Chenopodium Bonus-Henricus.

GOODYERA — *Rattlesnake Plantain* (Goodyer'a; Good'yera). These Orchids are grown chiefly for their ornamental leaves, which are in clusters near the soil, oval in shape, and marked with various colors—green, purple, red, yellow or white. Spikes of greenish flowers are produced, but they are inconspicuous. The name Goodyera was given to this plant in honor of J. Goodyer, a British botanist.

Culture. These Orchids should be planted in a well-drained semishady position on the rockery or elsewhere in April, in a compost of equal parts of peat, leaf mold and sand. Water must be given freely during dry weather. Propagation is by inserting cuttings in sandy soil in April; the cuttings are placed under a bell jar and set in a cold frame until rooted.

The chief kinds, North American natives, are: G. decipiens (Menziesii), leaves dark green, with whitish markings; and G. pubescens, with velvety green, silvery veined leaves. G. repens has deep green, mottled leaves and spikes of small yellow or white flowers.

GOOSEBERRY. Gooseberries are of two types, the English Gooseberry, Ribes Grossularia, a native of Europe from which many varieties have been developed, and the American Gooseberry, R. hirtellum, which has given us several varieties, either as selections of that species, or as hybrids with the English Gooseberry. Gooseberries have been cultivated in Europe since the 16th century, but only within the last 100 years in America, and in limited quantities. In recent years very few have been planted and not many nurseries offer them. Gooseberries are an excellent home garden fruit. They are used in the same way as Currants and bear heavy annual crops, requiring only weed control and pruning.

The English Gooseberry has been very popular abroad, where hundreds of varieties have been known and elaborate schemes of classification designed to account for them. They come in green, white, yellow, and red colors with several shapes and skins smooth, downy or rough.

The English Gooseberry in many varieties has been grown in America, but in spite of its much larger size, it is rarely grown now and a few va-

Gooseberries are delicious bush fruits, well adapted for growing in home gardens.

Gooseberries should be pruned in late winter.

Pruning consists of thinning out the older branches and cutting thin side shoots back close to their bases.

rieties of the American type are all that are available. The susceptibility of the English varieties to downy mildew, to which disease the American sorts are resistant, is in part responsible for the lack of interest in English Gooseberries.

English Varieties. Chautauqua, large, green, and one of the best English varieties grown in America; Fredonia, large, red, late.

American Varieties. Clark, large, greenish-yellow with reddish-blush, popular in Ontario, where it originated; Downing, medium sized, pale green, very productive; Oregon Champion, medium sized, green, very productive, and popular on the West Coast; Pixwell, small, pinkish, very productive, and promising for the Great Plains region; Poorman, large, bright red, very good quality, very vigorous and productive, and the best variety for the northeastern United States; Glenndale, a very vigorous, medium-sized variety that is heat resistant and suitable for the area south of the region where the other varieties do well.

Propagation. Gooseberries may be propagated by hardwood cuttings handled the same as for Currants, but as some varieties do not root well, mound layering is preferred. The plants are cut back severely in the dormant season before mounding. This severe pruning stimulates the development of many vigorous new shoots. In mid-July the soil is heaped up around these shoots, leaving the upper portions exposed. By fall the American sorts will be well rooted and are cut away from the parent plant for planting in the nursery, to be grown for another season. The European varieties require two years for satisfactory rooting.

After pruning, a Gooseberry bush should consist of a number of branches so spaced that ample light and air reach the foliage.

Culture. Climatic, soil and cultural requirements are the same as for Currants, which see. For additional information regarding Gooseberry, see Ribes.

GOOSEBERRY, BARBADOS. See Pereskia.

GOOSEBERRY, CAPE. Physalis peruviana, which see.

GOOSEBERRY, CEYLON. See Dovyalis.

GOOSEBERRY, HILL. See Rhodomyrtus.

GOOSEBERRY, OTAHEITE. See Phyllanthus.

GOPHER. See Pests and Diseases.

GORDONIA—*Loblolly Bay* (Gordo'nia). Flowering shrubs and trees from North America, China, and Formosa, which belong to the Camellia family, Theaceae. They are camellia-like shrubs, and have large, oval, shiny leaves, and white, sweet-scented flowers, 3 in. in diameter, in summer. The name Gordonia commemorates James Gordon, an English nurseryman. These plants are also known by the name Franklinia.

These shrubs are only generally hardy in mild districts, although G. alatamaha is hardy into southern New England. They should be planted in April or May in a well-drained border in fairly moist, peaty soil. Pruning is not required except to shorten an extra vigorous shoot or two after flowering.

Propagation is by layering in early autumn and by seeds. Cuttings are difficult to root.

The chief kinds are G. alatamaha, deciduous, up to 30 ft., white cup-shaped flowers in August–September, rich autumn foliage tints; G. axillaris, an evergreen shrub from China and Formosa, hardy only in mild climates and winter-flowering; and G. Lasianthus (Loblolly Bay), an evergreen tree, flowering in July–August.

GORSE. See Ulex.

GORSE, SPANISH. Genista hispanica, which see.

GOSSYPIUM—*Cotton*. Shrubs of considerable size or even small trees, widely distributed in tropical countries, and though actually perennial are often treated as annuals. Some kinds are of very great commercial importance, for it is the floss that surrounds the seeds that is the raw cotton.

When cotton was first used is unknown, but it is recorded as in use in India in 800 B.C. Herodotus, 450 B.C., wrote of India as having "wild trees that bear fleeces as their fruit," and Theophrastus, 350 B.C., wrote of cotton under cultivation, "They set them in the plains in rows, so as to look like Vines at a distance."

Care of the Plants. Except for plants cultivated in botanical collections or as items of special interest for educational purposes, Cotton is not a horticultural crop. When grown in pots for these purposes, the seeds are sown in spring in well-drained containers in sandy, fertile soil in a temperature of 70-75 degrees. As soon as the young plants have formed their second pair of leaves they are potted individually into 3-in. pots containing light fertile soil and are grown in a humid greenhouse in full sun, where the night temperature is 60-65 degrees and the day temperature somewhat higher. As soon as the roots begin to mat around the sides of the soil in the 3-in. pots, the plants are transplanted to pots of 5-in. size and later to 6-, 7- or 8-in. containers, as growth demands.

Cotton plants must not be allowed to suffer for lack of water, but constant saturation of the

The white flowers of Gordonia altamaha, a beautiful deciduous shrub, are produced in August-September.

soil is to be avoided. When the final pots are filled with roots, a program of feeding weekly with dilute liquid fertilizer should be instigated. Syringe the plants freely, daily, during bright weather until such times as the bolls (seed pods) begin to open and display the cotton within.

Kinds. Of the many species of Gossypium the following are among the most important: G. barbadense, Sea Island Cotton, a native of tropical America that grows to a height of 8 ft. and has yellow flowers tinged with purple; G. hirsutum, Upland Cotton, a native of tropical America that grows about 5 ft. tall and has white or light yellow flowers which assume pink or purplish coloring as they age. Varieties of these species are cultivated commercially for the production of cotton.

GOURD. Gourds are varieties of several kinds of plants belonging in the Gourd family, the Cucurbitaceae. There are many ornamental varieties which are valued for their fruits of quaint and curious shapes and bright colors. Some of these, if trained over a pergola, arch, or trellis, are interesting and decorative during the summer months, and the fruits, when dried and waxed or varnished, make attractive winter decorations in the home.

The plants belong to several different genera including Cucurbita, Lagenaria, Tricosanthes, Benincasa, Luffa, Cucumis, Coccinia.

Ornamental Gourds. Some of the most attractive of the ornamental Gourds for training on poles, trellises and arches are the Apple-shaped, Pear-shaped, Gooseberry Gourd, Golden Ball, Orange Gourd, Turk's-Cap, Egg-shaped and Turban.

Stronger-growing ornamental kinds, suitable for arbors, include variously colored Turk's-Caps, the Musk Gourd, the Snake Gourd and the Dishcloth Gourd.

Gourds Are Very Easily Grown. As soon as the weather is warm, seeds should be sown where they are to grow, in a light, rich soil in a sunny location. They do not transplant well. The fruits should be picked, when ripe, in early fall. They may be dried and preserved as ornaments.

Preserving Gourds. Thin-shelled Gourds of the dipper kind turn brown, become lighter in weight and begin to harden their shells at maturity. They are gathered as soon as the vines are killed by frost; before they are fully mature the insides are removed through a hole made for the purpose, or the top of the Gourd is sawed off, the insides removed and the top replaced. They are then cured by being hung in a well-ventilated cool place for six months or more. Gourds having thick flesh are gathered before the first frost, but after the rind has hardened and the stems have begun to shrivel. Handle them carefully to prevent bruising, wipe them with a soft cloth and apply a thin coat of ordinary floor wax to their skins.

Do not remove insides from this type of Gourd.

GOURD, SERPENT. See Trichosanthes.

GOURD, SNAKE. See Trichosanthes.

GOUTWEED. Aegopodium Podagraria, which see.

GOVERNOR'S PLUM. See Flacourtia.

GRADING: CONTOURING THE GROUND
How to Carry Out This Important Basic Work

Grading is the first problem to be met by the maker of a garden. The amount to be done depends on the topography of the site. It may vary from none to elaborate operations. For large areas a topographical survey is necessary. It may be checked and measured with proposed new requirements and both shown on the plan. Estimates of all quantities of cut and fill and measurements in connection with any operations desired can then be made.

On small places where little change of the original contours is needed, the grading can be done without a plan. A few long stakes, a line level, some strong twine, a pick and shovel, a wheelbarrow and a little common sense are all that are needed.

A simple way of determining levels is to drive a number of stakes into the ground and then, by means of a carpenter's level and 12- or 14-ft.-long straightedge, a series of levels can be established. Alternatively, a line level may be employed to establish levels. On larger areas a surveyor's transit is usually used.

The Grade. The surface or slope of a ground surface is called "the grade." Grading is the handling of the earth and the shaping of the ground surface to produce pleasing and practical contours.

The permanent grade of a walk, drive, lawn or other surface is the "finish grade." The working grade that is established beneath this during the construction period is the "subgrade," or lower grade. All contouring is done on the subgrade before the material that is to form the finish grade is added.

Drainage. In all grading operations drainage of the surface water must be planned so that rain and melting snow will not collect and cause damage to plants, grass, the soil, or to buildings or driveways. Also, it must be remembered that unless water that soaks into the earth drains away quickly, the soil may become saturated and unsuitable for the growth of plants and its surface soft and muddy. Drainage of lawn surfaces may be effected by sloping the grade to gutters surfaced with sod, brick, or stone flagging. The slope of cultivated land should be sufficiently gentle to allow the soil to absorb the water.

How to Grade. When grading is to be done, the topsoil is first removed and piled in a convenient place, to be used later to bring the surface up to the finish grade. The subgrade is then changed either by filling to raise it or by the removal of subsoil to lower it. The depth of soil or other material that is placed over the subgrade (and hence the depth below the finish grade at which the subgrade must be established) depends upon the purpose for which the final surface is to be used. A lawn requires a depth of 6-8 in., or more, of topsoil; perennials require 12-24 in.; and shrubs and trees a still greater depth. Where a considerable depth of added soil is necessary, it is customary to excavate a hole for each shrub or tree, then fill it with topsoil, rather than to fill the whole area to the maximum depth.

When grading near buildings, it is desirable to have the ground immediately surrounding the building slope away from it to carry away the surface water. A fall of half an inch in a foot will in most cases be satisfactory. When large surfaces are graded for lawn purposes, the

For areas of considerable size a surveyor's level is used to determine grades.

A carpenter's or mason's level is a practical aid in establishing grades over small areas.

A line level is a simple instrument for checking grades. It is hooked over the approximate center of a line stretched between two points.

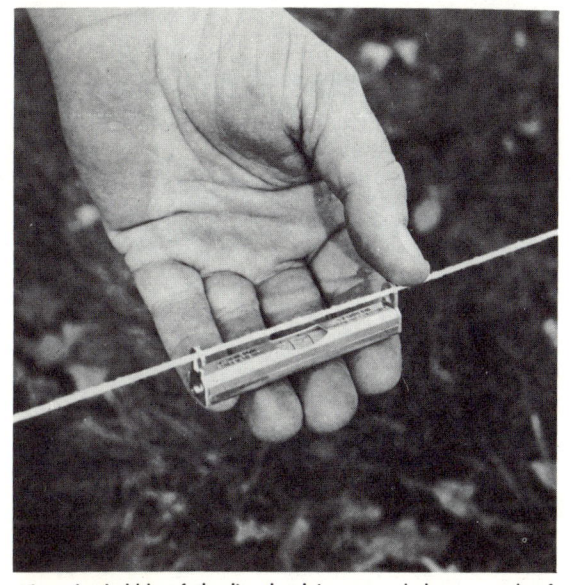

When the bubble of the line level is centered the two ends of the line are in a level plane.

Before grading operations are begun, all good topsoil should be piled to one side.

contours may, usually with advantage, blend gradually with those of the surrounding ground unless, of course, a level terrace or similar formal feature is the objective.

Near the House. When the house is located near the street, grading is determined by the difference in the grade level of the outside walk and the grade line of the house. When both levels are practically the same it is often best to grade the lawn so that it slopes down slightly from the outside walk and then rises to the house. When the house is below the street level the lowest point in the lawn should be some distance from the house, so that water drains away from it; from there it may rise in a curve to the sidewalk. If the house is above the level of the street the ground may be graded in a gentle curve from the street to the house. Any considerable difference of level between the house and the street that occurs in a comparativly short distance—in other words, if the rise is steep—makes the use of retaining walls and terraces or banks and terraces usually necessary.

Terraces near the house may be considered as a part of the house. The slope of their supporting banks should conform to that of steps used to ascend them. The maximum slope for this purpose is 1 to 2—that is, a 1-ft. rise in a horizontal distance of 2 ft. Quite often slopes of 1 to 3 are constructed. These give less rise to the approach steps but allow the grass on the terrace banks to be trimmed by a lawn mower, which is extremely difficult with steeper slopes.

Terrace embankments which do not conform to steps may be as steep as 1 to 1, which is the

After grading is completed, the topsoil is distributed evenly over the subgrade.

maximum at which most soils will maintain themselves. The steeper the terrace the more damage there is apt to be from erosion by surface water. With high banks it is often necessary to place a gutter at the top to catch surface water from the terrace area and so reduce the danger of erosion of the bank. It should be remembered that grass banks are hard to maintain, and where they are not necessary they should not be installed.

It is practically impossible to place soil in such a way that it will not settle. Consequently, when grading calls for filling, this must be taken into consideration and the finish grade must be brought higher than that level at which it will stabilize, to allow for settlement.

Grading should be done when the soil is workable, not when it is wet and sticky. Fills made from frozen soil will settle more than fills made from soil that is not frozen. All fills will settle in proportion to their depth and the nature of the soil. Where considerable filling is done, the surface is usually brought to a rough subgrade

A well-graded terrace. The slope of the bank is the same as that of the steps.

During grading operations trees that are to be retained should be protected against accidental damage.

and this is allowed to settle so that it can be finished properly before the application of the surfacing material.

Protection of Trees. In grading operations for which heavy equipment is employed, trees that are to be saved should be protected either by heavy guard stakes or rocks piled a little away from their bases. No earth should be cut from over the roots of trees that are to be saved. When a tree is located in a cut area, and the cut is

[5—4]
*Gentian
(Gentiana)*

[5—4a]
*Geranium
grandiflorum variety*

[5—4b]
Geranium sanguineum prostratum

[5—4c]
Geranium subcaulescens

[5—5]
Gardenia jasminoides

[5—5a]
Gazania Pavonia

[5—5b]
Glory Lily
(Gloriosa)

[5—5c]
Guzmania Berteroniana

not too deep, the tree may be left and the finish grade gently sloped downwards from the base of its trunk, leaving the tree on a slight mound. Where only shallow fill is used, trees may be protected by arranging loose stones about their bases to the depth of the fill. Earth in contact with the bases of trees above its normal level may kill the trees.

If the fill around a tree is deep, it is necessary to build a well around the trunk, 18-24 in. away from it and to the height of the fill. Wells may be made of an encircling wall of brick, stone, or concrete. Should a tree with this construction around it occur in a low spot where surface water will drain into it, install several lines of 4-in. draintile so that they extend from the trunk to the outer tips of the branches like the spokes of a wheel. Cover these tiles with stones and gravel before the extra fill is placed in position.

Where it is necessary to raise the grade above the roots of a tree, a well of masonry should be built around the trunk to keep the fill away from it.

GRAFTING: AN IMPORTANT MEANS OF PLANT PROPAGATION
There Are Many Different Ways of Doing It

Grafting is the art of inserting a piece of one plant into another plant, part of another plant or into another part of the same plant, in such a way that the parts brought into contact may be expected to grow together and form a permanent union. Most commonly, grafting is used as a method of propagation but it is also employed to repair injured trees, strengthen weak

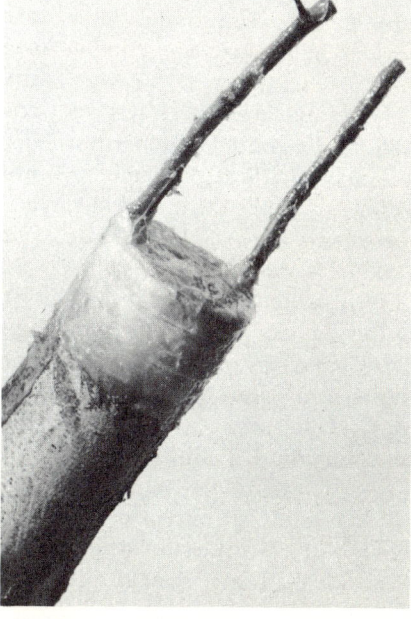

Left. An old Apple tree cut back and top grafted. Right. A close-up. Two scions have been inserted by rind grafting. The scions and the top of the stock are then covered with grafting wax.

crotches in trees, join together branches in certain methods of training trees and vines, to establish a branch that bears male flowers on a tree or shrub that normally develops only female flowers, and thus encourage fruiting, and to produce specimens that consist of more than variety growing on a common rootstock.

When grafting is done, as it usually is, by inserting a part of a stem or shoot that has no roots and is not expected to develop roots into a rooted plant, part of a plant that is expected to form roots or into a piece of root, the part that is inserted is called the scion; the plant or part of a plant into which the scion is inserted is called the stock or understock. When the scion consists of one bud only the grafting operation is called budding. When two plants both of which have roots are grafted together and each is permitted to retain its roots until after the graft is united, the special type of grafting involved is called approach grafting or inarching.

In general, only plants belonging to the great groups botanists call dicotyledons and conifers can be successfully grafted because to those groups belong all plants that possess a continuous cambium layer just beneath the bark and such a layer of cambium tissue is necessary for grafting to be successful. Plants belonging in the group known to botanists as monocotyledons (here belong such plants as Bamboos, Lilies, Palms and Orchids) have no continuous layer of cambium tissue and hence are not suitable for grafting.

Compatibility. Plants that are not closely related botanically can not be grafted together but not all plants that are botanically closely related can be grafted one upon the other. Usually, grafting is done between varieties of the same species or species of the same genus. In a few cases, plants of different genera may be successfully grafted together as, for instance, Pears (Pyrus) on Hawthorns (Crataegus), Pears (Pyrus) on Quinces (Cydonia) and Lilacs (Syringa) on Privet (Ligustrum). Grafting between plants belonging to different botanical families is not practicable.

In many cases it is possible to obtain a successful union between a stock and scion which, because of incompatibilities other than a disinclination of the tissues to unite, are not suitable for grafting together. Thus, if stock and scion are of kinds that grow in girth at markedly different rates the result is not likely to be permanently satisfactory. Experience and established practices that have resulted from trial and error methods are the only true guides in determining the likelihood of compatibility between a particular stock and scion.

An Ancient Art. Grafting is one of the oldest of gardening practices. Pliny the Elder, the Roman naturalist, described cleft grafting in the first century A.D. and undoubtedly it was practiced long before that. In China grafting has been done since remote times.

There is little doubt that the art of grafting developed as a result of man's observation of natural grafts, which are by no means uncommon. Natural grafts are likely to occur where two branches of the same tree or of different individuals come into close contact and are held tightly together until the barks of both are worn through and the cambium layers are in contact. Natural grafts are more likely to occur with thin-barked trees, such as Beeches, than with rough-barked kinds. Natural grafting between roots is also very common.

There are numerous forms of grafting, but in every case success depends upon placing the cambium layers of the understock and of the scion—the shoot to be used and grafted—in close contact. The cambium is a thin layer of tissue situated immediately beneath the inner bark or rind of a shoot or stem; this tissue is constantly dividing and multiplying, so that when the cambium of the scion and stock are placed together at a suitable time of year and under suitable conditions, the tissues intermingle and a complete and lasting union is formed.

Grafting Apples and Pears. For these fruits the operation is carried out in spring, when the sap is rising freely; this is usually from the middle of March to early in May, according to the locality, the variety and kind of tree to be grafted and the earliness or lateness of the season. The exact time to choose is when the buds on the stock or branch are just beginning to grow, but before the buds on the scions or grafts have started into growth. If the scions have already started into growth when grafting is done, the buds may wilt and die before a union is effected with the stock or branch.

Scions Must Be Retarded. For this reason it is important that the scions shall be practically dormant when required for grafting, certainly much less advanced than the stock. To retard them they must be cut off in the month of January or early February and laid in a trench, covered two thirds their length with soil, in a shady part of the garden, there to remain, alive but inactive, until the time comes for grafting in March or April.

The scions or grafts must be well-ripened shoots of the previous year's growth, furnished with sound wood buds. Weak, spindly shoots, or growths from diseased, unhealthy trees, or shoots containing only fruit buds, are unsatisfactory.

When young stocks for propagating new trees are planted in spring or fall, they should stand for a year before being grafted. Stocks planted in fall and grafted the next spring are insufficiently established to give good results. It is important to employ the correct stocks for the different kinds of fruit and various forms of trained trees (see Apples, Pears, and Stocks). The stocks are usually most suitable for grafting when one or two years old and with stems little more than half an inch in diameter.

Whip and Tongue Grafting. When grafting small stocks, with stems about the same thickness as, or very little thicker than, the scions, the method known as Whip and Tongue grafting may be employed.

The stock is first cut down to within about 4 or 5 in. of the ground, this being a suitable height at which to operate. All side growths from the stock are cut clean off. Then on one side of the shortened stock, make a clean, sloping upward cut with the knife, about 1½ in. long. Across the middle of this sloping surface make a thin "tongue" by a clean downward cut. No wood is cut out to make this "tongue"; just a clean cut with the knife is required. The cut should begin one-third of the way down from the top of the sloping surface.

Preparing the Scion. Next, prepare the scion. Select a stout, sound shoot from the bundle of one-year-old shoots, cut off and heeled in the ground a month or two previously, to retard their development. The scion should contain four good buds and is best cut from the middle part of a longish shoot. Cut it off immediately above a good bud and make the bottom cut about ¾ in. below the lowest of the four buds. At the bottom end of the scion and on the side opposite the lowest bud make a long sloping cut about 1½ in. long, and a "tongue" across the middle to correspond exactly with that on the

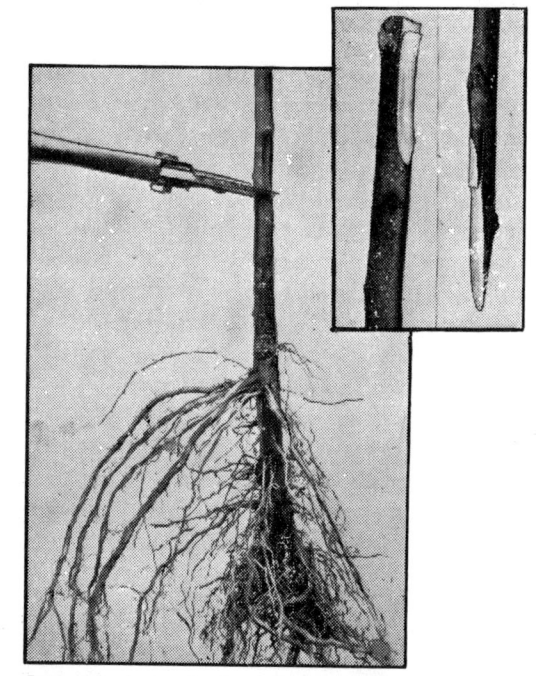

Cutting back an Apple stock for grafting. The smaller picture shows the stock and scion prepared for whip and tongue grafting.

prepared stock. Begin the cut to form this "tongue" one-third of the way up from the bottom of sloping cut surface of the scion, and make the cut in an upward direction.

To ensure accuracy and a good fit, the unpracticed operator should lay the scions against the prepared stock and mark the exact positions for the cuts on the scion, before any wood is removed at all. He should fit the scion on the stock, pushing the tongue of the scion well down behind the tongue on the stock, so that they interlock and make a close, tight fit.

The most important detail is to see that the inner bark or rind, and the cambium layer of the stock and scion, come into close contact on both sides, if possible, but at least all along one side. If the scion is much smaller in diameter than the stock, it may have to be placed on one side of the prepared cut on the stock to ensure that the inner bark is in close contact at least along one side. If when using a scion smaller than the stock, the scion is placed in the center of the prepared cut, so that its inner bark at no point coincides exactly with the inner bark of the stock, then the graft will fail to unite and will die.

The scion is bound in place with raffia or soft string, leaving the bottom bud on the scion free and the whole is then covered completely with grafting wax to make an airtight union. Many propagators now use a specially prepared grafting tape or adhesive tape to cover the union in place of the raffia tie and the covering of wax or clay. It is important to work quickly and make clean, smooth cuts, and during the cutting and fitting the grafts should be kept covered with a damp sack to prevent their drying out.

Splice grafting is even simpler and is performed in the manner described except that no tongue is made in the stock or scion. A long sloping cut is made on the stock as before, a corresponding cut on the scion, and the two are fitted together, being held in position with the raffia or string. This does not make such a firm and strong union as when the Whip and Tongue method is employed.

Top Grafting Old Trees. When it is desired to graft shoots on old established trees, with thick branches, the Whip and Tongue method is quite unsuitable and a different method must be employed. An old, unsatisfactory Apple or Pear tree can be rejuvenated by grafting shoots of a better variety on the cut-back branches and within a few years a new head of fruiting branches will be formed on the old framework. So long as the trunk and lower half of the main limbs are sound and healthy, a tree up to 25 years or more old will support a new head of branches and remain vigorous and fruitful for many more years. This method of treatment is known as top grafting, and may be employed to rejuvenate old Apple and Pear trees. Plums and Cherries can be top-grafted, but not always with satisfactory result. Top grafting is sometimes referred to as top working.

Cutting Back the Branches. The usual and best practice is to cut back the tree in January or February, in readiness for regrafting in April, but in an emergency this can be done immediately before grafting is carried out. The branches

Side grafting Azalea. *(Left)* Inserting scion *(Center)* Tying scion in position *(Right)* The completed graft.

GRAFTING

A Privet stock being prepared for splice-grafting Lilac upon it.

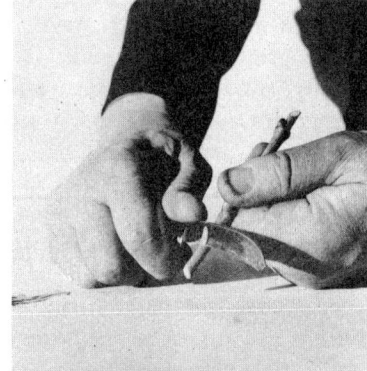

The Lilac scion is prepared with a sloping cut to fit the Privet stock.

Stock and scion are fitted together and bound with a rubber band.

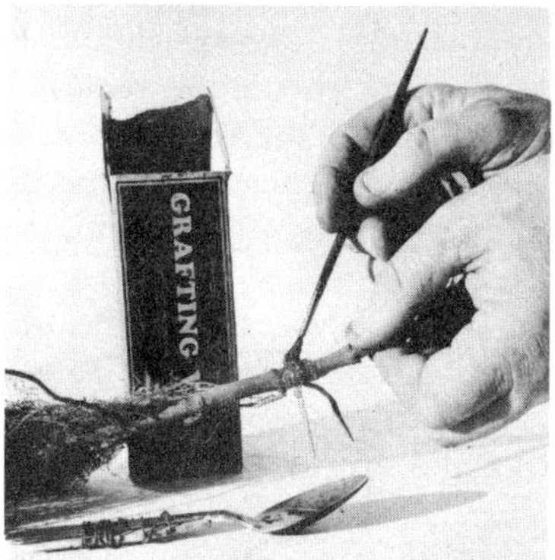

Melted grafting wax is painted over the pointed union.

Some months later, when stock and scion have united.

to be operated upon should be shortened to within about 2 ft. of where they join the trunk or main limb; it is important to saw them off at a point where there is live, clean bark in which to insert the grafts. Very old trees with rough and thick bark should not be cut hard back, close to the trunk, but to a point where they are little more than 5 or 6 in. in diameter. The branches must be sawed off carefully to avoid splitting or cracking. Big branches crowding the middle of the tree should be cut clean away and five or six well-placed branch stumps left to receive the grafts. If the tree is a vigorous grower, a small branch should be left intact to act as a "safety valve" and draw off the rush of sap in spring which might otherwise flood out the grafts before they have united with the branch.

Each branch stump is then treated as a separate stock. On a branch stump only 2 or 3 in. across, one graft, or scion, is sufficient, but on a stump wider than that there is room for two scions, one on either side. On very big branches, 6 in. and more in diameter, three grafts, or scions, could be inserted, though two are usually sufficient.

At grafting-time, the weathered end of the branches sawed off in the previous January should be freshened up by sawing off a further couple of inches and paring the surface smooth and even with a sharp knife.

Crown or Rind Grafting. There are two or three methods of top grafting in practice, but the one most generally used, and the best and simplest, is that known as Crown, or Rind, grafting.

To carry out this method, decide upon the spot where each graft is to go, choosing places where the bark is clean and healthy, usually on the outer side of the branch, and at that point make a downward cut in the bark with the knife point. Start from the surface of the branch stump and run the knife point down just deep enough to penetrate the bark so that it can be raised slightly on either side. The cut should be about 2 in. long. No bark should be removed; just make a long, knife-point slit and then prize up the edges of the bark on either side of the slit slightly, so that the prepared graft, or scion, can be slipped down between.

To prepare the scion, or graft, select a healthy shoot from the bundle of shoots which were laid in the ground to retard development, and from the middle part of this, cut a piece with four buds on it, being careful to make the bottom cut about 1 in. below, and the top cut immediately above, a sound bud. On the lower part of this and on the side opposite the bottom bud make a long, sloping cut, smooth and flat, about 1½ in. long, so that this wedge-shaped, flat end will fit down between the bark of the 2 in. cut on the branch stump and lie tight against the inner wood of the branch.

Push the prepared scion, or graft, gently down beneath the slightly raised bark of the branch so that the top of the long cut surface comes just level with the end of the branch. Bind it in place with raffia, or soft string. If there are two or more grafts to go on one stump, fix them all in this way, then bind them in place with the raffia and finish by covering the top of the branch and all exposed cuts with grafting wax to make the unions completely waterproof and airtight.

Cleft Grafting. Another method is known as cleft grafting. This is sometimes employed when the tree is old and the bark is tough and thick. The branch end is split across with a chisel and the grafts, or scions, prepared with a wedge-shaped end, are slipped into the opening. To enable the scions to be slipped easily in position, a small wedge of wood may be driven into the cleft made in the stump to hold the crack apart; this is afterwards withdrawn. The scions must always be fitted on the side or edge of the cleft made, so that their inner bark is in contact with the inner bark of the thick branch. Two, or sometimes four, scions may be inserted in each branch. It is important when cleft grafting is employed to cover the surface with a good thickness of grafting wax else disease may enter and the branch die.

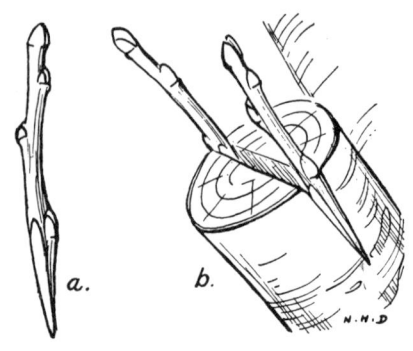

In cleft grafting, the scion (a) is inserted into a split in the stock (b). The cut surfaces are then covered with grafting wax.

Care of Grafted Fruit Trees. When the grafted shoot is growing strongly in late spring the wax and the raffia or string ties must be removed to prevent the growth from being strangled and seriously injured. The raffia tie should be replaced, being more loosely fastened and the growth then supported with a stake or cane. On the top-grafted branch, the supporting cane should be tied to the branch stump and the growth secured to the cane throughout the summer and autumn days, or it may be broken out during a gale.

All growths from the small stock or branch stump below the grafted shoot should be rubbed off.

Stub Grafting. Instead of heading back old fruit trees and crown or cleft grafting them as described above, some modern growers have adopted the practice known as "frameworking" as a means of rebuilding the head with another variety. This practice is used largely in Australia and Tasmania and it is claimed that the extra skill and labor required are compensated for by having the tree come quickly into bearing.

Of several methods employed, that known as stub grafting is the simplest. In this method numerous scions, each carrying 6 or 8 buds, are inserted along the whole length of the branches, each in a well-placed lateral or spur, the remainder of which are removed.

The base of the scion is cut wedge-shaped, with the cut on one side rather longer than the other. An oblique cut is then made ½ in. from the base of the lateral, on the inside, and long enough to take the wedge of the scion. The lateral is bent back to open the cut and the scion inserted, whereupon the lateral, on being released, springs back to grip it firmly, and it remains then only to cover the union with grafting wax.

Bridge Grafting. If the trunk of a fruit or other tree is so damaged by, say, rabbits gnawing the bark, or by canker, that the life of the head of the tree is endangered, it can be saved by what is known as bridge grafting. In the case of rabbit or similar damage, the upper and lower edges of the bark are pared clean. If canker is the cause of the damage, all diseased tissue should be cut clean away. One-year-old growths are then cut from any compatible tree—any kind of Apple for an Apple tree, Pear for Pear, Maple for Maple, and so on—long enough to span the damaged area comfortably.

The scions are prepared, both top and bottom, by making a sloping cut about 1½ in. long to go on the inside, and another cut 1 in. long on the opposite side, so that the ends are wedge-shaped. To insert them, a vertical cut is made in the bark of the trunk, 1 in. long from the clean edge, the knife being then turned to make a cut to the right, at an obtuse angle, so that when this piece of bark is lifted, with the thin handle of a budding knife or other suitable implement, a flap is formed.

The ends of the scions are inserted under the "flaps," the bark pressed back, and the whole secured firmly by driving small thin nails through bark and scion into the wood. In large wounds, several scions may be inserted 2 in. or so apart, and the job is completed by sealing the points of insertion with grafting wax.

Other Methods of Grafting. It must be remembered that grafting is not limited to the propagation of fruit trees. Many choice ornamental plants are grafted on to seedlings, or roots, of commoner kinds, and specialized methods of grafting are used for some of these.

Rhododendrons newly propagated by veneer grafting, before removal of the tops of the understock.

Here is shown a veneer graft after the top of the stock has been cut away and the ties have been removed.

Side Grafting and Veneer Grafting. The side graft is commonly used for evergreens and other ornamentals in greenhouses. The stock plant is not cut down until after the scion has united with it. The opening to be made in the stock for the reception of the scion consists of a slicing, shallow, downward cut of an inch or so. The base of the scion is prepared by tapering it with two sloping cuts made on opposite sides of it, of such lengths and sizes that the exposed surfaces will fit closely and completely against those of the stock. The prepared scion is slipped into the cut in the stock, and stock and scion are bound firmly together and placed in a close propagating case until union occurs.

A variation of the side graft, used for similar purposes, is the veneer graft. In this, a thin slice of stem is removed from the stem of the stock and a similar slice from one side of the stem of the scion. The two surfaces are then bound together and the newly grafted plant is placed in a close propagating case until union takes place.

Side grafts and veneer grafts are usually not waxed if they are placed in a humid atmosphere to unite. However, if the atmosphere is not well charged with moisture, waxing of the grafts is beneficial.

The ties should be watched carefully to make sure they do not cut into the swelling bark; before they do this, old ties should be removed and new ones installed. After union has taken place and the scion is well established and growing, the top of the stock is cut off.

Saddle Grafting. Although this method can be used in the open, it is usually employed for hard-wooded subjects, particularly Rhododendrons, the seedling stocks of which have been potted. It is a simple method. The stock is cut upwards on both sides to form a wedge shape, the base of the scion is slit up, the inner surfaces pared if necessary to make a close fit, and the scion then fitted on the stock in saddle fashion, bound with raffia, and waxed.

Approach Grafting or Inarching. This method is used for greenhouse Grape vines when it is desired to change the variety, occasionally for Walnuts, and some greenhouse hard-wooded plants. Both stock and scion are on their own roots; a thin layer of bark, down to the cambium, is removed from both at the point it is desired to join them, and the cut surfaces are then bound together. When union is complete the scion is severed below the graft, and the stock, above. For further details see Inarching.

Soft Shoot Grafting. This is a method in which young, actively growing stocks and scions are employed, usually under glass so that rapid growth conditions can be maintained. It is employed for some kinds of Cacti, and for rare Pines that are not easy to propagate otherwise. The latter are best grafted in late spring, when young soft shoots are available, and the method is the opposite of saddle grafting. The terminal bud and leaves are removed from the stock, which is then split down to receive the scion, cut to wedge shape, after which they are bound with

Cacti are easily grafted. A wedge or cleft is cut in the stock. The scion is shaped to fit it and is secured in the cleft with a cactus spine, which pins scion and stock together.

Mammillaria, a species of Cactus, is shown here thriving after being grafted upon an entirely different kind of Cactus.

Scions of Bignonia grafted on to pieces of root of the same species. The cleft graft is shown here.

a soft string sealed with wax, and kept shaded until union is complete. With Cacti, stock and scion may be held in place by pinning them together with large spines removed from a Cactus plant.

Root Grafting. Large numbers of woody plants are propagated by grafting shoots on to pieces of roots, under the warm, close conditions of a greenhouse propagating case. Cleft or saddle grafts are usually made, and the method is commonly employed for the large-flowered Clematis, Tree Peonies, Wisteria, Bignonia, and double-flowered Gypsophila paniculata. Apples are sometimes root-grafted under cover in winter, the grafts being then kept in moist soil for planting in March.

Budding. Although it is actually a form of grafting the art of budding (using a single bud as a scion) is usually considered separately. See Budding.

GRAMINEUS. A Latin term meaning grass-like; graminifolius means with grassy foliage.

GRAMMANTHES — *Letter Flower* (Gramman'thes). Annual flowering plants, which grow wild in South Africa and belong to the family Crassulaceae. The only kind in cultivation, G. gentianoides, grows about 4 in. in height, has opposite narrow leaves and orange, yellow and red flowers, each with a V-shaped mark, in summer. The name Grammanthes is derived from *gramma*, writing, and *anthos*, a flower, and refers to the marking on the flower. An alternative name for this genus, favored by some botanists, is Vaucanthes.

For the Rock Garden. This plant requires a sunny position on the rock garden, and does best in light, well-drained soil. The seeds are sown in pans of light soil in March, and set in a greenhouse with a minimum temperature of 45 degrees. The seedlings are pricked out in a box, 2 in. apart, and after being hardened off are planted in the rockery in May 6 in. apart.

GRAMMATOCARPUS VOLUBILIS (Grammatocar'pus). A climbing annual with opposite, divided leaves and yellow, tubular flowers, produced in the axils of the leaves in summer. It is a native of Chile and belongs to the family Loasaceae. The name is from *grammata*, letters, and *karpos*, fruit, and refers to the markings on the fruit.

For Covering a Trellis. This plant is raised from seeds sown in pots of sandy soil in spring in a warm greenhouse, and the seedlings are potted separately in 3-in. pots. They are gradually hardened off and planted out of doors in early June against a trellis or other support. They will grow in ordinary garden soil and benefit from occasional doses of liquid fertilizer when established.

GRAMMATOPHYLLUM (Grammatophyl'lum). Evergreen epiphytal Orchids found wild in New Guinea, Borneo, and the Philippines. The flowers are not brightly colored, but curiously marked. One section of these Orchids has tall stems covered with long, strap-shaped leaves, the other section has clustered pseudobulbs. The name is from *grammata*, letters, and *phyllon*, a leaf, and has reference probably to the markings on the flower leaves. Grammatophyllum belongs to the family Orchidaceae.

For a Warm Greenhouse. All these Orchids must be grown in a very warm greenhouse. Those with pseudobulbs may be placed in a slightly cooler glasshouse when growth is complete, but the winter temperature should never fall below 65 degrees. The tall-stemmed kinds take more than a season to finish their growth and the minimum winter temperature for them should be as near 70 degrees as possible. A suitable compost consists of osmunda fiber cut into small pieces or of Fir bark.

Noteworthy Kinds. G. speciosum, from Malaya, of which the growths will reach a height of 10 ft., bears many large blooms which are ochre yellow, curiously marked with purple-red. G. papuanum, from New Guinea, is very similar, but has smaller, more brightly colored flowers. G. scriptum, from the Moluccas, has yellow flowers spotted with red.

Of those kinds which have pseudobulbs, G. Fenzlianum, from Amboina, is typical. The flower stems are 3-4 ft. long with numerous flowers, over 2 in. across, green, shaded with yellow and blotched with dark brown red or chocolate. All bloom in summer.

GRANADILLA. A name used for the fruits of two or more kinds of Passion Flower, Passiflora quadrangularis and P. edulis. The fruits are. yellowish green or purple, variable in size, and contain numerous seeds embedded in sweet pulp. Granadillas are grown in most tropical countries. As they are climbing plants they are usually secured to stakes, or trellises, but are sometimes grown on trees, always in sunny positions with a free circulation of air. They are raised from seeds or cuttings, require rich soil and a generous rainfall. After an adequate number of fruits are set, the shoots are pinched to direct food material to the fruits rather than to the production of more branches. The names of Sweet Cup, Pomme d'Or and Bell Apple are applied to these or allied fruits.

GRANDIFLORUS. A botanical term which means large-flowered; it is commonly used in describing varieties of plants which bear larger flowers than the original species or wild types.

GRAPE: THREE DISTINCT TYPES, MANY VARIETIES
Complete Cultural Guide for All Grape-growing Sections

The Grapes cultivated in North America are of three distinct types. Each type includes many varieties, and their climatic adaptations and cultural requirements vary. The European or Old World Grape, Vitis vinifera, is the one that is cultivated in California, and to some extent in Arizona and Oregon. It is the Grape of the Mediterranean region and of most other grape-growing parts of the world. It probably was originally a native of the Caucasus.

The other great group of Grapes cultivated in North America encompasses those derived from V. Labrusca, the Fox Grape, a native of eastern North America. These include varieties of the Fox Grape and hybrids between them and V. vinifera. Such hybrids are grouped under the name V. Labruscana. They are typified by the variety Concord.

Muscadine Grapes, varieties of the native American Vitis rotundifolia, form yet another distinct group of Grapes. They are cultivated in the South.

Fox Grape Varieties and Hybrids

Early Grape growers in eastern America attempted to grow the European varieties by European methods. They failed because of the susceptibility of these kinds to low winter temperatures, diseases and insects. Soon after the year 1800, hybrids between European varieties and native American species appeared, and in 1849 Concord first fruited. The development of the Grape industry in the eastern states and in Ontario then proceeded rapidly.

The commercial Grape industry of the East is located near large bodies of water where the moderating effect of the water delays the frosts of autumn until the crop has ripened and retards vine growth in the spring until the danger of late frosts is past. Important producing regions are near Lake Erie in New York, Pennsylvania and Ohio; along Lake Ontario in western New York and Ontario; and southwestern Michigan near Lake Michigan. Other important areas are the Finger Lakes region and the Hudson Valley in New York; Arkansas and Missouri are other commercial grape regions. In these regions Concord is the principal variety.

Grapes in suitable varieties are grown for home use and to a very limited extent commercially in many other eastern states.

The Best Site. Grapes, except near the Great Lakes, should be on elevated sites to provide suitable air circulation, important for frost protection, a factor in disease control. "Frost pockets" or low areas surrounded by higher ground are wholly unsuitable for Grapes. Some of the vineyards in the Finger Lakes region of New York are on steep slopes which are suitable from the standpoint of climate, but very difficult to manage because of soil erosion.

The Best Soil. Grapes may be grown on a wide range of soils from coarse sands to heavy clays, but deep, fertile sandy or gravelly loams are considered best. Good subsoil drainage is important as the vines are short-lived where the water table is high. The subsoil should be such that the roots can penetrate to a depth of 5 or 6 ft.

Propagation. These American Grapes of the Labrusca and Labruscana varieties are propagated rapidly and cheaply by hardwood cuttings which root easily. The cuttings are made from well-matured wood of the previous season's growth that is between $\frac{1}{4}$ and $\frac{3}{8}$ in. in diameter.

The cuttings are made in late fall and early winter. They are made about 9 inches in length with 3 buds, the basal cut being made just below the basal bud, and the top cut an inch above the top bud. The cuttings are then tied in bundles, facing the same way, and buried butt ends-up in a trench with about 3 in. of soil over them. The trenches should be mulched with several inches of straw during the winter, this being removed as the weather warms up in the spring.

In the spring the cuttings are planted 6 in. apart in nursery rows with the top bud just above the surface of the ground. If on good soil and well cared for, the vine should be ready for field planting after one year in the nursery.

Layering may be used to reproduce a few varieties that do not root readily from cuttings, or to fill a vacancy in a vineyard where newly planted vines do not start well. A hole is dug where the vine is wanted and a cane from the adjacent vine is bent so that the bend is in the hole with two buds above the surface. The portion of the cane in the hole is covered with soil. After two years the layer is well rooted and may be severed from the mother plant.

Grafting. Grafting is not commonly practiced with these kinds of Grapes, as they propagate so readily from cuttings. However, they are easily cleft-grafted and undesirable varieties may be top-worked with more desirable sorts.

Rootstocks for Grapes. Labrusca and Labruscana Grape varieties have been experimentally grafted on various rootstocks and have been compared with the same varieties growing on their own roots. The plants on other rootstocks in some cases have greatly outyielded the plants on their own roots. The differences in performance are thought to be due to the resistance of the rootstocks to Grape Phylloxera, a widely distributed insect that infests the roots of many Grape varieties. Propagation methods that will make these grafted Grapes available in large numbers at prices that will permit extensive planting are under investigation. For the time being, Grape growers who may wish to take advantage of the superior vigor and productiveness of Grapes grown on Phylloxera-resistant rootstocks will have to plant these rootstocks and do their own grafting. Information concerning the best rootstocks and sources of propagating wood may be obtained from Agricultural Experiment Stations.

A modern variety of a Labruscana Grape.

Varieties of V. Labrusca and V. Labruscana. The commercial culture of the American Vitis Labrusca and V. Labruscana Grapes is based on the Concord variety in the eastern states, where it makes up 85 per cent of the plantings. Niagara, Catawba and Delaware are also important in some areas. There are a number of other excellent varieties for home use that ripen earlier and later than Concord. The range of flavor, color and texture is great and some varieties may be kept two or three months in storage in good eating condition.

Concord is the leading Grape for commercial planting and is also first choice for the home garden. The flavor appeals to many and the fruit is excellent for unfermented juice, jelly and jam. It is also used for wine. The berries are large, black with a heavy bloom, giving it a blue appearance, sweet and good. The vines are hardy, vigorous and reliably productive.

Niagara is the leading white, or green Grape, and it is a popular home garden variety. Its commercial usefulness is limited as it is not used extensively in processing, the principal outlet for eastern Grapes. The berries are large, white, sweet and good. The vine is vigorous, hardy and productive.

Catawba is the standard red Grape. Its principal use is in making wine for champagne. It is also an excellent table Grape, but requires a season two weeks longer than Concord to mature its crop. The berries are large, red and sweet. The vine is vigorous, hardy and productive, but rather susceptible to fungus diseases.

Delaware is a delicious Grape that has long been the standard of quality among this type of Grape. It is highly prized as a table Grape and in great demand by the wine-makers for the manufacture of high quality wines and champagne. The berries are small, red, sweet and with a very characteristic delicious flavor. The vines are of medium vigor, hardy and productive, but require a fertile soil.

Black-fruited Varieties. Varieties chiefly of value for the home garden are: Fredonia, a black Grape of Concord type that ripens 2 or 3 weeks before Concord; Van Buren, of Concord type, but ripens a week before Fredonia; Buffalo, a high-quality Grape of excellent keeping quality that ripens 10 days before Concord; Worden, very similar to Concord, but a week earlier; Steuben, a high-quality Grape that ripens with Concord and keeps very well; Sheridan, a late-keeping Grape that ripens after Concord.

Red-fruited Varieties. Dunkirk, midseason, small berries, good quality and very reliable; Yates, late ripening, keeps well, fine quality.

White-fruited Varieties. Portland, very early, sweet, type of Niagara; Ontario, very early, sweet; Seneca, very early, California type of grape, highest quality and an excellent keeper; Golden Muscat, late, large berries and clusters, excellent quality, may overbear and should be pruned more closely than other varieties.

Seedless Grapes. New seedless varieties of the type of Thompson Seedless, but hardy in the East, are Interlaken, Himrod and Romulus. They are of excellent dessert and keeping quality. Concord Seedless is of Concord flavor but small berried. It makes a fine Grape pie.

Late-keeping Grapes. The Grape season may be extended considerably by growing some of the varieties that are much superior to Concord and Niagara in keeping quality. Seneca, Interlaken, Himrod, Romulus, Buffalo, Steuben, Sheridan, Yates, Agawam and Salem are excellent keepers.

Wine Grapes. Varieties for red wine are Ives and Clinton. For white wines the following are used: Delaware, Elvira, Catawba, Iona and Seibel 1000. Other Seibel numbers and various French hybrids are promising, and detailed information as to the best of these may be had from the New York State Agricultural Experiment Station at Geneva, New York.

Very Hardy Grapes. For Minnesota and colder regions where other varieties are not winter hardy, the following black Grapes, which are better for juices and jelly than for dessert, should be grown: Alpha, Beta, Hungarian and Janesville.

For the Southwestern States. In addition to the varieties already mentioned, several of Texas origin are useful for planting in the southwestern states. Black varieties are Beacon, Carman, Fern Munson and Manito. Red varieties are Brilliant, Captivator, Ellen Scott and Headlight. White varieties are Gold Coin, Hidalgo, Rommel and Wapanuka. Some others of value in the deep South are Herbemont and Lenoir, both black.

Soil Preparation. Grape vines are normally long-lived plants and the soil should be well prepared at the start. An abundance of organic matter is desirable and this may be supplied by a heavy application of manure or compost, or by turning under a heavy grass or legume sod that has been growing for several years.

Planting Stock and Planting. The best grade of one-year-old vines should be used for planting. Older vines are less satisfactory.

Grape vines are commonly planted in the spring, but fall planting is satisfactory if soil is mounded up or plowed up to the vines after planting, to prevent them from being heaved out of the ground by frost action during the first winter.

The vines are spaced 8-9 ft. apart in the row and 8-9 ft. between rows. Vines to be trained on an arbor should be 8-10 ft. apart, depending on the vigor of the variety.

The vines are set the same as any other fruit plant. The hole is dug large enough to accommodate the roots without crowding. The soil should be packed firmly about the roots leaving no air spaces; stepping heavily on the soil as it is filled into the planting hole insures a good planting job. Fertilizer should not be used at planting time.

At this time the vine is usually cut back to two buds. Another practice is to leave 8 to 10 buds on the best cane and remove other canes. When the new growth from these buds is 1 in. long all except the two topmost shoots are broken off.

The Trellis. The Grape is a vine that must be grown on a trellis or arbor to provide the support necessary to keep the fruit off the ground. The vine is attractive enough to be grown on an arbor where it is decorative as well as fruit producing. It may also be grown along a boundary on a fence or trellis.

For fruit production, the trellis commonly used by vineyardists is satisfactory. It consists of two wires, the lower $2\frac{1}{2}$-3 ft. above the ground, and the upper 3 ft. higher. No. 9 wire is used for the top wire and No. 10 or 11 for the bottom wire.

The posts should be of a durable wood or treated with a preservative as they will be needed for many years. The end posts should be well braced if the rows are long.

Methods of Training. Grapes must be trained according to a definite system and the training and pruning that goes with it must be done

Before pruning—Grape Vine trained according to the single-stem, four-arm Kniffen system.

After pruning—Grape Vine trained according to the single-stem, four-arm Kniffen system.

systematically each year, or the vine soon becomes an unmanageable thicket of little use for fruit production.

Many methods have been devised, but they fall into two groups, those with the shoots drooping, and those with the shoots upright.

The method in which the shoots droop is easier to manage and the vines are usually more productive. The shoots hang down from the wire, and they are injured less by wind than with the upright method in which the shoots are tied to the wires above as they develop.

The single stem four-arm Kniffin system is the most widely used and is perhaps the best method for fruit production. It consists of a single trunk which reaches to the top wire to which it is firmly fastened. Four canes, two for each wire, grow to the right and left. Sometimes more canes are left on vigorous vines.

To train a vine according to this system, a cane is brought to the top wire as soon as it is vigorous enough to reach it, which may be the first, second, or third year after planting. Lateral buds supply the canes for each wire.

Pruning the Vine. Pruning is performed to reduce the crop to the quantity the vine can properly mature and to produce sufficient cane growth for a good crop the following year. The majority of the crop and canes depends primarily on the ratio of healthy leaf surface to the weight of the crop. If the vine overbears, the fruit does not ripen well and is of poor quality; cane growth is weak. If the vine bears less fruit than it is capable of maturing, the clusters of some varieties do not set fruits well and cane growth is overvigorous, resulting in "bull canes" which are less fruitful a year later than canes of medium vigor.

The best canes to leave for fruiting on Concord are those $1/4$ in., or slightly greater, in diameter, and which have internode lengths of 5-8 in. between the fifth and sixth buds. The canes should arise as near the trunk as possible, but if canes too far from the trunk must be saved, then short renewal spurs should be left near the trunk to provide for next year's canes to keep the vine from spreading out too far on the trellis and getting in the way of neighboring vines. The canes which are left for fruiting should have from 8-16 buds, the higher number being for the best canes.

The best way to learn how many buds a vine can support, and thus how many should be left, is to weigh the prunings until one is able to estimate from the appearance of the vine the weight of the wood which grew the previous season.

The pruner estimates the wood of an unpruned vine at 3 pounds and prunes it to leave 60 buds. The wood removed is weighed. If the prunings weigh 2 pounds, the number of buds is reduced to 40, if they weigh $3\frac{1}{2}$ pounds, then 55 buds are left. With Concord and Delaware 30 buds are left for the first pound of prunings and 10 buds for each additional pound. With Fredonia 40 buds are left for the first pound and for Catawba the number is 25 buds. This method of pruning has proved very effective in commercial practice and has resulted in substantial yield increases over the old method of guessing at the number of buds to leave.

Pruning is done at any time during the dormant season. After the prunings have been stripped from the trellis, the trunk and canes are retied to the wires. The canes are tied twice, loosely near the base and tighter near the tip. The trunk should be retied if necessary and it should be kept as straight as possible.

Vines on arbors may be pruned by this method, but the canes left will be longer and should be arranged to cover as much of the arbor as possible.

Pruning during the growing season, or summer pruning, should not be done, as any reduction in foliage at this time may result in poor ripening and reduced cane growth.

It is desirable to renew the trunk every 10 to 15 years by bringing up a sucker from the base. In about 3 years it will be in full bearing, at which time the old trunk is removed.

Surface Cultivation. Cultivation of the surface soil is necessary to control weeds. Experience has shown that Grape vines do not perform well in sod. However, deep cultivation injures the roots and too frequent cultivation results in excessive losses of organic matter. On slopes, erosion is encouraged by cultivation.

Surface tillage, therefore, should be as infre-

Grapes trained with their shoots tied vertically against a trellis.

Young canes of a Grape trained vertically against a trellis and budding out after pruning.

quent and as shallow as possible and yet sufficient to control weeds. On slopes a method of tillage which leaves considerable vegetation on the surface, yet discourages it to the point where it does not offer serious competition with the Grapes, is essential to reduce soil losses from erosion.

Cultivation should start early and continue until late July when a cover crop is sown to occupy the ground during the fall and winter. Rye Grass is one of the best cover crops, but Rye, Winter Wheat and Barley are also suitable.

It is also desirable to spread waste hay, straw, Grape pomace and manure in the vineyard at the rate of 2-3 tons to the acre after the last cultivation.

Mulching in the home vineyard is a satisfactory practice and may take the place of sowing a cover crop.

Fertilizers. Nitrogenous fertilizers have demonstrated their value in increasing the vigor and size of crop of Grape vines. The amount to be used depends on the vigor of the vines and ordinarily should range from 40 to 80 pounds of nitrogen to the acre. This may be had from 125 to 150 pounds of ammonium nitrate, or twice that amount of nitrate of soda. Grapes are not likely to respond to phosphorus and only rarely to potash. Fertilizers are more effective on soils well supplied with organic matter than on badly eroded soils low in organic matter.

The cover crop may need fertilization to ensure vigorous growth, and for this purpose 400 pounds of a 10-10-10 fertilizer per acre should be used. It is not likely that the cover crop will need fertilizing every year.

The pH (acid-alkaline reaction) of the soil should be maintained at 5.5, or above, for the cover crop.

Harvesting Grapes. Grapes should be fully ripe when harvested as they do not improve in sugar content and flavor after they are removed from the vine. The seeds become brown as the Grapes ripen, and separate more easily from the pulp. Each variety develops its characteristic flavor and aroma.

The clusters should be cut off with Grape shears, as many varieties have tough stems, the breaking of which injures the fruit and the vine.

Varieties in which the Labrusca characteristics dominate—as they do in Fredonia, Van Buren, Concord, Niagara, Portland, Kendaia, Athens, Lucile and Caco—do not keep well on or off the vine, and should be used promptly if their best quality is to be enjoyed.

Varieties in which the vinifera characteristics are dominant are of excellent keeping quality on the vine and after harvest, and they may be kept in good eating condition for 2-3 months after they are ripe. They should be stored in shallow trays with the fruit one layer deep in a temperature as cool as possible down to 32 degrees F.

Muscadine Grapes

The Muscadine Grape, Vitis rotundifolia, is native to the southeastern states, being found wild from Delaware to the Gulf of Mexico and westward to Missouri, Kansas and Texas. In the hot, humid southeastern region it is much better suited for culture than other types because it is usually not troubled seriously by the disease and insects which make difficult the culture of the European and American varieties. The fruit is used for wine, dessert and unfermented juice.

The Muscadine varieties in cultivation may be injured by minimum winter temperature of zero F. and should not be grown in regions where temperatures frequently go below 10 degrees above zero.

Propagation. The Muscadine varieties are commonly propagated by layering, as cuttings root with difficulty. The layering may be done at any time, but is commonly done in midsummer. Canes of the current season's growth are bent down and covered with earth, the tips being left uncovered. By fall the cane will have developed roots, and it is severed from the parent plant.

The Muscadine varieties are all selections of V. rotundifolia as no satisfactory hybrids with other species have been produced. Until recently the varieties were all pistillate-flowered and required staminate vines nearby to provide the pollen. Recently six perfect-flowered varieties resulting from breeding work of the United States Department of Agriculture have been introduced, and these should be planted instead of the staminate vines as they will pollinate the pistillate flowered varieties and produce a crop themselves.

Varieties. The older varieties are all selected wild plants, but in recent years the Georgia Agricultural Experiment Station and the United States Department of Agriculture have introduced a number of varieties, some of which are promising, but they have not yet established themselves as standard varieties.

Scuppernong. This is the oldest, and most widely planted Muscadine variety, having been established in North Carolina before 1760. The berries vary from green to reddish in color, are soft, sweet and of good quality. The clusters bear 2-6 berries. The variety is excellent for wine.

Thomas. This very productive variety is considered the best all-around variety. The berries are dark wine-colored, very sweet and richly flavored. It is the best variety for unfermented juice and preserving.

James. The berries are deep purplish-black, very large, meaty and of medium quality. The vine is very productive.

Mish. The berries are nearly black with tender, juicy flesh and very fine quality. The vine is very productive. It is considered a good wine Grape.

Flowers. The vine is very productive. The berries are purplish-black with meaty, tough flesh, not very juicy and of only fair quality. The variety is good for wine and various culinary purposes such as conserves and catsup.

Varieties from the Georgia Agricultural Experiment Station that appear promising are Hunt, black; Yuga, light bronze; Creek, reddish-purple; Dulcet, reddish-purple; and Lucida, greenish to bronze. Hunt is possibly the best, but all have merit.

The United States Department of Agriculture has introduced 15 varieties from its breeding work at Willard, North Carolina. Six of these, Burgaw, Duplin, Pender, Tarheel, Wallace and Willard are perfect flowered and should be used in place of the staminate varieties to pollinate the pistillate varieties. Others of promise are Morrison, Stanford, Creswell and Topsail.

Soils. The Muscadine Grapes grow well on a wide range of soils but best results are obtained from well-drained sandy loams. They do not do well on low, wet ground or eroded clay hills.

Planting. In the Piedmont region, March is the preferred planting time, but southward earlier planting is preferred. Strong, 1-year-old

[5–6]
Globe Amaranth
(Gomphrena globosa)

[5–6a]
Sunflower
(Helianthus)

[5–6b]
Blood Lily
(Haemanthus Katharinae)

[5–6c]
Ginger Lily
(Hedychium)

[5—7a]
Primulinus Grandiflorus Gladiolus

[5—7]
Large Flowered Gladiolus

[5—7c]
Greenhouse with Succulent Plants

[5—7b]
Greenhouse with Geraniums

vines are best, but 2-year-old vines may be used.

The spacing depends on variety, vigor and type of trellis used. For vines on a vertical trellis the rows should be 10 ft. apart with the vines 15-20 ft. apart in the row. For overhead horizontal trellises the spacing is 15 ft. each way.

Soil Management and Fertilization. Clean cultivation with a cover crop is practiced in commercial vineyards. Cash crops may be grown between the rows in young vineyards or in vineyards with the overhead trellis and after the crop is harvested the cover crop is sown to be turned under when it reaches flowering size. Austrian Winter Peas and Vetch are used.

Home vineyards are often maintained in sod, but yields are not so heavy as with clean cultivation. Heavy nitrogen fertilization and mulching are desirable in the sod vineyard. Sod culture works better with the overhead trellis.

Nitrogenous fertilizers, or complete fertilizers high in nitrogen, are recommended. Nitrate of soda at the rate of $\frac{1}{2}$ pound for a 1-year-old vine, 1 lb. for a 2-year-old vine, and 2 lbs. for a 3-year-old vine is suggested. Other materials to supply the same amount of nitrogen may be used. Phosphorus and potash are not likely to be profitable except as they may be needed for the cover crop. Vine vigor should be the determining factor in deciding the material and amounts to use.

Training and Pruning. Two systems of training are used, the upright or vertical and the overhead, or horizontal system.

In the upright system, a 3-wire trellis is used, the lower wire being 2 ft. from the ground, and the others 2 ft. apart. On the trellis the arms may be horizontal along the wires or fan-shaped from a low trunk. With this system the cane is taken to the top wire the first year or when vigorous enough, and then topped to make it branch. The resulting laterals are trained along the wire to make the arms.

The overhead trellis has the advantage of permitting cross cultivation and easy access for intercropping. It also provides more bearing surface per vine. The vines form a complete canopy about 7 ft. from the ground. The vines are trained to a single trunk 7 ft. tall with the arms radiating from the top of the trunk like the spokes of a wheel. A mature vine has about 8 arms.

The trellis has a substantial post 7 ft. above ground for each vine. Extra-heavy posts are set at the ends of each row on all sides of the vineyard. The wires run from north to south and east to west. After the vine is 2 years old, diagonal wires are run each way. These wires support the 8 arms of the vine.

During the first 3 years the vine with its trunk and arms is established on the trellis. Thereafter pruning consists of cutting back the canes along the arms to 3 or 4 bud spurs. As the arms age, they decline in vigor and must be renewed. This is done by cutting the arm back to the trunk and replacing it with a strong shoot. Only one or two arms a year should be renewed to avoid substantial yield reductions in any one year. Some judgment is necessary in pruning to prevent overbearing with decreased vine growth, or underbearing with excessive vine growth.

Harvesting. The Muscadine Grapes are commonly harvested for the winery by jarring them on to canvas sheets spread under the vines. The debris coming down with the berries is removed by hand-picking or with a fanning mill, after which the berries are put in bushel baskets or lugs to go to the winery. The berries of some varieties drop easily; others cling and must be picked. The jarred berries require prompt handling to prevent spoilage. Fruit for table use and shipping is hand-picked.

The European Grape

The European Grape, Vitis vinifera, is the Grape to most of the world except eastern North America. It is thought to have originated in western Asia in the Transcaucasian region, where its cultivation began several thousands of years ago. (Noah planted a vineyard and drank wine.) Its culture spread westward to France and northern Africa. As the European peoples settled the world, the Grape went with them. The Franciscan fathers introduced it into California during the latter half of the seventeenth century, where it found conditions to its liking. All attempts to grow the European Grape in eastern North America were a failure.

Ninety per cent of the cultivated Grapes of the world are varieties of V. vinifera and 80 per cent of the Grape acreage of the United States is in California, where the industry is based on varieties of this species.

Climatic Requirements. The European Grape requires long, hot, dry summers and cool, but not cold, winters. Rains are desirable in the winter, but not in summer and fall. In California some varieties are restricted to very small areas where the climate is suitable for their best development. The famous wine Grapes of Europe are often limited to very restricted areas where the climate and soil are most suitable for them.

Soil. Grapes grow on a wide range of soils from light sands to clay loams. The intermediate types are to be preferred. The more fertile soils produce heavier crops, but some table and wine varieties are of better quality on the less fertile soils. Good drainage and freedom from excess salts are essential in a good vineyard soil.

European Grape Varieties. The European Grapes may be divided into groups based on their use as follows: table Grapes, wine Grapes, raisin Grapes and canning Grapes. Some varieties have several uses.

Important table Grapes are Flame Tokay, Emperor, Malaga, Red Malaga, Ribier, Muscat of Alexandria, Thompson Seedless and others of lesser importance.

Raisin Grapes are Muscat of Alexandria, Thompson Seedless and Black Corinth.

The principal black wine Grapes for making red wine are Zinfandel, Carignane, Alicante Boushet, Petite Syrah, Mataro, Cabernet, Sauvignon, Grenache, Mission and a few others.

Varieties for white wine are Palomino, Burger, Semillon, Sauvignon Blanc, Johannisberger Riesling, Franken Riesling, and others.

Thompson Seedless is the principal canning Grape.

The best black-fruited varieties are the following:

Black Hamburg. Heavy-yielding, meaty, sweet. The best-known European Grape, it is grown extensively in greenhouses, especially in Europe.

Carignane. A heavy-yielding red wine Grape.

Black Corinth. A productive, small-berried, seedless variety that has long been grown in Greece for making currants. The vines must be girdled to be productive.

Muscat Hamburg. A very high-quality muscat-flavored table Grape of great merit for home use.

Mission. The first variety planted in California by the Jesuit Missionaries. It is grown chiefly for sweet white wines.

Petite Syrah. A medium-sized Grape for making red wine.

Scarlet. A new Grape with bright red juice, this was introduced for making jam and jelly. The foliage turns bright red in the fall.

Zinfandel. A heavy-yielding Grape for red wine. It is the leading wine Grape of California.

Ribier. A large-berried handsome table Grape of only fair quality.

The best red-fruited varieties are the following:

Cardinal. A new, very early attractive high-quality variety that appears to have considerable promise in California and Arizona.

Emperor. A very productive, firm, late-ripening, shipping Grape of only fair quality.

Flame Tokay. A very attractive large-clustered, very firm, fair quality, midseason variety grown for shipping.

Red Malaga. Very large clusters, neutral flavor, tender-skinned, early midseason.

The best white-fruited varieties are the following:

Delight. A new variety of Thompson Seedless type that is superior in flavor and better for canning.

Franken Riesling. The principal Rhine wine type grown in California.

Johannisberger Riesling. The Rhine wines of Germany are made from this variety, which is also grown in California.

Muscat of Alexandria. A very old variety from North Africa that is prized for its rich, muscat flavor that gives it top rank among high-quality Grapes. It is important for raisins and for making muscatel wine. The vine is very productive. The color is unattractive.

Palomino. This is an important sherry Grape in Spain and California.

Pearl of Csaba. A very early-ripening muscat-flavored variety valued chiefly for its quality and earliness.

Perlette. A new, very early seedless variety ripening about two weeks before Thompson Seedless, to which it is superior in size, but inferior in quality.

Sauvignon Blanc. The most important Sauterne wine variety grown in California.

Semillon. One of the great wine Grapes of the world, it is used for the fine Sauternes of France.

Thompson Seedless. In California about one third of the Grape acreage is of this variety, which is the principal raisin Grape of California and the world. It is also the leading table Grape of California, an important white wine variety, and the chief canning Grape. The vine is very vigorous and very productive. The Grapes are of medium size, seedless, firm, very sweet, are borne on large well-filled clusters and ripen early.

Planting Stock. European Grapes are susceptible to serious injury from the Phylloxera, an insect which attacks the roots. The only control measure is to use Phylloxera-resistant rootstocks wherever this insect is present. In some areas the insect is not present and Grapes may be grown on their own roots. Own-root plants are raised from hardwood cuttings.

Plantings made in areas where the Phylloxera is present should be grafted on resistant rootstocks, of which there are many. Among those used in California, Rupestris St. George is highly resistant and extensively used. Aramon x Rupestris No. 1 is less resistant, but vines grafted on it surpass Rupestris St. George in vigor and productivity. It is suitable for deep moist soils. Solonis x Othello 1613 is moderately resistant to Phylloxera and very resistant to the Root Knot Nematode. It is considered the best rootstock for fertile, irrigated sandy loam soils. Dogridge and Salt Creek are very vigorous stocks for soils of low fertility.

Propagation. Hardwood cuttings made while the vines are dormant are commonly used to propagate the European varieties. These are made 14 to 18 in. long, or a little longer if of the Phylloxera-resistant rootstocks. The cuttings are planted as soon as possible in the nursery row to the depth of the second bud from the top and are completely covered with soil. The cuttings are spaced from 2-4 in. apart. The ridges of soil are removed after the cuttings have started to grow. After one year in the nursery the plants are ready for vineyard planting.

Grapes that are to be grown on Phylloxera-resistant rootstocks are propagated by chip budding or by grafting. The cuttings are planted in the spring and budded in August or September. A chip bud is taken with a bit of wood in it and inserted in a notch, then tied. It is covered immediately with moist soil. The bud unites to the stock within a month, but remains dormant until spring when the top of the stock is cut off. A sleeve of paper 9 in. long is placed over the end of the stock and bud to protect the scion shoots and to force them to grow upright to facilitate training. As soon as the shoot grows out of the sleeve it is tied to the stake. All suckers from the root and roots from the scion should be removed promptly.

The stocks of buds that do not take or that make a weak union are whipgrafted or cleftgrafted in the spring so that the stock will not be lost.

Planting. The roots are cut back to 3-4 in. before planting and are planted at the same depth as they grew in the nursery. With grafted vines the union should be 4-5 in. above the soil to prevent scion rooting. Planting distances vary according to the soil and the vigor of the variety, ranging from 7 by 7 to 8 by 12 ft. Power tools require considerable room.

Cultivation. Cultivation is for weed control only and should be shallow and just often enough to eliminate weed growth. When the soil becomes too dry for weed seed germination cultivation is discontinued.

Winter cover crops are used to prevent erosion. They may be native vegetation or sown crops. A mixture of Oats or Barley and Purple Vetch is commonly used, and it is drilled in a strip between the rows.

Fertilizers. Nitrogen is the only element to which the Grapes may be expected to respond profitably and it should be tried at rates of 40-80 pounds to the acre. Manure is also excellent if available at a low price.

Irrigation. Irrigation is desirable and often essential as the European Grapes are grown mostly where the summers are long, hot and dry, and the moisture from winter rainfall is insufficient to produce maximum crops. Several irrigations are necessary, the first being applied when most of the available water in the soil has been used by the vine in the spring. In very hot regions an irrigation may be necessary after harvest.

Training. The European Grapes are trained in two general forms, headed and cordon vines. The head-pruned vine has a trunk, 1-3 ft. high, which is fastened to a stake. At the top of the trunk is a ring of arms on which are spurs to produce the shoots that will bear the crop. Head training is used for wine and raisin Grapes and some table varieties.

The cordon-pruned vine is supported by a trellis of two wires, the bottom one 34 in. from the ground and the top wire 48 in. above the ground. A short trunk extends nearly up to the bottom wire where it divides into two branches which extend along the wire in opposite directions. Spurs arise from upright arms at regular intervals on the horizontal trunk. Cordon pruning is used for the Malaga, Red Malaga, Ribier and Emperor varieties.

Pruning. With the head-pruned vine all but 3-6 of the strongest canes are removed. These are cut back to 2, 3 or 4 buds, depending on cane vigor. As the vine grows older more spurs are retained until an old vine may have from 10-20 spurs. These are distributed uniformly around the trunk at one height. If the vine overbears, fewer spurs should be left; if overvigorous, more spurs should be left.

With the cordon-trained vines the fruiting spurs are spaced 8-12 in. apart along the arm of the cordon. The spurs are cut to 2 or 3 buds depending on the vigor of the canes. The shoots which grow from these spurs are tied to the upper wire during the summer. During the summer, suckers arising on the trunk should be removed as they appear.

Thinning. Thinning of table Grapes is practiced. Flower-cluster thinning is used on table Grapes that produce loose clusters, or with varieties that produce many small berries. This is done as soon as possible after the flower clusters appear. Cluster thinning is done soon after the fruit is set and it gets rid of small and poorly set clusters as well as reducing the load on vines that have set too-heavy a crop.

Berry thinning is removal of part of the cluster by cutting off the end and some of the branches. It is done when the clusters are too compact and it promotes good color and quality. It is done soon after the berries set.

Girdling. Girdling, or ringing, is the removal of a ring of bark $3/16$ in. wide from the trunk or an arm or a cane. It causes the carbohydrates elaborated in the leaves to accumulate in the

A Grape vine trained as a double horizontal cordon against a fence.

Immediately after pruning—a Grape vine trained as a double horizontal cordon against a fence.

fruit, thus increasing berry size, color and quality. If done while the vine is in bloom, girdling increases berry set.

The Black Corinth variety, a seedless Grape, is always girdled; otherwise the clusters are small and straggly with very small seedless berries. The Thompson Seedless variety is girdled a week or two after bloom to greatly increase berry size. Girdling of some table Grapes is sometimes practiced to improve color and hasten ripening. It is done just as the fruit begins to color and works best on vigorous vines with a light crop.

The girdle is made with double-bladed tools designed for the purpose. The ring of bark only is removed and the wood should not be injured. The girdle is bridged across with new growth during the growing season or the vine would die from starvation of the roots.

Irrigation should be increased while the wounds are open and girdled vines should not be allowed to bear more than two thirds of the crop that they could bear if they had not been girdled.

Harvesting. Grapes for market should not be picked until fully ripe. Standards of maturity have been set up. The sugar is determined by the hydrometer and the acid by titration. The pickers must exercise judgment when picking and determine maturity by the color and condition of the stem, the flavor and color of the berries. The Grapes ripen unevenly and must be gone over two or more times to get most of the crop harvested at the proper stage of maturity.

GRAPEFRUIT. See Citrus.
GRAPE HYACINTH. See Muscari.
GRAPE, OREGON. See Mahonia nervosa.
GRAPE, TAIL. See Artabotrys.
GRASS. See Lawns.
GRASS, BEACH. Ammophila, which see.
GRASS, BENT. Agrostis, which see.
GRASS, BERMUDA. See Cynodon, and Lawns.
GRASS, BLUE. Poa, which see.
GRASS, BLUE-EYED. See Sisyrinchium.
GRASS, BOTTLE BRUSH. See Hystrix patula.
GRASS, CARPET. See Axonopus compressus.
GRASS, CENTIPEDE. See Eremochloa ophiuroides.

GRASS, CITRONELLA. See Cymbopogon Nardus.
GRASS, CLOUD. See Agrostis nebulosa.
GRASS, COTTON. Eriophorum, which see.
GRASS, EEL. Vallisneria, which see.
GRASSES, LAWN. See Lawn.
GRASSES, ORNAMENTAL. Many of these are useful to cut and dry for winter decoration indoors. The chief kinds are: Agrostis, Briza, Bromus, Cortaderia, Eragrostis, Festuca, Hordeum, Lagurus, Lamarckia, Pennisetum, Stipa, and Tricholaena. Reference should be made to each of these particular headings for details of cultivation.
GRASS, FEATHER. See Stipa and Eragrostis.
GRASS, FOUNTAIN. See Pennisetum Ruppelii.
GRASS, HARE'S-TAIL. See Lagurus.
GRASS, HOLY. See Hierochloë.
GRASSHOPPER. See Pests and Diseases.
GRASS, KOREAN. See Zoysia japonica.
GRASS, KOREAN VELVET. Zoysia tenuifolia, which see.
GRASS, LEMON. See Cymbopogon citratus.
GRASS, MANILA. See Zoysia Matrella.
GRASS, MEADOW. Poa, which see.
GRASS-OF-PARNASSUS. See Parnassia.
GRASS, PAMPAS. Cortaderia, which see.
GRASS, RIBBON. See Phalaris arundinacea var. picta.
GRASS, RYE. Lolium, which see.
GRASS, ST. AUGUSTINE. See Stenotaphrum secundatum.
GRASS, SILK. See Agrostis hiemalis.
GRASS, SQUIRRELTAIL. See Hordeum jubatum.
GRASS, STAR. Aletris and Hypoxis, which see.
GRASS, SWEET VERNAL. See Anthoxanthum odoratum.
GRASS, VELVET. See Holcus lanatus.
GRASS, WHITLOW. See Draba verna.
GRASS, ZEBRA. See Miscanthus sinensis variety zebrinus.
GRAY MOLD. See Pests and Diseases.
GREAT LAUREL. See Rhododendron maximum.
GRECIAN FIR. Abies cephalonica, which see
GREENBRIAR. Smilax, which see.

GREENHOUSES FOR AMATEURS
Full Details of Types and How to Manage Them

A greenhouse may be defined as a structure, chiefly of glass, in which plants may be raised and grown with protection from adverse weather conditions. It provides the gardener with an environment in which he can control many factors of plant growth—light, warmth, moisture, ventilation and soil—more precisely, thus enabling him to rear plants in advance of, or out of their normal season, or without regard to their native clime.

A small or moderate-sized greenhouse may easily double the amateur gardener's pleasures and production. It makes 12 months of growing possible instead of, in the North, the usual 5 or 6. From it may be had fresh flowers and perhaps some vegetables all winter long, potted plants to embellish the home, husky seedlings to start the outdoor spring garden, and rooted cuttings of decorative shrubbery to grow to mature size for later planting outdoors. The possibilities for fun, plants and flowers that a greenhouse of modest size offers are endless.

For as little as the cost of a low-priced car, most excellent small prefabricated home green-

A cool greenhouse at Chrysanthemum time.

In an intermediate-temperature greenhouse a wide variety of plants can be grown. This amateur's greenhouse is well stocked with flowering and foliage pot plants, including Campanula isophylla *(in front)*, Begonia metallica, Canna, Maidenhair Fern and Coleus.

houses may be purchased; and their upkeep and operational costs are correspondingly modest.

Larger greenhouses of the conventional construction favored by commercial greenhouse men are more expensive than prefabricated types and are of sturdier construction, but the best prefabricated types (which may be erected by the amateur without highly skilled labor) are most satisfactory.

To meet special requirements it is sometimes desirable to have a custom-built greenhouse designed and erected if it must fit some special spot and blend in harmony with surrounding buildings.

Whether the greenhouse be prefabricated and erected without highly skilled help, of conventional construction and erected by skilled greenhouse builders or specially designed and custom-built by craftsmen, it is essential that design, materials and construction be good. To ensure this it is important to deal with a reliable firm that specializes in the manufacture and erection of greenhouses. Home-manufactured greenhouses and those built by mechanics unfamiliar with the special needs of greenhouse construction are very likely to be unsatisfactory and disappointing.

Modern building methods and materials make possible the finest greenhouses in the history of gardening. These materials include time-tested California redwood that lasts for years and years without repair; aluminum, alloyed for greatest strength and resistance to corrosion; and stainless steel. Modern greenhouses, either of good redwood or metal, last well without painting. There is nothing to wear out. By choosing a greenhouse manufactured by a company with a dependable reputation good value and a safe investment are assured.

When selecting a greenhouse it is advisable not only to check thoroughly the materials of which the superstructure is made, but to be sure that the fastenings—bolts, screws, nuts, and fittings—are rust-proof or at least rust-resistant. A greenhouse is no stronger than its fastenings. Black steel, cadmium plating and electroplating soon rust. Hot galvanized steel or, better yet, stainless steel or aluminum, last a lifetime and longer. Copper becomes brittle and snaps. Zinc oxidizes over the years.

There are numerous styles of standard greenhouses which may be had in a wide variety of sizes in both prefabricated and conventional construction. The small home gardener who wants a practical structure he can put up himself, does well to choose one of the prefabricated types that go together in sections. These may be obtained made of wood or aluminum construction and are fitted together with bolts and screws.

To grow many kinds of plants well a greenhouse must be light, airy, well ventilated, tight and free from condensation drip. It must be light to admit a maximum of sunshine, especially in winter when the arc of the sun is low. Wide panes of glass with slender structural members are a big advantage.

Of course, there are other important functions necessary to make a greenhouse right. It must carry off all water condensation that forms on the glass when it is warm inside and cold outside. Unless proper provisions are made, the water that forms will drip on the plants, cause disease and soon kill them. Reliable manufacturers design a series of small drip gutters in the bars and use a system of continuous curves along which the water flows to the ground.

A tight greenhouse structure is easily attained with modern greenhouse glazing. There are several methods by which it is assured. In greenhouses of prefabricated wood construction, the glass slides into deep glazing grooves and is held weathertight with a special caulking rope. In aluminum greenhouses, the glass is set in tough extruded rubber channels and protected on the outside with aluminum barcaps. The best method for conventional greenhouses is to bed the glass in special glazing compound and seal it with aluminum barcaps. With all these methods, the glass is held tightly once and for all. There are no leaks, the glass can't slip and the aluminum never needs paint.

Size of Greenhouse. The kind and number of plants to be grown, the size of the garden it is to serve as a propagating station, cost, and personal ambitions, will influence the size of the individual greenhouse. It is obvious that the larger the house, the cheaper it is per cubic foot capacity. As a large house can always be managed more easily than a small one, and gives the best results, it is always wise to build as big as reasonable limits will allow. Small greenhouses fluctuate in temperature, humidity and aeration more quickly than large ones during weather changes. A house 12 ft. by 8 ft. is probably the minimum worth considering.

Lean-to vs. Span-roofed Greenhouses. A span-roofed greenhouse has a roof like a tent and receives light from both sides. A lean-to greenhouse is half of a span-roofed greenhouse with one side connected to another building. Since light enters only from one side of the lean-to, the plants tend to reach out and bend toward the sunshine. The structure is also more difficult to heat evenly because the wall absorbs and holds the sun's heat and tends to become too warm.

The span-roofed greenhouse can be built free-standing out in the garden or joined at one of its ends or by a connecting corridor to an existing building. There is an advantage in having the greenhouse connected to your home. You

A span-roof greenhouse can be attached at one end to a house.

can enter it day or night, without bundling up to go out of doors. With such conveniences, you are sure to do more gardening. The connected greenhouse is also easier to heat, as described later.

Where to Build It. The greenhouse should be built where it gets a maximum amount of sunshine, especially morning sun. If connected to another building, an eastern or southeastern exposure is best. Maximum exposure to light, at least in winter, is essential to nearly all flowering plants. Lack of light is one of the limiting factors to plant growth during the fall and winter months when there is a large proportion of dull cloudy days. Only a few plants succeed in winter without direct sunlight. These include African Violets, and other Gesneriads, Orchids and Ferns, with which good results can be had from a greenhouse with a westerly or even northerly exposure.

Foundation. Walls of masonry with footings extending below frost are always advisable. The depth is usually 2½ ft. in climates like those of New York City and Chicago. It may be 3-4 ft. further north and less in the South. Without a firm foundation, a greenhouse may heave with the freezing and thawing of the ground.

Greenhouses attached to other buildings should always have a firm masonry footing or they will pull away from the building to which they are attached. Above grade, walls may be of concrete block, brick, poured concrete, wood or shingle siding, etc., to match the main house.

Erecting the Greenhouse. Home greenhouses of prefabricated types are produced in sections

A small lean-to greenhouse affords opportunity to grow a wide variety of plants.

at the factory so that any handy man can do the building. It is just a question of following printed and illustrated instructions. In a well-prefabricated greenhouse, there are no parts to cut and fit, no glass to cut, no putty glazing. It is just a matter of assembly.

Types of conventional design are framed and cut for assembly at the factory but do require some skill in carpentry to put up. It is advisable to find out how much work must be done before deciding upon a definite type.

Different Designs. Greenhouses with curved eaves are extremely attractive. The graceful lines blend well with almost any style of architecture.

Straight-sided colonial styles are preferred by many and harmonize well with the angular lines of modern architecture.

The English style of greenhouse with slanted sides has both structural and functional advantages. The slanted sides capture the direct rays of the sunshine. Plants grow well in them and there is structural strength in this self-supporting shape. On the other hand, sides that slant at too sharp an angle interfere with the growth of tall plants close to the side glass. A happy medium between the two is, undoubtedly, best. All types—curved-eave, straight-eave, and slant-sided—are made in span-roofed and lean-to styles.

Ventilation. Ample-size roof-ventilating sash is a necessity for healthy plant growth. Sash on both sides of the roof is always prefabricated. Side ventilation is also needed on wider greenhouses and desirable on smaller houses in the summer. Greenhouses designed with ventilators that are too small give disappointing results.

Automatic ventilators are almost a must for the home greenhouse gardener. Motor-driven units that open and close the roof sash by thermostatic control are available. When the sun comes out and heats the greenhouse, the ventilating sash opens. If it becomes cloudy and cooler the sash closes. Automatically, fresh air is admitted as required. See Ventilation.

Benches (tables on which potted plants are stood or which contain soil in which plants are planted) should be fitted at a height of about 2 ft. 9 in. For pot plants, they may be of slatted wood or metal shelves, or of asbestos sheeting, slate or tiles covered with 3 in. or so of fine gravel, broken shell, limestone chippings or screened cinders. To grow plants in soil in benches, a solid stage of corrugated iron, slate, tile, rot-resistant wood or sheet asbestos is needed. A small portable potting bench, consisting of a tray 3 ft. by 6 ft. with back and sides 12 in. high, is very handy for use in small greenhouses.

Deep greenhouse benches like this one need not be used just for potted plants. The benches may be filled with soil and the plants set directly in them.

Wooden lath shades that may be rolled up and down are used to protect plants from excessive sun.

Shades are valuable both for minimizing damage to plants which cannot stand direct strong sun and as insulation against night cold in winter. Permanent shades of wood laths roll up to the ridge, and are the best type. They are not usually fitted to greenhouses unless Orchids, Ferns, Begonias, tropical foliage plants or other kinds that need considerable shade are being grown. Even then it is not unusual to omit installing permanent shades and to use instead a coat of whiting and gasoline or some similar mixture on the outside of the glass.

Heating

There are several ways to heat a greenhouse. The one you select should be as automatic and trouble-free as possible. Location, cost, and availability of fuel as well as cost of the installation are influencing factors.

The most convenient and least expensive method to use, when possible, for the small home greenhouse is to heat it from the same system that furnishes heat to the house or some other building. This can usually be done, no matter whether the system is hot water, steam, or hot air. When extending a steam or hot-air system, the radiation in the greenhouse is usually best accomplished by means of fin tubes or pipe coils. Fin tubes (pipes fitted with metal fins set closely together along their lengths) are excellent since one line has radiation equal to 5 lines of pipe coils. Hot water is drawn off the boiler and circulated by means of a circulator or pump. The circulator is controlled by a thermostat in the greenhouse. In the case of a steam boiler, the water is drawn from below the water line in the boiler. Such systems are practical when the greenhouse is located within 35 ft. of the boiler.

If the house is heated by hot air, a duct having a built-in fan may be run into the greenhouse. The fan is controlled by a thermostat in the greenhouse.

Most usually a separate cast-iron hot-water boiler with gun type of oil burner or natural gas burner and connected with a fin type of radiation system in the greenhouse, is by far the most satisfactory means of greenhouse heating.

Less expensive are pot type of oil burners such as the Duo-Therm, Sears Roebuck, Coleman and Perfex. In deciding on such a heater, it is well to be sure that you can get oil, kerosene, or No. 2 fuel oil, that is refined by the "distilled process." Oil that has been cracked by the catalytic process soots up the burner with the result that the pilot light goes out. Many greenhouses are heated most satisfactorily by such heaters when the proper oil is available, but if proper oil is not used serious trouble may result. It is well to check with your oil supplier before deciding upon a pot type oil heater.

Natural gas heaters are excellent where this fuel is available, but you should check to make sure that artificial or mixed gas will never come into the line. Artificial gas is sure death to plant life. Most gas companies know this and would not run an artificial gas line anywhere near a greenhouse. Always be sure to use a vented natural gas heater where you are growing tender flowering plants. This is the type of heater that draws the air for combustion from outside the greenhouse and expels the products of combustion outside.

Bottled gas can be used instead of natural gas with any of the gas heaters. It is inexpensive in most localities, and the service company will supply the tank and run the gas line to the heater for a reasonable charge. When purchasing the heater, however, be sure to tell the manufacturer which kind of gas will be used, bottled or natural gas.

Electric space heaters provide the most efficient kind of heat for a greenhouse. Nothing is wasted, but they are only practical where electric rates are low, say 1½ to 2¢ a kilowatt. These heaters are thermostatically controlled; in an experiment in a greenhouse near New York City it was found that temperatures that did not vary ½ degree could be maintained without difficulty. The cost to heat a 13- by 18-ft. greenhouse in Tarrytown, New York, to 45-50 degrees night temperature was about $150 through a cold winter in 1954-55. The heaters should be of 2- or 4-kilowatt capacity and be connected by a line directly to the meter.

Coal-burning stoves can also be used to heat greenhouses. They require more attention than other heaters and great care must be taken that coal gas does not enter the greenhouse. Many farmers use coal stoves but they have adequate flues and know how to handle the fire. If they are mismanaged they are likely to be unsatisfactory.

Potting Shed or Workroom. A special workroom or building attached to a greenhouse is most useful. In it potting, seed sowing, soil mixing and many other operations connected with the culture of the plants can be done and tools, soils, pots, flats, stakes, sprays and other supplies can be stored.

A potting shed should be furnished with a sturdy bench for potting, bins in which soil, leaf mold, peat moss, sand, etc., can be kept, a closet (preferably one that can be locked) in which to keep insecticides, fungicides and similar materials and a rack designed to accommodate flowerpots and flats in such a way that they will not be broken and are stored separately according to their sizes.

Provision should also be made in the potting shed for the orderly keeping of stakes, tools and other items needed for the operation of the greenhouse. Adequate lighting (the fluorescent kind is good) should be provided over the potting bench so that work may be done without strain in dull weather and, if necessary, at night. A sink with running water (if possible both cold and hot) is needed for washing pots and other purposes.

Greenhouse Management

The art of maintaining conditions of growth at their best in a greenhouse calls for good judgment of weather conditions and their effects.

Temperature Control. Plants can tolerate fairly wide fluctuations of temperature without harm, but the gardener should be aware of the limits for the species being grown. A good maximum and minimum thermometer should be used to record the highest and lowest temperatures between readings in a given interval of time as a guide to control.

The brighter the light, the higher the temperature can be with advantage rather than harm to the plants. At night, plants require temperatures of 10 degrees or so less than the highest temperature (taken in the shade without the sun shining on the thermometer) of the day. Older plants resist both unduly low and high temperatures better than young ones. Seeds usually need higher temperatures when germinating, than do the seedlings. Although generally preoccupied with maintaining temperatures high enough, the gardener must not forget that too-high temperatures can also be damaging.

Ventilation. The objects are to prevent temperatures rising too high, to introduce fresh air, to dry and circulate the air. There are no hard and fast rules, but normally it is sound practice to open ventilators progressively on days of increasing warmth in the mornings, closing down in the afternoons or early evenings ahead of serious temperature falls. Top ventilators are opened first, and then the side ones, if necessary. It must be done without causing drafts and as gradually as possible. On windy days, ventilators are opened carefully on the lee side. Automatic ventilators, motor-driven and thermostatically controlled, eliminate the need for constant attention, especially during the changeable spring weather, which is needed when ventilators are hand-operated.

Watering. Plants vary according to their kind, age, condition, vigor, and season, in their water requirements. The more active the growth, the more water is needed, so that more watering must be done on sunny, warm days than on cool, dull ones. As plants mature, less water is needed, and when they are dormant, little or none is required. Seed and potting soils and benches, beds and borders should be well soaked after planting is completed. Thereafter, the aim should be to allow the soil to approach a condition of dryness and then to thoroughly soak it again. This soak-and-let-dry principle is to be preferred to more frequent, superficial sprinklings and to repeated soakings given while the soil is yet sufficiently wet.

Plants in pots, tubs and benches need more frequent watering than those in borders and ground beds. In warm weather heavy watering should be done in the late afternoon or early evening, supplemented with morning watering if needed, in cold weather, give water in the

In the greenhouse, watering needs regular attention.

mornings when temperatures are rising. The aim must be to have the foliage dry by nightfall. The water should be applied in the form of a spray with watering can or hose.

Damping Down. This is needed in heated greenhouses to keep the atmosphere humid. It is done by wetting the paths, walls, benches and beneath the benches. More damping down is needed on bright days than on dull days; when the greenhouse ventilators are open than when they are closed; when temperatures are high than when they are low; and for tropical plants that need high humidity than for kinds like Carnations and Cacti that prefer a drier atmosphere. On bright, warm days the plants themselves can be syringed lightly with clear water to prevent wilting. Damping down and syringing should be completed early enough in the day to ensure the plant foliage being dry by nightfall.

Shading. This reduces light and heat, and is often very useful in summer and for plants liking cool, shady conditions. Movable shades, of lath, are most satisfactory since they can be raised or lowered at will.

Hygiene. Cleanliness is of the utmost importance in greenhouses. If this is not maintained, diseases and pests soon take serious toll of the plants. Paths and floors, particularly under benches, should be kept free of weeds and debris. If dead leaves, old pots, flats, stakes and suchlike materials are allowed to accumulate they are likely to serve as breeding grounds for organisms that cause diseases and for insects and other pests.

Once a year all glass, woodwork and other washable surfaces should be scrubbed clean with strong soap and hot water and all wall surfaces should be painted or whitewashed. Every second or third year interior surfaces should be painted.

Cleanliness in the greenhouse is important. At periodic intervals all woodwork, glass and other surfaces should be cleaned.

A keen lookout must be maintained at all times for the first signs of pests and diseases and when they are noticed measures must be taken to eradicate them. The competent greenhouse gardener never allows a pest or disease to become really established; he either takes effective control measures promptly or, if these are not feasible, he discards the plants that are affected.

One common cause of uncleanliness in greenhouses is overcrowding. Where this occurs it is more important than ever to maintain hygienic conditions because crowded plants get insufficient light and are likely to be somewhat weak and more susceptible than ever to pests and diseases.

Plants for the Greenhouse

When selecting plants to be grown in a greenhouse, it is obviously important to choose kinds that thrive under similar conditions. Some greenhouses are devoted to the cultivation of one kind of plant only, Carnations, Roses or Cattleya Orchids for example; in others a succession of plants is grown, such as Chrysanthemums followed by Easter Lilies and these in turn by young annuals to be planted later outdoors. Either of these plans makes it easy to regulate conditions to suit the plants that occupy the greenhouse at any particular time.

Most often the amateur wants a mixed house. He wishes to grow a variety of kinds of plants, at the same time, under essentially the same conditions, in one greenhouse. This can be done with real success provided care is taken in making the selection.

The choice of plants to grow should be based chiefly on the temperatures that are to be maintained. And when considering temperatures in this regard the greenhouse operator refers to the night temperatures that are kept during the fall-to-spring season when artificial heating is usually required. Summer night temperatures normally will be above these. Daytime temperatures, on dull days, are permitted to rise 5-10 degrees above the night temperatures, 10-15 degrees higher on sunny days.

When a gardener speaks of a "50-degree house" or a "60-degree house" he means a greenhouse in which the night temperatures, except when outside temperatures are higher, are maintained at the levels indicated.

The Cool Greenhouse (night temperature 45-50 degrees). This greenhouse affords opportunity to grow a wide selection of plants. It is ventilated more freely than warmer ones and the atmosphere should never be so moist that it is oppressively humid. In winter special care must be exercised not to overwater and not to damp down too much; more damping and watering are required from spring to fall.

In a cool greenhouse may be grown for winter and spring display many garden annuals such as Asters, Calendulas, Forget-me-nots, Pansies, Stocks, Nemesias, Clarkias, Godetias, Gypsophila, Sweet Peas, Annual Chrysanthemums, Snapdragons, Salpiglossis, Leptosynes and Larkspurs. Nicotianas, Carnations, Chrysanthemums, Piquerias (Stevias) as well as Primulas, Cinerarias, Cyclamens, Calceolarias, Schizanthus and the winter-flowering Buddleias asiatica and Farquhari.

Shrubby plants such as Cytisus, Azaleas, Camellias, Acacias, Fuchsias, Plumbago capensis, Pelargoniums (including Geraniums), Raphiolepis, Oleanders, Myrtus, and Daphne odora and Gardenia florida prosper under these conditions.

A great variety of bulbs thrive in a cool greenhouse. Notable are Freesias, Eucomis, Babianas, Nerines, Ixias, Sparaxis, Tulbaghias, Ranunculus, Ornithogalums, Anemones, Lachenalias and Calla Lilies. Hardy bulbs such as Narcissi, Tulips, Hyacinths, Crocuses, Grape Hyacinths and Scillas can be bloomed in spring and so, too, can a number of hardy perennials including Lilies-of-the-valley, Bleeding Hearts, Astilbes and Polyanthus Primroses.

Among foliage plants suitable for the cool greenhouse are English Ivies, Fatshederas, and Eucalyptus globulus.

The cool greenhouse is also very useful for raising young plants of annual flowers and vegetables for later transplanting to the outdoor garden.

The Intermediate or Warm-Temperate Greenhouse (night temperature 55 degrees). This greenhouse should always be comfortably warm and the air fairly moist, but never oppressively so. In summer it is ventilated freely and shaded. In winter and spring it is ventilated less freely than a cool greenhouse.

Here may be grown such plants as Achimenes, Begonias, Gloxinias, African Violets, Impatiens, Clerodendrums, Boston Ferns, Eupatoriums, Bouvardias, Streptosolens, Gloriosas, Abutilons, Haemanthus, Hoyas, Jacobinias, Pentas, Rivinas, Strelitzias, Vallotas, Hippeastrums, Asparagus Ferns, Calla Lilies, Clivias, Manettias, Browallias, Passion Flowers, Coleus as well as Cacti and many other succulents.

The intermediate greenhouse is also very useful as a place to start seeds and in which to grow, during their young stages, many annuals and some vegetables, such as Tomatoes in preparation for later planting outdoors. In it, too, may be forced into bloom early hardy bulbs such as Narcissi, Tulips and Hyacinths.

The Tropical Greenhouse or Hothouse (night temperature 60-70 degrees). The atmosphere in this greenhouse should be kept humid by frequently damping down the paths and other surfaces and by syringing all plants that will stand this treatment whenever the weather is sunny and the foliage will dry before nightfall. In the depth of winter rather less watering and syringing are required than at other times but at no season must very dry conditions prevail. Less ventilating will be required than within cooler greenhouses but more shading. Most plants grown in a tropical greenhouse require more or less shade from mid-February to early November.

Plants suitable for growing under these conditions include many foliage plants such as Dieffenbachias, Codiaeums, Acalyphas, Dracaenas, Fittonias, Marantas, Calatheas, Pandanus, Maidenhair Ferns, Pileas, Caladiums, Palms, Philodendrons, and Cissus discolor. Other plants that may be expected to thrive under these conditions are Anthuriums, Eucharis, Episcias, Columneas, Bromeliads, Brunsfelsias, Bougainvilleas, Ardisias, Allamandas, Thunbergias, Passion Flowers, Ixoras and Hymenocallis. The tropical greenhouse provides excellent propagating facilities for a wide variety of tender plants.

GREEN MANURE. See Fertilizers including Manures.

GREENOVIA (Greeno'via). Tender succulent plants closely related to Sempervivum and Aichryson. They belong in the Crassula family, Crassulaceae, and were named in honor of a geologist, George Ballas Greenough. They are natives of the Canary Islands and are suitable for growing outdoors in California and in similar mild climates and for cultivating in greenhouses and window gardens.

The kinds most likely to be grown are G. diplocycla, which has 10-in.-wide rosettes and attains a height of 8 in.; and G. dodrentalis, which grows slightly taller but has much smaller rosettes, and which makes offsets freely, which G. diplocycla does not do. Cultivation and propagation are the same as for Aichryson and Sempervivum, which see.

GREEN ROSE. See Rosa chinensis var. viridiflora.

GREENWOOD. A term applied to shoots and branches, particularly those used for propagating. It means shoots, normally furnished with leaves and of the current season's growth, that have not yet hardened and become woody. Greenwood is used in contrast to hardwood. Greenwood does not consist of firm, woody tissues but of softer and sappier growth, the outer bark of which is usually, but not necessarily, green in color.

GREVILLEA — *Silk Oak* (Grevil'lea). Flowering and ornamental foliage shrubs and trees from Australia, which belong to the family Proteaceae. They are cultivated outdoors in California and similar climates, G. robusta being much used as a street tree. They thrive in ordinary soil in sun.

Most of them have small, narrow tomentose (woolly-coated) leaves. G. robusta, which has finely divided, fernlike foliage, does not flower

Grevillea Thelemanniana.

in a small state, being chiefly grown as a foliage plant, but other kinds, especially G. Thelemanniana and G. rosmarinifolia, produce flowers when grown in small pots. The flowers are in clusters on the ends of the branches, and are tubular, about ½ in. in length and red, pink, or yellow. The name Grevillea commemorates Charles Greville, a founder of the Royal Horticultural Society of England.

Greenhouse Flowering Plants. Those grown in a greenhouse for the sake of their flowers require a minimum temperature of 45 degrees, and the best potting compost consists of equal parts of turfy loam, peat, and sand. They are repotted in March, when a little of the old soil is removed, and are set in slightly larger pots. Large plants may be grown in tubs or planted out in a prepared bed of soil in the greenhouse. Pruning consists of slightly shortening the shoots after flowering. They require full sunlight and free ventilation. From October till April they are watered moderately and during the summer the soil is kept always moist.

Propagation is by inserting young shoots with a "heel" of old wood attached in sandy peat in summer. The pots of cuttings are placed under a bell jar in the greenhouse until roots are formed, when the young plants are potted separately in 3-in. pots.

A House Plant. Grevillea robusta is most serviceable as a house plant when from 12-24 in. in height. It is raised from seeds sown in a pot of sandy soil in spring in a propagating case in the greenhouse. The seedlings are potted separately in small pots and, later on, in 5-in. pots; when well rooted in these they are used for decorating the greenhouse or house, or they may be used in summer flower beds.

The chief kinds for the greenhouse are G. alpina, 4 ft., red and yellow, May; G. Thelemanniana, 5 ft., yellow, green and red, spring; G. Banksii, 20 ft., red, June; G. robusta, fernlike foliage, does not flower in a small state.

Other kinds are G. rosmarinifolia, 7 ft., rose-red, May; and G. juniperina, 6 ft., yellow, May.

GREWIA (Grew'ia). Mostly tender trees and shrubs that are natives of the warmer regions of the Old World. One, G. biloba, is hardy into southern New England. Grewia is named after Nehemiah Grew, a botanist interested in the anatomy of plants; it belongs to the Linden family, Tiliaceae.

Grewia thrives in any reasonably good soil and is propagated by seeds and cuttings. G. biloba is a shrub about 8 ft. tall that has pale yellow flowers and orange or red-colored fruits. Its variety, parviflora, differs in that its stems and leaves are hairy. G. caffra, a small tree or shrub from South Africa and G. occidentalis, a shrub from the same region, are planted in California; both have purple flowers. G. biloba and its variety parviflora are natives of China and Korea.

GRIFFINIA—*Blue Amaryllis* (Griffin'ia). Tender bulb plants from Brazil with ornamental flowers, which belong to the Amaryllis family, Amaryllidaceae. The bulbs produce leaves about 9 in. in length and 3 in. wide, which are rounded at the base and the leafstalk is channelled; the clusters of blue flowers about 2 in. in diameter are on stout stalks 2 ft. in height. The name Griffinia was given in honor of W. Griffin, who introduced these bulbs from Brazil. G. hyacinthina is also known as Hippeastrum procerum.

These plants require a winter temperature of 55 degrees and the best potting compost consists

The Blue Amaryllis, Griffinia hyacinthina.

of two parts stone chips, one part soil, a small quantity of well-decayed manure, and a free sprinkling of sand. Repotting is done in midsummer, but it is not necessary more than once in every 3 or 4 years as the plants flower best when pot-bound. They are kept growing vigorously by top-dressing them annually in March. Water is applied freely to the soil during the summer, but very little is required from October until April, sufficient only being given to keep the bulbs from shriveling.

Propagation is by offsets removed at potting time or seeds may be sown in pans of sandy soil in March.

The chief kinds are Griffinia hyacinthina, 15 in., blue, July, and G. ornata, 12 in., lilac, March.

GRINDELIA—*California Gum Plant* (Grinde'lia). Biennials and perennials, natives of North America, which belong to the Daisy family, Compositae. They are rather coarse-growing plants, about 3 ft. in height, with large, saw-edged, lance-shaped sessile leaves, and bear bell-shaped,

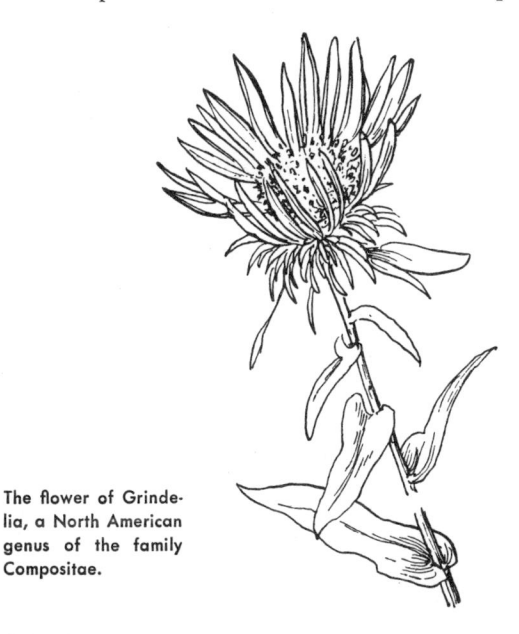

The flower of Grindelia, a North American genus of the family Compositae.

daisy-like yellow flowers, about 2 in. in diameter. The name Grindelia commemorates David H. Grindel, a German botanist.

For a Sunny Border. Seeds are sown each year to produce flowering plants the following season. They succeed in any ordinary soil, in full sun, and should be planted about 2 ft. apart.

The chief kinds are G. squarrosa, 2-3 ft., yellow, August, and G. hirsutula, 18 in., yellow, August.

GRISELINIA (Griseli'nia). Two evergreen shrubs, G. littoralis and G. lucida, natives of New Zealand, and remarkable for their handsome, glossy green leaves are suitable for gardens in California and similar mild climates. They thrive in ordinary, well-drained loamy soil.

Both are easily increased by cuttings in July; these are set in a frame kept close. G. littoralis is the hardier. In order to produce fertile seeds it is necessary to have both male and female plants, for the inconspicuous flowers of different bushes are unisexual.

Griselinia belongs to the Dogwood family, Cornaceae, and the name commemorates an eighteenth-century Italian botanist, Franc Griselini.

G. littoralis may form a large, shapely bush or a small tree, 15-25 ft. high, with a wide spread: the glossy yellowish-green leaves are about 3 in. long and 2 in. wide. It is an excellent evergreen for seaside gardens and forms a good hedge.

G. lucida has much larger and darker colored leaves, about 7 in. long and $3\frac{1}{2}$ in. wide; the variety macrophylla has even larger leaves.

GROMWELL. See Lithospermum.

GROUND CEDAR. Lycopodium complanatum. See Lycopodium.

GROUND CHERRY. Physalis, which see.

GROUND COVER. A designation used by gardeners for low plants that are useful for

Planted in broad sweeps, Euonymus Fortunei coloratus is an effective ground cover for shaded places.

The Japanese Spurge, Pachysandra terminalis, is a popular ground cover.

covering considerable areas of ground and that persist and create pleasing carpeting effects without requiring much maintenance. Wisely used, ground covers do much to reduce the cost of garden upkeep and they are effective in place of lawns in many places where grass can not be easily grown, as in dense shade, in competition with surface rooting trees, on steep banks, etc. Many different plants are adaptable as ground covers. Some of the best and most widely used are listed in the following paragraphs.

For Sunny Locations. Phlox subulata and other creeping Phloxes, Rosa Wichuraiana, Rose Max Graf, Thymus Serpyllum, Mazus reptans, Arctostaphylos Uva-ursi, creeping Junipers and many kinds of Sedum.

For Shaded Places. Pachysandra terminalis, Vinca minor, Euonymus Fortunei coloratus, Ajuga reptans, Ophiopogon japonicus, Hedera Helix, Convallaria majalis, Asarum europaeum, Hypericum calycinum, and many kinds of Epimedium.

GROUND HEMLOCK. Taxus canadensis, which see.

GROUND IVY. See Nepeta hederacea.

GROUND NUT. See Apios americana and Peanut.

GROUND PINE. See Lycopodium obscurum.

GROUNDSEL. See Senecio.

GROUNDSEL BUSH. See Baccharis.

GROW HARD. This is a gardening term that refers to maintaining environmental conditions that encourage the production of firm leaf and shoot growth, rather than forcing the production of soft growth as may be done if greenhouses and frames are not well ventilated or if the temperatures inside them are kept too high. Lack of sufficient light and the excessive use of nitrogenous fertilizers tend to produce soft growth.

GROW ON. A gardeners' term meaning to promote continued growth and progress towards maturity. It is used in such expressions as "transplant the seedlings and grow them on in a warm, moist greenhouse" and "the young plants should be grown on in a nursery until large enough to be set out in permanent locations."

GROWTH RINGS. In trees grown in temperate countries transverse sections of trunks and branches are marked with definite rings. These rings are caused by the wood produced during a single growing season being of two distinct densities; the elements of that produced during the early part of the season are less densely arranged than those of the wood produced later in the season. Thus the former is lighter colored than the latter and the denser and darker colored autumn wood forms a distinct break between the spring or summer wood of the two years.

The way to ascertain the true age of a tree is to count these annual rings. Now and then false annual rings are formed, but they are unusual. By an examination of the rings it is easy to realize the difference in rate of growth at different periods of the life of a tree.

GRUBBING. A gardening term for chopping out trees and shrubs by the roots, for which job the most handy implement is a mattock, sometimes called a "grubber." This is a double-bladed tool, with one broad, flat blade, and the other axlike for chopping through roots; it is fitted to a stout ash handle like a pick-ax.

GRUBS. See Pests and Diseases.

GRUSONIA (Gruso'nia). A small group of Cacti with cylindrical stems and their spines borne on ribs, closely related to Opuntia. They belong to the Cactus family, Cactaceae, and are natives of Mexico. The name honors Herman Gruson, a Cactus specialist of Magdeburg.

For the cultivation of these easy-to-grow plants see Cacti. Kinds are: G. Bradtiana, erect, 7 ft. tall, flowers yellow; G. Hamiltonii, erect, G. Santamaria, low spreading, spines purple, flowers pink.

GUAIACUM—*Lignum Vitae* (Guaia'cum). A group of about 8 small trees and shrubs, natives of South America and the West Indies; one, G. sanctum, occurs naturally on the Florida keys. Guaiacum belongs in the Caltrop family, Zygophyllaceae. The name is derived from Guaiac, a South American name. These trees are propagated by seeds and by cuttings.

Guaiacum officinale is known by the name of Lignum Vitae and it is of considerable importance in trade. It is very hard, one of the heaviest woods known, and is tough and oily. The heartwood is black or dark brown, the sapwood yellow; the heartwood only is of value.

For Warm Climates. In southern Florida and southern California these trees are sometimes planted for ornament. G. guatemalense attains a height of about 16 ft. and has blue flowers followed by fruits that are reddish or orange; G. officinale grows 15 to 30 ft. tall and has blue or white flowers and yellow fruits.

GUANO. This was the name originally applied to the consolidated excrements of sea birds, collected in equatorial countries, for the most part, and used as a fertilizer. Until supplies began to run short at the end of the last century, huge amounts were imported by European countries annually. The original Peruvian guano is now scarce and expensive. See Fertilizers including Manures.

GUAVA. See Psidium.

GUELDER-ROSE. See Viburnum Opulus roseum.

GUERNSEY LILY. See Nerine sarniensis.

GUINEA CHESTNUT. See Pachira aquatica.

GUINEA-HEN FLOWER. Fritillaria meleagris, which see.

GUM. A substance exuded from the trunks and branches of various trees, shrubs, and herbaceous plants. Gums differ from resins in the following particulars: Gums are soluble in water and not soluble in alcohol; resins are soluble in spirit or oil, not in water. True gums are decomposed products of cellulose, whereas resins appear to be elaborated from certain constituents of essential oils. There are, however, intermediates between the two, called gum resins, just as there are intermediates between oils and resins, called oleoresins.

Gum Tragacanth. This is obtained from Astragalus gummifer, a dwarf spiny shrub of Asia Minor, Persia, Syria, and Greece, and from other allied kinds, and is important in the arts and pharmacy. It is also used as a mucilage for stiffening crepe, calico, and other textiles, also in the manufacture of straw hats. Other gums used for similar purposes are Kutira Gum, obtained in India from Cochlospermum, Gossypium, and from Sterculia urens.

Gum Arabic. Another set of Gums is furnished by several kinds of Acacia, notably A. Senegal, from which Gum Arabic is obtained. This shrub, or often scrubby tree, is found in dry regions in India, Arabia, Egypt, and tropical and South Africa. Suakin and Talca Gum are produced in the Nile Land, and Palestine by Acacia Seyal.

Other Gums. Gum Galbanum is a gum resin with medicinal properties obtained from the roots of Ferula galbaniflua and F. rubricaulis, both herbaceous plants of Persia, and Gum ammoniacum, also of medicinal value, is obtained in Persia and Afghanistan from stems of an herbaceous plant, Dorema ammoniacum.

Gum Benjamin or Gum Benzoin is a fragrant substance collected in Sumatra, Java, and Borneo from a shrub or small tree, Styrax Benzoin, and from S. tonkinensis in Siam. This gum is of medicinal value.

Gum Guaiacum is another medicinal gum. This is obtained from the wood of Lignum Vitae (Guaiacum officinale), a South American tree. Gum Olibanum is a second name for Frankincense, a fragrant gummy or resinous substance obtained from a shrub, Boswellia Carteri.

GUM, BLUE. See Eucalyptus globulus.

GUMBO. See Okra.

GUM CISTUS. Cistus ladaniferus, which see.

GUM, SWEET. See Liquidambar styraciflua.

GUNNERA — *Prickly Rhubarb* (Gunn'era). A group of moisture-loving herbaceous perennials that are not hardy in the North. Several have immense leaves and are suitable for waterside planting; others are attractive in the bog garden and low-lying positions in the rock garden. About twenty-five species or kinds are known. They are natives of South America, South Africa, New Zealand, Tasmania, Abyssinia, Java and Hawaii. The name commemorates J. Ernest Gunner, a Swedish bishop and botanist. The Gunneras belong to the family Haloragidaceae. The thick, succulent leafstalks of two kinds, G. manicata and G. chilensis, are eaten by natives of South America, either raw or cooked; they are known as "Pangue."

Giant-leaved Plants. The large-leaved Gunneras thrive in deeply cultivated ground in which compost or rotted manure has been dug: each year in spring the soil should be top-dressed with similar material. A fairly sheltered position should be chosen to prevent damage to the leaves. These giant Gunneras are admirable plants for the waterside and for moist places in woodland or on a lawn. They should be given protection in winter by covering the crowns with dry leaves and litter which are kept in position by tree branches.

The Chief Kinds. Gunnera manicata from Brazil is the giant of the family; its huge leaves, sometimes 6-10 ft. across, are borne on prickly stems 5-8 ft. long. The Chilean Rhubarb, Gunnera chilensis, which grows 4-5 ft. high, has large leaves; its small flowers on large club-shaped spikes, 3-4 ft. or more in height, open in spring.

G. magellanica, from southern Chile and the Falkland Islands, is a free-growing plant which spreads quickly, forming a carpet of small leaves 3 or 4 in. high. It is suitable for bog gardens. G. Hamiltonii is similar.

GUZMANIA (Guzman'ia). Tropical flowering plants, with ornamental foliage, from tropical America; they belong to the Bromeliad family, Bromeliaceae. They grow 18 in. in height, have stiff, leathery, sword-shaped leaves in the form of a tube close to the soil, and terminal spikes of yellow or white flowers, surrounded by yellow, red or green bracts. The leaves are also striped with brown or white lines. The name Guzmania commemorates A. Guzman, a Spanish botanist.

Greenhouse Plants. They are grown in well-drained pots in a hothouse with a minimum winter temperature of 55 degrees. Repotting is done in March and a compost of fibrous peat and turfy loam with sand added is used. Water is ap-

A handsome, giant-leaved plant for the waterside, Gunnera manicata.

plied freely to the soil during the summer, but less is required in winter.

Propagation is by inserting offshoots in pots of sand and peat moss in spring or summer.

The chief kinds are G. monostachya (tricolor) variegata, with white flowers and purple bracts, leaves streaked with white; G. lingulata, flowers yellowish and purplish, bracts red; G. Berteroniana, flowers yellow, bracts scarlet, leaves wine-red or fresh green. G. musaica, flowers yellowish, bracts yellow and rose, leaves banded dark green above, purple beneath; G. Zahnii, flowers yellow, bracts scarlet.

GYMNOCALYCIUM (Gymnocaly'cium). Dwarf Cacti (family Cactaceae) of cylindrical form, strongly ribbed, the ribs having prominent tubercles, each with a "chin" beneath the areole or cluster of spines. The flowers are white or pinkish. All are natives of South America. The name is from *gymnos,* naked, and *kalyx,* bud, and refers to the naked flower buds. For cultivation see Cacti.

Gymnocalyciums are easy to grow and bear attractive blossoms.

Notable species include G. denudatum, white or pinkish; G. gibbosum, pink; G. Kurtzianum, white, with reddish base; G. Leeanum, greenish-yellow; G. multiflorum, pale pink; G. Mihanovitchii is brownish green and produces yellowish green flowers.

G. Mihanovitchii Friedrichiae Ruby Ball is a curious and remarkable plant. It is bright orange-red and is devoid of chlorophyll. Because of this, it must be grafted on to another Cactus in order for it to exist. When so grafted it somewhat resembles a Tomato on top of a green stake. This variant was raised in Japan about 1941.

GYMNOCLADUS — *Kentucky Coffee Tree* (Gymno'cladus). Hardy leaf-losing trees which have stout branches, ornamental leaves, small, not very attractive flowers, and long, narrow pods.

Only two species are known, one a native of North America, the other of China. They belong to the Pea family, Leguminosae. The name is from the Greek *gymnos,* naked, and *klados,* a branch, referring to the stout branches without twigs. The name Kentucky Coffee Tree originated from the fact that the Indians of Kentucky and Tennessee at one time roasted and ground the seeds to make a coffee-like beverage.

Planting and Pruning. These trees thrive in ordinary, well-drained, loamy soil in sunny places. Planting may be done in fall or spring. Little pruning is necessary except to prevent the side branches from extending so far as to restrict the development of the main stem; it should be done in winter. Propagation is by seeds sown out of doors.

Gymnocladus dioica is a tree of slow growth, reaching an ultimate height of 100 ft. The tree usually branches rather low down and is distinct in its long, twigless branches. The bipinnate leaves, pinkish when unfolding, are 2-3 ft. long and 1-2 ft. wide. The tree is dioecious, male and female flowers being borne on different trees; the flowers are greenish.

The Chinese Soap Tree, Gymnocladus chinensis, is apparently not so hardy as the Kentucky Coffee Tree. Growing 30-40 ft. high, it has smaller leaflets than G. dioica, and male and female flowers are borne on the same tree.

GYMNOGRAMMA. Pityrogramma, which see.

GYNERIUM (Gyner'ium). A small group of tropical American Grasses belonging to the Grass family, Gramineae. The name is derived from the Greek *gyne,* female, and *erion,* wool, and refers to the hairy spikelets of the female plants.

G. sagittatum, the Uva Grass, is sometimes grown for garden decoration in the far South and in tropical countries. Under favorable conditions it attains heights of 12-40 ft., and its arching flowering panicles may be 5-6 ft. long. Unlike the Pampas Grass, Cortaderia, which is sometimes grown under the name of Gynerium, this plant bears leaves along the entire length of its stems; the leaves of Cortaderia all arise from the base of the plant.

For its most successful cultivation Gynerium sagittatum requires a rich, moist soil and a sunny location. Propagation is by division and seeds.

GYNURA (Gynu'ra). Tropical plants grown in greenhouses and window gardens. Gynura belongs to the Daisy family, Compositae. The name is derived from *gyne,* female, and *oura,* tail, and refers to the long, rough stigma.

Gynuras are easily propagated by cuttings set in sand or vermiculite, or in a mixture of peat moss and sand. They grow well in a temperature of 60 degrees at night with a 5- to 10-degree increase in the daytime and need light shade from strong sun. The soil should be rich, well drained and moist, but not waterlogged. Specimens that have filled their pots with healthy roots benefit from feeding at weekly intervals with dilute liquid fertilizers.

Gynura aurantiaca grows to a height of 2-3 ft. and bears orange-colored flowers in winter or early spring. G. sarmentosa has twining stems and coarsely toothed leaves. G. bicolor has leaves gray-purple above, rich purple on their under surfaces.

GYPSOPHILA—*Chalk Plant, Baby's-Breath* (Gypsoph'ila). Hardy annual and perennial plants of great value in the herbaceous border, rock garden and as cut flowers. They belong to the Pink family, Caryophyllaceae, and grow wild in various parts of Europe chiefly. Gypsophila is derived from *gypsos,* gypsum, and *philos,* loving, and alludes to the plants' preference for gypsum rock.

The favorite kind is the vigorous hardy perennial Gypsophila paniculata, which reaches a height of 3 or 4 ft. and bears a profusion of small white flowers in July. It is very beautiful when in full bloom and most useful for cutting. The variety named Bristol Fairy is finer than the old double variety, flore-pleno. Flamingo is a pretty lilac-pink double variety, and Rosy Veil, 12-15 in., double, is good for the front of the herbaceous border.

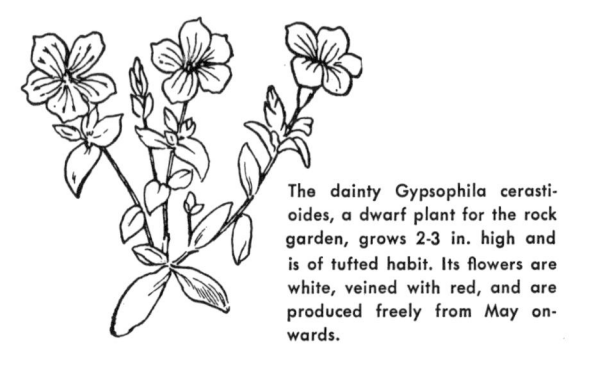

The Velvet Plant, Gynura aurantiaca, has leaves covered with purple hairs.

The dainty Gypsophila cerastioides, a dwarf plant for the rock garden, grows 2-3 in. high and is of tufted habit. Its flowers are white, veined with red, and are produced freely from May onwards.

This plant dislikes being disturbed, and the long thick roots should be planted where they can remain indefinitely. They should be covered with an inch or two of soil. Deeply dug, ordinary garden soil, enriched with compost or manure, is needed to ensure large floriferous plants. The roots should be set about 4 ft. apart for well-grown plants take a lot of room. Propagation is by sowing seeds in sandy soil in a frame in spring. The double varieties are grafted on roots of G. paniculata.

For the Rock Garden. Several charming low-growing, creeping kinds of Gypsophila are suitable for planting in the rock garden, where they will give little trouble if set in well-drained sandy, loamy soil in a sunny place. Gypsophila repens, with white flowers, and G. repens rosea, pale rose, are very attractive. Another rock garden Gypsophila is G. cerastioides, which has pale pink flowers. The pretty kind with delicate pink flowers that is grown as G. fratensis appears to be a compact variety of G. repens.

The perennial Gypsophila repens is a trailing kind suitable for rock gardens.

Gypsophila elegans is a dainty white-flowered hardy annual, 12 in. high, which is useful for cutting or for sowing near the front of the herbaceous border or flower bed. Seedsmen offer colored strains in shades of pink and rose. The seeds are sown out of doors early in April to furnish summer bloom.

Greenhouse Cultivation. Gypsophila elegans is useful for growing in greenhouses for cut flowers and as an attractive pot plant. It is very easily cultivated. Seeds may be sown in pots or flats of porous soil any time from late summer to late winter. The young seedlings are transplanted 2-3 in. apart in deep flats or 4-in. or 5-in. pots and are grown on in a sunny, airy greenhouse where the night temperature is 45-50 degrees and daytime temperatures are a few degrees higher. Any fairly fertile, porous soil suits them. Under favorable conditions the plants are in full flower in a few weeks.

GYPSUM. This is the name given to commercial calcium sulphate (sulphate of lime). A chemical of considerable value as a soil conditioner, this also supplies the fertilizing elements calcium and sulphur. Gypsum is of especial value on alkali soils, on soils that have been flooded with sea water and on heavy clay soils that have assumed a pasty, impervious condition as a result of being worked while they are wet. Gypsum does not reduce acidity but, on the contrary, under some circumstances, has an acidifying effect. Consequently, it may be used as a soil conditioner for acid-soil plants, for which purpose lime and limestone are totally unsatisfactory.

H

HAAGEOCEREUS (Haageocer'eus). A genus of Cacti (family Cactaceae) that are natives of Chile and Peru and are night bloomers. They are closely allied to Borzicactus and some kinds were previously known as Cereus. Among the kinds cultivated are H. acranthus, flowers white or pale pink; H. decumbens, flowers white, fragrant; H. laredensis, flowers white; H. pseudomelanostele, flowers white; and H. versicolor, flowers white or cream. For cultural details see Cacti.

HABENARIA—*Butterfly Orchid; Fringed Orchis* (Habena'ria). A large and varied group of Orchids, found wild in tropical, subtropical and temperate countries. All are terrestrial and tuberous-rooted, with strap-shaped, deciduous leaves, usually arranged in a rosette from the center of which springs an erect leafy spike. The sepals and petals are small and the lip may be entire, or deeply lobed.

Habenaria is represented in North America

by a number of native varieties. It belongs to the family Orchidaceae.

Habenaria is derived from *habena,* a strap, and the name refers to the strap-shaped flower spur of some kinds.

Greenhouse Orchids. The exotic kinds require a warm greenhouse having a tropical temperature and moist atmosphere in summer. When dormant, in winter, the plants should be kept in a temperature of 60-65 degrees; they must not be watered unless there is danger of the tubers shriveling. When these Orchids are in full growth they should be watered liberally. A suitable compost is provided by three parts of loam fibre, two parts of osmunda fibre and one part of sphagnum moss with the addition of sand and finely broken brick.

The Best Kinds. All these flower in the summer and autumn: H. carnea, from Penang, with beautifully spotted leaves, bears bluish or rose-colored flowers; H. Susannae, found wild from India to Malaya, stems 2 ft. high and white flowers.

Hardy Kinds. The hardy native kinds are not easy plants to establish in the garden and it is useless to attempt to grow them unless the special environmental conditions they need can be provided. Acid soil is needed by the White Fringed Orchis, Habenaria blephariglottis; the Yellow Fringed Orchis, H. ciliaris; the Small Purple Fringed Orchis, H. psycodes; and the Large Purple Fringed Orchis, H. psycodes grandiflora (H. fimbriata). The White and the Yellow Fringed Orchises must be grown in bogs on raised hummocks above the water level; the two Purple Fringed kinds named will thrive either in bogs or in moist soils. Roots obtained from reliable dealers in native plants afford the best means of establishing these plants. Specimens that are thriving should not be disturbed unnecessarily.

HABERLEA (Haber'lea). Haberlea rhodopensis, closely related to Ramonda, is a beautiful hardy perennial rock plant from the Balkans. It belongs to the family Gesneriaceae and was named in honor of Karl K. Haberle, a professor of botany at Pesth.

This plant forms rosettes of evergreen leaves, and eventually tufts of these rosettes. The flow-

A charming plant for a shady crevice in the rock garden is Haberlea rhodopensis.

ers resemble small Gloxinias or Streptocarpus, are pale lilac, and are borne two to five on 6 in. stems. There is a very lovely white-flowered variety named virginalis. H. Ferdinandi-Coburgii, from the Balkans, is similar to H. rhodopensis, but larger.

For a Shady Crevice in the Rock Garden. Like Ramonda, the Haberleas require a northern exposure, and are best planted in crevices among rocks in a soil rich in vegetable humus, in such a position that little or no sun reaches them. They flower in May and June.

Haberleas are most easily increased by division, in September, carefully detaching the leafy rosettes, with roots. It is possible to root the leaves as cuttings in the same way that Begonia leaves are rooted, and plants may also be raised from seed. The seed is exceedingly fine, and requires very careful shading and watering in the early stages. Seedlings develop slowly and care must be taken that they do not become smothered by moss and liverwort.

HABIT. This word is commonly used by gardeners in referring to the natural forms in which trees and plants grow. The term "habit of growth" is frequently employed; the "habit of growth" may be low, tall, erect, spreading, trailing, bushy, and so on.

HABITAT. The place in which a plant is found growing wild.

HABLITZIA TAMNOIDES (Hablitz'ia). A herbaceous climbing plant, 6-8 ft. high, with oval or elliptic leaves, and clusters of greenish-yellow flowers during summer and early autumn. It is a native of the Caucasus and belongs to the family Chenopodiaceae. The name Hablitzia commemorates C. von Hablitz, a traveler and author.

For Covering a Trellis. The roots are planted in autumn or spring in deep, rich, loamy soil. The plant requires abundance of water during the summer, but stagnant moisture is fatal to the roots in winter. The shoots, which die down in the autumn, may be trained to a trellis to form a screen in summer.

Propagation is by inserting shoots, 3 in. long, in pots of sandy soil in spring. They are kept in a cold frame until roots are formed and then planted out where they are to remain.

HABRANTHUS (Habran'thus). Tender bulbous plants mostly from South America, which belong to the Amaryllis family, Amaryllidaceae. They grow about 18 in. in height, have strap-shaped leaves and bear showy, trumpet-shaped flowers in summer. They may be grown outdoors in the South. The name Habranthus is derived from *habros,* delicate, and *anthos,* a flower.

A flower spray of Habranthus cardinalis, a half-hardy bulbous plant for the foot of a south wall.

When to Plant. The bulbs are planted 4-6 in. deep in spring in a well-drained, sunny position in the rock garden, or in a sunny border. Ordinary garden soil enriched with compost or sandy loam is suitable. As a protection against frost a layer of ashes, 6 in. in depth, is spread over the ground in autumn where winters are cold. This is removed in April and replaced by a mulch of leaf mold. Propagation is by lifting and replanting the offsets in April. In cold localities they are best grown in a cool greenhouse.

The best kinds are H. Andersonii, yellow or coppery; H. cardinalis, bright red; H. brachyandrus, lavender-pink; robustus, rose-red; and texanus, yellow and reddish. H. texanus is a native of Texas.

HABROTHAMNUS. Another name for Cestrum, which see.

HACKBERRY. See Celtis.

HACKMATACK. Larix laricina, which see.

HACQUETIA EPIPACTIS (Hacque'tia). A dwarf hardy perennial flowering plant suitable for the rock garden. It is a native of the Eastern Alps and belongs to the Parsnip family, Umbelliferae. This plant grows about 6 in. tall, has small palmate, deeply lobed leaves, close to the soil, and bears umbels of small yellow flowers in spring. The name Hacquetia commemorates B. Hacquet, a botanist.

For the Rock Garden. Planting is done in spring, when the plants are set in a sunny position in sandy loam. After planting they should not be disturbed until they show signs of deterioration, as they dislike being moved. Propagation is principally by dividing the roots in March. H. Epipactis is the only species.

HAEMANTHUS—*Blood Lily* (Haeman'thus). Tender bulbous plants which have showy flowers; they are natives of tropical and South Africa and belong to the Amaryllis family, Amaryllidaceae. Over 50 species are known, but only a few are in cultivation. They are of two distinct types.

The Blood Lily named Haemanthus Katherinae, a striking bulbous plant for the amateur's greenhouse. It is also a good house plant.

H. albiflos and H. coccineus have roundish bulbs about the size of tennis balls, from which their wide, leathery, stalkless, leaves arise and flop over on either side alternately, like the pages of an open book. From the center of the bulbs, the flower spikes are produced; these are about 12 in. in height and bear at their tips closely packed heads of scarlet or white flowers, of which the stamens are the most conspicuous feature.

Haemanthus albiflos has white flowers that are followed by red berries. It is a most attractive plant for a cool, sunny window.

Other kinds, principally H. Katharinae and H. natalensis, produce stout succulent stems, about 2 ft. in height, annually; they have large ovate leaves, and the flowers are on separate stalks rising straight from the bulbs. The name Haemanthus is derived from *haima*, blood, and *anthos*, a flower, and refers to the color of the flowers of some kinds.

For the Greenhouse. These plants require a compost of equal parts sandy loam, peat moss or leaf mold and coarse sand. When in growth, they require a minimum temperature of 50-55 degrees, a few degrees less when resting. Repotting is done in February or as soon as signs of new growth are evident, the bulbs being buried to half their depth in well-drained pots, and the compost is made firm. Repotting is not necessary every year as the bulbs flower best when the pots are well filled with roots. No shading is required except for newly potted plants. During the summer months water is applied liberally to the soil and dilute liquid fertilizer is given once a week to established plants.

The deciduous (leaf-losing) kinds are gradually dried off after flowering and are stored, in their pots, under the greenhouse benches during the winter. Those with evergreen leaves are not dried off completely; sufficient water is applied in winter to prevent the leaves from shrivelling.

Propagation is by removing and potting the small bulblets in spring. Seeds may also be sown in pots of sandy soil in spring, the seed pots being covered with a pane of glass and set in a propagating case in the greenhouse. When the seedlings have formed two leaves they are potted separately in 3-in. pots.

The chief kinds are H. coccineus, 12 in., scarlet, September; H. albiflos, 12 in., white, July; H. natalensis, 18 in., green and orange; H. Katharinae, 2 ft., orange scarlet, August. The last-named has star-shaped flowers and is quite distinct from the others, in which the colored stamens or bracts are the most conspicuous feature.

HA-HA. A boundary fence or wall concealed in a ditch below the normal ground level so as not to obstruct the view. It was used extensively by that great English landscape gardener, "Capability" Brown.

HAIR GRASS. See Deschampsia.

HAKEA (Ha'kea). Tender, evergreen shrubs from Australia which belong to the family Proteaceae. In their native country they grow from 10-30 ft. in height and produce clusters of white, sometimes fragrant, flowers. They are well suited for cultivation in California and similar dry climates. In some kinds the leaves are ovate and about 3 in. long, while those of other kinds, especially H. suaveolens, consist of only stiff, prickle-like main vines. The name Hakea commemorates Baron von Hake, a German patron of botany.

These plants require a well-drained soil and sunny location. Propagation is by inserting well-ripened shoots in pots of sandy peat in August; the pots of cuttings are placed under a bell jar in the greenhouse until roots are formed.

Favorite kinds are H. suaveolens, fragrant, 10 ft., and H. saligna, very fragrant, 8 ft.

HALESIA—*Snowdrop Tree, Silver-Bell Tree* (Hales'ia). Leaf-losing trees of moderate size with

Halesia diptera, growing near Philadelphia, Pennsylvania.

This white-flowered Silver-Bell Tree is the native Halesia carolina.

spreading branches, bearing beautiful, pendent, white or delicate pink flowers in spring. They are mostly natives of North America. The name was given in commemoration of Dr. Stephen Hales, a botanist of the sixteenth century. Halesia belongs to the family Styracaceae.

Halesias are not difficult to cultivate. They can be raised from seeds sown in sandy soil in greenhouse or frame as soon as ripe, and they thrive without trouble if planted in well-drained, loamy soil and given a position that is sheltered from sweeping winds.

H. carolina is the best-known. It is native from West Virginia to Florida and Texas and may grow 20-40 ft. high, with a rounded, spreading head of branches. It bears dainty, bell-like flowers; the variety Meehanii is of shrubby growth and has smaller flowers. H. diptera may be a large shrub or small tree that occurs naturally from South Carolina to Florida and Texas. H. monticola, in North Carolina, Georgia and Tennessee, which is its native range, attains a height of about 100 ft., but in gardens elsewhere it is usually smaller; its variety rosea has pale pink flowers.

HALF-HARDY. A term used by gardeners in reference to plants which cannot be relied on to pass through the winter out of doors without protection. It is also sometimes applied to annuals that require a long season of growth and are started indoors early for planting outside later.

HALF-RIPE. Gardeners frequently refer to half-ripe wood and half-ripe shoots. When they do so they mean current season's shoots that are no longer soft and flabby but have not yet attained the woody maturity that characterizes them at the end of their first season.

Half-ripe shoots of many kinds of plants are favored as cuttings to be used for summer propagation.

HALF-STANDARD. This term, when applied to Rose trees, denotes a tree with a stem clear of branches, about 2 ft. high. Half-standard fruit trees and ornamental trees have stems free from branches, about 4 ft. high.

HALIMIUM (Halim'ium). Sun-loving shrubs, natives of the Mediterranean regions and western Asia, closely related to Helianthemum and included in that genus by some botanists. These shrubs are of slender growth, and cultivation is

This native American Witch Hazel, Hamamelis virginiana, produces its yellow flowers in late fall.

the same as for Cistus, which see. The name is from the Greek *halimos*, and alludes to the similarity in foliage to Atriplex Halimus. Halimium belongs to the Rock Rose family, Cistaceae.

Popular kinds are H. halimifolium, from the Mediterranean region, 3-4 ft., yellow flowers, with tiny dark spots at base of each petal; H. lasianthum, a species from Portugal, up to 3 ft., golden-yellow, with conspicuous dark blotches which, however, are absent in the variety concolor; H. Libanotis, from Spain and Portugal, 2-3 ft., yellow; H. ocymoides, from Spain and Portugal, 2-3 ft., rich yellow, with purple at base of petals; and H. umbellatum, 1½ ft., from the Mediterranean region, with rosemary-like foliage and white flowers.

HALIMOCISTUS (Halimo'cistus). A small group of hybrids between Halimium and Cistus, and intermediate in character between the two. They are showy evergreen, downy-leaved shrubs for sunny positions in well-drained loamy soil and are propagated by cuttings of the young shoots inserted in sandy compost in a closed frame or under a bell jar in July–August.

There are three kinds in cultivation: H. Ingwersenii, 2 ft., white; H. Sahucii, 1-1½ ft., white; and H. wintonensis, 1½-2 ft., white, with maroon and yellow markings. All bloom in early summer.

HALIMODENDRON — *Salt Tree* (Halimoden'dron). Only one kind is known, H. argenteum, sometimes called H. halodendron, a leaf-losing hardy shrub from Siberia, growing 5-7 ft. high, with spiny branches, gray or blue-green leaves divided into several silky leaflets, and purplish or pinkish, pea-shaped flowers, produced several together from side buds in June–July. The variety purpurea has rosy-purple flowers.

A sunny position in light, well-drained, loamy soil suits it, and it is most easily increased by seeds sown out of doors or in a frame in September. As it grows slowly, the plant is sometimes grafted on stocks of Laburnum or Caragana. If planted in the higher parts of the rock garden it is effective; it also thrives near the sea.

Halimodendron belongs to the Pea family, Leguminosae, and the name is from the Greek *halimos*, maritime, and *dendron*, a tree.

HAMAMELIS — *Witch Hazel* (Hamame'lis). These are very attractive hardy winter-flowering shrubs and small trees. They lose their leaves in autumn, and bear yellow, golden or lemon-colored flowers in profusion in fall, winter or early spring. They are found wild in North America, China and Japan, the Asiatic kinds being the more decorative. A peculiarity of several of the Witch Hazels is seen in the narrow twisted petals, which give the flowers a spidery appearance. Hamamelis gives its name to the family Hamamelidaceae, and the name is said to be taken

The lemon-yellow-flowered Witch Hazel, Hamamelis japonica Zuccariniana, is one of the finest of flowering shrubs.

from the Greek *hama,* together, and *mela,* fruit, owing to flowers and fruits being sometimes found on plants at the same time.

Raising Seedlings. When seeds are available they should be used for propagation. They frequently lie two years in the soil before germination takes place. There is no difficulty in procuring seeds of the North American H. virginiana, and seedlings of this may be grown in pots to provide stocks on which to graft the more ornamental kinds from China and Japan. Grafting is carried on in a greenhouse in spring. Branches can be layered in spring, but cuttings are difficult to root.

Planting and Pruning. Well-drained, loamy soil, on the light rather than the heavy side, is most suitable, and it is wise to mix in some peat or compost at planting time. If it is desired to rear trees with a short trunk, it is necessary to keep the leading shoot tied to a stake and check the side branches for a few years. If, however, bush plants are desired, little or no pruning is necessary. As the best kinds flower in midwinter, it is wise to choose a sheltered position exposed to the south, and to provide a dark background. The flowers are not injured by light frosts extending over several days, and the wood is rarely damaged by cold.

The Best Witch Hazel. H. mollis, the Chinese Witch Hazel, is the best of all. It forms a spreading bush or small tree and may eventually grow more than 20 ft. high. Its leaves are larger than those of other kinds, being 3-5 in. long and 2-3 in. wide. The golden-yellow flowers are very fragrant, the odor being reminiscent of Primroses. This shrub can be distinguished from other kinds by the narrow petals having hooked ends instead of being twisted.

The Japanese Witch Hazel. H. japonica, the Japanese Witch Hazel, is the next most useful kind. It varies a good deal in habit of growth, and although in Japan it grows as large as H. mollis does in China, it is usually smaller here. Its flowers are freely produced, slightly fragrant and yellow, with narrow, twisted petals. There are two very beautiful varieties, arborea, which is more vigorous than the type and has darker colored flowers, and Zuccariniana, with lemon-yellow flowers. Another variety of H. japonica, called flavo-purpurascens, has petals of a curious reddish shade.

The Virginian Witch Hazel. H. virginiana, the Virginian Witch Hazel, is less decorative than the others, the flowers being much smaller, and as it blooms in autumn before the fall of the leaves, they are not well seen. The leaves, however, turn to a pleasing golden shade before they fall. It is found wild in eastern North America. The variety rubescens has reddish petals. A closely allied kind is H. vernalis, also a native of eastern North America. This flowers in spring and spreads by suckers.

Economic Uses. The bark and leaves of H. virginiana contain a medicinal oil with astringent, tonic and sedative properties. It is much used in proprietary preparations in pharmacy, and is known as witch hazel.

HAMATOCACTUS (Hamatocac'tus). A small group of Cacti, family Cactaceae, natives of southern Texas and Mexico. They take their name from *hamatus,* hooked, and Cactus; the name refers to the hooked spines that some kinds possess.

The commonest one cultivated is H. setispinus, which grows to 6 in. tall and has yellow flowers with red throats. H. hamatacanthus grows to 2 ft. tall and has yellow flowers. H. uncinatus has reddish-brown flowers and attains a height of about 8 in. These plants require the same culture as Echinocactus. See Cactus.

HAMBURGH PARSLEY. The cultivation of this vegetable is dealt with under Parsley, which see.

HAMELIA (Hamel'ia). A group of evergreen shrubs that are natives of the warmer parts of the Americas and belong in the Madder family, Rubiaceae. The name honors the French botanical writer Henri Louis du Hamel du Monceau. In the United States Hamelias may be grown outdoors in southern Florida and southern California only.

These handsome evergreens thrive best in soils that are rich and fairly moist. They are propagated by seeds and by cuttings made from half-ripe shoots inserted in a warm greenhouse.

Hamelia erecta, the Scarlet Bush, occurs naturally from Florida to Brazil. It grows to a maximum height of 25 ft. and has red or orange flowers. H. sphaerocarpa, a native of Peru, grows up to 12 ft. tall and has orange-yellow flowers.

HAND LIGHT. A small portable glass case with detachable top, used for the purpose of protecting seedlings or special plants coming into bloom (the Christmas Rose for example) and for rooting cuttings. A hand light is usually square and one of ordinary size measures 18 in. by 18 in. The lower part of the hand light is 12 in. high, and the removable top has four sloping sides meeting at a point in the center. Cuttings of many hardy plants and shrubs will form roots if, in summer and early autumn, they are put in sandy soil and covered with a hand light.

HAND WEEDING. A certain amount of hand weeding is always necessary in a well-ordered garden, although it can be reduced to a minimum in the vegetable and cut flower garden by sowing in rows to permit the use of the hoe. Lawns can be kept free of weeds by the use

Hand weeding is a necessary garden chore in some parts of the garden.

of selective weed killers, and paths by dressing them with ordinary weed killers. But weeds are sure to appear between the plants in the rows of vegetables, among the plants in the herbaceous border, in the rock garden, and elsewhere, and for these hand-pulling, with the aid of a broken kitchen knife, or hand fork, is the only remedy. This work is best done when the soil is moist, as the weeds can then be removed easily with less chance of disturbing the rightful occupants of the site.

HANGING BASKET. Suitable plants for cultivation in hanging baskets are given under the heading of Basket Plants, which see.

HAPLOCARPHA (Haplocar'pha). Tender perennial flowering plants from South Africa which belong to the Daisy family, Compositae. The name is derived from *haploos,* single, and *karphe,* scale. They form woody rhizomes from which rise the short-stalked, lance-shaped leaves; these are about 6 in. in length and covered on the undersides with small, white hairs. The yellowish, daisy-like flowers, 2 in. in diameter, are borne singly on slender stems in summer.

For Light Soil and a Sunny Place. In mild climates such as that of California the plants may be grown permanently outdoors; elsewhere they are put out in April in a sunny border, which is well drained and of light, sandy soil. They are lifted in autumn, set in shallow boxes of soil and kept in a cold frame or greenhouse.

Propagation is by sowing seeds in sandy soil in summer in a cold frame. When the seedlings are an inch or so high they are pricked out. They can also be increased by cuttings of the young shoots inserted in a close frame.

The chief kinds are H. Leitchlinii and H. scaposa, yellow, 12-18 in., summer.

HARBINGER-OF-SPRING. Erigenia bulbosa, which see.

HARDENBERGIA. (Hardenber'gia). Tender evergreen climbing plants with showy flowers. They are natives of Australia and belong to the Pea family, Leguminosae. These plants, which climb 10 ft. in height by their twining stems, have pinnate leaves and long racemes of purplish, pea-shaped flowers in early summer. The name Hardenbergia commemorates Franziska, Countess of Hardenberg. They are suitable for growing outdoors in southern California and in similar mild, dry climates.

A Greenhouse Climbing Plant. The plants are set in large pots or tubs or planted in a prepared bed in the greenhouse. The minimum winter temperature should be 45 degrees, and the best compost consists of equal parts of loam and peat with sand added. Water is applied freely from April to September, but during the remainder of the year the soil is only moistened when it becomes dry.

Pruning and Propagation. Pruning consists of cutting back the straggling shoots and thinning out old, worn-out branches in March. Shade is afforded from the fiercest rays of the sun only. Propagation is by inserting young shoots about 3 in. in length in April. The cuttings are placed under a hand light and, when roots are formed are potted separately in 3-in. pots and subsequently in 5-in. pots, from which they are set in their permanent position.

The chief kinds are H. Comptoniana, 10 ft., violet blue, April; and H. violacea (monophylla), 10 ft., purple, April.

HARDENING OFF. A gardening term used to describe the practice of gradually inuring tender plants to a lower temperature and more airy conditions before they are planted out of doors. If plants which have been grown in a heated greenhouse are set out of doors without an intermediate stay in a cool greenhouse or frame they will almost certainly suffer and will lose many of their leaves. When plants are removed from a warm greenhouse they should be placed in a cold frame which must be kept close for a few days. Subsequently it should be ventilated slightly if the weather is mild, the ventilation being increased gradually during the following weeks; finally, the frame is kept fully open during the day, and at night, if the weather is mild, for a few days before the plants are set out of doors. Hardening off is practiced chiefly in the management of summer bedding plants and tender annuals which are propagated by seeds and cuttings in a heated greenhouse and must therefore be kept in a cold frame for a few weeks before they are planted out.

HARDHACK. Spiraea tomentosa, which see.

HARDPAN. A hardpan is a hard layer of material in the ground. The soil there is hard and rocklike; this prevents the free passage of water into the subsoil, and the layer of soil above the hardpan becomes, like undrained land, wet and sodden. As a result it sours and plants grown in it become sickly; deep-rooting plants and shrubs cannot penetrate the hard stratum and languish. The hardpan is caused sometimes by salts of iron and lime which are washed down by rain water to a certain depth; at that depth the iron or the lime changes into insoluble compounds which, uniting with the soil there, act like cement and harden. Good cultivation requires the breaking up of hardpan before planting is done.

HARD-WOODED. A term used by gardeners in describing certain hardy and greenhouse shrubs, and more particularly Azalea, Boronia, Chorizema, Correa, Erica, Epacris, Eriostemon, Leschenaultia, Metrosideros and Rhododendron. All have hard wood and very fibrous roots, and thrive best in sandy, peaty soil.

HARDY. This term is applied to plants of all kinds which will pass safely through the winter out of doors. However, plants that are hardy in one locality may not be hardy in another. Not only temperatures, but the type of soil, amount of exposure to drying winds and winter sun, the condition of the plants when they enter the winter and other factors are often significant in determining whether or not critical kinds will survive. Hardiness often can only be stated approximately. In this work plants said to be hardy, without other qualification, may normally be expected to withstand winters outdoors in the North except, possibly, where extreme cold occurs.

HARDY AGERATUM. Eupatorium coelestinum, which see.

HARDY ANNUAL. Plants which are raised from seeds sown out of doors in autumn or early spring, which bloom within a year and perish after they have flowered. Familiar kinds are Candytuft, Shirley Poppy, Clarkia and Godetia. See Annuals.

HARDY GLOXINIA. Incarvillea Delavayi, which see.

HARDY ORANGE. Poncirus trifoliata, which see.

HARDY PERENNIAL. This term is correctly applied to any tree, shrub or plant which lives on from year to year and is hardy, but in gardening it is mostly applied to plants of which the top or leaf growth dies down annually in autumn, but the rootstock lives on from year to year.

HAREBELL. See Campanula rotundifolia.

HAREBELL POPPY. See Meconopsis quintuplinervia.

HARE'S-EAR. See Bupleurum.
HARE'S-FOOT FERN. See Davallia.
HARE'S-TAIL. Lagurus ovatus, which see.
HARLEQUIN FLOWER. See Sparaxis.
HARPALIUM. Helianthus rigidus, which see.
HARRISIA (Harris′ia). A group of South American night-flowering Cacti, previously included in the genus Cereus, which appreciate rather warm conditions, but otherwise require treatment as outlined under Cacti.

The genus is named after W. Harris, superintendent of the Public Gardens, Jamaica. The plants have slender, weak stems, with rounded ribs and furnished with long spines, the large, funnel-shaped flowers being produced singly near the ends of the branches.

The principal kinds include H. adscendens, H. Bonplandii, H. Martinii, and H. tortuosa, all with white flowers; and H. eriophora, purplish.

HART'S-TONGUE FERN. See Phyllitis Scolopendrium.

HARTWEGIA PURPUREA (Hartweg′ia). A small epiphytal Orchid, found wild in Mexico. The slender stems, which take the place of pseudobulbs, are 2 or 3 in. in height and each bears a fleshy, gray-green leaf. Short spikes, produced from the junction of the stem and leaf, have small rose-purple flowers at various seasons of the year. The name commemorates Theodor Hartweg, a collector for the London Horticultural Society. Hartwegia belongs to the family Orchidaceae.

A moderately warm greenhouse with a moist atmosphere suits this Orchid during summer, the season of growth; it should be wintered in a temperature of 55 degrees. A suitable potting compost consists of cut osmunda fiber or of Fir bark or other bark used for potting Orchids. Repotting should be done in early spring when necessary. When the plants are in full growth they must be kept moist at the roots, but during winter far less water is needed, though the soil should not be allowed to become dry.

HASTATE. A botanical term meaning shaped like a spear head.

HAULM. A term applied to the stem and leaf growth of Peas, Beans and Potatoes.

HAUTBOIS STRAWBERRY. Fragaria moschata. See Strawberry.

HAW. A term applied to the fruits of the Thorn or Crataegus.

HAWKWEED. Crepis and Hieracium, which see.

HAWKWEED, YELLOW. See Tolpis.

HAWORTHIA (Haworth′ia). Tender succulent-leaved plants from South Africa, which belong to the Lily family, Liliaceae. These plants, which are similar in structure to Cacti and need the same treatment, form clusters of rosettes of leaves, generally close to the soil. The leaves are triangular, 2-5 in. long, soft and fleshy. Some are light-green, with dark green markings at the tips; others have raised, whitish lumps all over the surface. The small, inconspicuous flowers, which are tubular, white and green, or white striped with pink, are produced on slender stems sometimes 2 ft. in length. The name Haworthia commemorates an English botanist.

For a Cool Greenhouse. These plants require a minimum winter temperature of 45 degrees. No

Haworthia margaritifera granata.

shade is required. The best potting compost consists of two parts of loam and one part of broken bricks and sand. Repotting is done in April, but is not necessary every year, as the plants are slow growing. During the summer months the soil is kept moist, but throughout winter very little water is required, sufficient only being given to prevent the leaves from shriveling.

The plants are suitable, too, for growing in a sunny window, where they require essentially the same care as in the greenhouse.

[5–8]
Loblolly Bay
(Gordonia Lasianthus)

[5–8a]
Blue Amaryllis
(Griffinia hyacinthina)

[5–8b]
Rose of Sharon
(Hibiscus syriacus varieties)

[5–8c]
Hibiscus Rosa-sinensis variety

[5—9]
English Ivy
(Hedera Helix variety)

[5—9a]
Heliotrope
(Heliotropium arborescens variety)

[5—9b]
Hibiscus Rosa-sinensis variety

[5—9c]
Hylocereus undatus

Among the best succulents for growing in window gardens are the Haworthias.

Outdoor Culture. In mild climates that are almost or quite frost-free, such as that of southern California, Haworthias may be grown outdoors in well-drained soils under the same conditions as those that suit Aloes.

Propagation is by removing and potting the rosettes in small pots in spring or summer. The

Haworthia setata.

seeds are lightly covered with soil and a pane of glass is set over the seed pot until germination has taken place. When two leaves have formed, the seedlings are pricked out 1 in. apart in a flower pan of fine soil and, later on, potted singly in 2-in. pots.

The chief kinds are H. albicans, 4 in.; H. arachnoides, 12 in.; H. laetevirens, H. margaritifera and varieties of it, 4 in.; H. Reinwardtii, 6 in.; H. setata, 3 in.; H. tessellata, and H. viscosa, 6 in.

HAWTHORN. See Crataegus.

HAWTHORN, INDIA. Raphiolepis indica, which see.

HAWTHORN, WATER. See Aponogeton.

HAWTHORN, YEDDO. Raphiolepis umbellata, which see.

HAY-SCENTED FERN. See Dennstaedtia.

HAZEL. See Corylus, and Filbert.

HAZEL, WINTER. Corylopsis, which see.

HAZEL, WITCH. See Hamamelis.

HEAD. A gardening term used to denote a bunch or cluster of flowers. For instance, the Agapanthus and Hydrangea are said to bear "heads of bloom."

The term is also used to refer to certain vegetables that form compact masses of leaves or, in the cases of Cauliflower and Broccoli, flower buds. Thus we speak of a head of Lettuce and a head of Cabbage.

The upper branching parts of trees such as Apples, and of standard (tree-trained) plants such as Roses, Heliotropes and Geraniums, are also called heads; when they are pruned severely, we call it heading them back or heading them in.

HEAD BACK AND HEAD IN. See Head, above.

HEARTNUT. See Walnut and Juglans.

HEARTSEASE. Viola tricolor, which see.

HEARTSEED. Cardiospermum, which see.

HEARTWOOD. If a transverse section of an Oak tree is examined it will be found that the wood is of two distinct colors; there is an area of pale-colored wood immediately within the bark and, within that again, darker wood extending to the center of the trunk. The darker colored wood is heartwood, the lighter colored wood sapwood. Heartwood may be separated from sapwood by a sharp dividing line or the two kinds may intermingle. In some trees, Laburnum, for instance, the difference is even more marked than in Oak; but in other trees, such as the Sycamore Maple, it is less pronounced, and in some woods the dividing line is difficult to determine.

Heartwood is much stronger and harder than Sapwood and resists decay better. From some kinds of lumber, Sapwood is excluded in specifications for various kinds of work. The darkening of Heartwood is brought about to some extent by the oxidation of chemical substances that take the place of water.

HEATH. See Erica.

HEATH, AUSTRALIAN. See Epacris.

HEATH, FALSE. See Fabiana.

HEATH, IRISH. See Daboecia.

HEATHER. See Erica and Calluna.

HEATH, ST. DABOEC'S. See Daboecia.

HEATING. There are many and various ways of heating a greenhouse: the method chosen must depend on the size of the greenhouse and the purpose for which it is intended, and the temperature which it is desired to maintain. This subject is dealt with fully under Greenhouses For Amateurs.

HEAVY SOIL. The term heavy as applied to soils refers to those that are of a clayey, tenacious character and thus are more difficult to work with tools and implements than are sandy soils. The latter are termed light soils.

HEBE (He′be). Mostly tender evergreen shrubs and small trees that are closely related to Veronica and at one time were included in that genus. Hebe belongs in the Figwort family, the Scrophulariaceae, and is named after the Greek Goddess Hebe.

In gardens Hebes are often called Veronicas. They are mostly natives of New Zealand and are well adapted for planting outdoors in mild climates such as those of California and the Pacific Northwest; they are also sometimes grown as pot plants in cool greenhouses. In favored climates Hebes are extremely valuable for seaside gardens. Although generally tender, one or two kinds have proved reasonably hardy, if given a sheltered location, even in the vicinity of New York City. Among these hardiest are H. Armstrongii and H. Traversii.

The Hebes include shrubs of rather diverse appearance. In one group the leaves are of ordinary appearance and the handsome flowers are carried in conspicuous racemes. These are showy flowering shrubs. In another group, generally known as the Whipcord Hebes, the leaves of plants that have passed their juvenile stage are ordinarily short and scalelike and are crowded on the stems so that the branches have something of the appearance of the Club Mosses, Lycopodium or of Cupressus. These kinds have quite inconspicuous flowers; they are grown primarily for their curious and interesting foliage.

It is reported that if plants of the Whipcord Hebes are grown in a moderately warm greenhouse, where the atmosphere is moist, they retain their juvenile type of foliage, which is larger and more ordinary-looking than the mature scalelike kind.

One of the richly colored hybrids of the shrubby Hebe speciosa.

Outdoor Culture. The Hebes are easy plants to grow in any suitable climate. They are sunlovers and stand exposure to wind well. Any reasonably good garden soil, provided it is well drained and not alkaline, suits them; they especially appreciate peat moss or other peaty material mixed in with the soil. Some kinds make good hedge plants and may be trimmed each spring. However, when not used as hedges, they require little pruning; all that is needed is the shortening back of any straggly shoots in spring, just before new growth begins.

Pot Culture. When Hebes are grown in pots, the soil mixture should consist of good loam, peat moss and coarse sand in about equal proportions with a little bone meal added. The pots must be well drained and plants should be potted in March and again in the early summer if their growth is sufficient to make such a move seem desirable. They need watering freely from spring through fall, moderately in winter. Speci-

Hardiest of all the Hebes, the white-flowered H. Traversii.

mens that have filled their pots with healthy roots benefit from occasional applications of dilute liquid fertilizer.

From the time when fall frost threatens until after all danger of spring frost has passed the plants should be accommodated in a cool greenhouse where a minimum temperature of 40-50 degrees F. is maintained. During the summer they may be plunged (buried to the rims of their pots) in a bed of cinders or sand in a sunny location outdoors; or, if preferred, fall-blooming kinds may be planted out of their pots in a nursery bed and left to grow there until the late summer, when they may be carefully dug up and potted.

Among kinds best suited for pot culture are H. speciosa and its hybrids, including H. Andersonii and its variegated-leaved variety.

Propagation. All Hebes are easily propagated by means of young branches prepared as cuttings and inserted in a bed of sand or sand and peat moss in a cold frame or cool greenhouse in summer. They may also be raised very easily from seeds. Self-sown seedlings often spring up in gardens where these shrubs thrive. The broad-leaved kinds hybridize freely, and many beautiful seedlings of intermediate coloring occur.

The Chief Kinds. H. Andersonii is a hybrid between H. salicifolia and H. speciosa. It grows 4-6 ft. tall and has oblong, fleshy leaves 3-4 in. long and 1-1½ in. wide. The flowers, bluish-violet fading to white, are in densely packed racemes 3-5 in. long. This kind blooms in late summer and fall. A variety named H. Andersonii variegata has leaves margined with white.

H. angustifolia is a distinct and ornamental shrub, 3-5 ft. tall, of slender, rather graceful habit. The conspicuous brown stems and twigs are clothed with long, narrow, willow-like leaves and, towards the summit, bear pairs of slender flower spikes, 3-5 in. long. The flowers are white with a faint tinge of lilac, and are produced abundantly from July till November.

H. anomala is one of the hardiest and most satisfactory sorts. It grows up to 4 or 5 ft. tall, has narrow pointed leaves and produces, in June and July, masses of white or pale pink flowers in clustered spikes or panicles. With age the plant grows somewhat lank and leggy but it is a fast grower and easily propagated, so that younger specimens can be raised to replace the old ones. It is native of the South Island, New Zealand, and was introduced to European gardens as long ago as 1883.

H. Armstrongii is a dwarf member of the Whipcord type, 1-3 ft. tall. It comes from the South Island, New Zealand, and is among the hardier sorts. The arrangement of the opposite pairs of leaves, jointed together in cuplike form, is interesting. The twigs have the appearance of a string of cup-shaped beads fitting down closely into one another. The flowers are white.

H. Balfouriana was raised at Edinburgh Botanic Gardens, Scotland, from seeds sent from New Zealand, and named in honor of Sir I. Bailey Balfour; curiously enough, the plant is not known wild in its native country. It is closely related to H. Traversii and its spikes of large, blue flowers are very handsome. It grows 2-3 ft. high.

H. Buchananii is a valuable dwarf evergreen shrub for the rock garden, 12 in. tall, branched and bushy, with closely set glaucous leaves and short spikes of white flowers. It is a mountain shrub from South Island, New Zealand, and flowers in June and July.

H. buxifolia is a valuable and attractive shrub, 2-4 ft. tall, neat in habit and quite hardy. The leaves are pale green and the flowers white.

H. carnosula is a neat and attractive dwarf shrub for the rock garden. It grows about 12 in. high, and is prostrate in habit, with white flower spikes crowded at the summits of the branches. The gray-green leaves are closely set in opposite pairs to form neat rows up the stems.

H. cupressoides, from South Island, New Zealand, is one of the most valuable of the Whipcord type. It forms a rounded neat bush, 2-4 ft. tall, with very much the appearance of some dwarf Cypress of gray-green color. It is a valuable shrub for the rock garden or the choice shrubbery. It flowers freely, covering itself with countless small, pale lilac flowers in June or July. The most remarkable feature of this first-rate shrub is its scent, which is like that of cedar wood; on warm, still days it will fill the air for yards around.

H. decumbens, from South Island, New Zealand, is an attractive shrub, 1-2 ft. tall, the dark purplish shoots of which are closely set with oval, rather fleshy leaves, dark green with distinctive reddish margins. The flowers are white, borne in congested racemes at the tips of the shoots. It is a valuable and attractive kind.

H. diosmaefolia, from North Island, New Zealand, is a branched shrub, evergreen and of neat, attractive appearance, 2-5 ft. high. The leaves are arranged in four rows, and the white or pale lavender flowers are borne in rounded heads near the ends of the twigs in June.

H. elliptica is native of New Zealand, Chile, Tierra del Fuego, and the Falkland Islands. It may be a tree 20 ft. high or, more often, a shrub 3-5 ft. high. It has oval leaves and few-flowered racemes of large, fragrant, white flowers, the largest of any of the Hebes. It is a very attractive shrub but one of the less hardy sorts. It was introduced to Europe by Dr. Fothergill in 1776 and again from the Falkland Islands by Clarence Elliott in 1909.

H. epacridea is an attractive and distinct plant of dwarf habit, with the recurved leaves arranged closely in pairs to form four lines up the stems. It is of neat prostrate growth and excellent for the rock garden. The flowers, in close rounded heads, are large and white. From altitudes of 3,000-5,000 ft. in South Island, New Zealand.

H. Hectori is an interesting evergreen Whipcord Veronica from altitudes up to 8,000 ft. in South Island, New Zealand, growing from 1-2 ft. tall. It is of erect branched habit with small scalelike leaves in opposite pairs clasping the stems; the color of the whole plant is a pleasing dark golden-green. The flowers are white or pinkish, in small terminal heads. This is a first-rate rock garden shrub of picturesque aspect.

H. Hulkeana is an extremely beautiful shrub of rather straggling habit, growing 3-6 ft. or even more. The leaves are ovate and slightly toothed, and the flowers, of large size, are soft lavender or lilac color, in large branched panicles 6 in. or more long. It is one of the less hardy kinds but it is well worth taking some trouble to secure its exquisite flowers.

H. ligustrifolia is an evergreen shrub, 2-3 ft. tall, of loose habit of growth. The white flowers are produced in slender spikes some 3 in. long from near the ends of the branches in July and August. It comes from North Island, New Zealand. It is an attractive shrub.

H. loganioides from South Island, New Zealand, is an attractive dwarf, evergreen, rock garden shrub, resembling a decumbent conifer, only 4-6 in. high. It is slightly hairy, and the rather large, white flowers, sometimes with pink veins, are produced in June and July.

H. lycopodioides is a pretty dwarf rock garden shrub, 1-2 ft. tall. It is one of the Whipcord group and resembles a Club Moss. The whole plant has a charming bronzy-golden tone which is especially welcome in winter. It is one of the hardiest and has white flowers with conspicuous blue anthers.

H. pimeleoides is a neat and pretty, prostrate, rock garden shrub, 6-9 in. high, with glaucous, boxwood-like leaves and short spikes of purplish flowers in June, July and August.

H. pimeleoides glauco-caerulea is a rather larger edition of the last, with larger leaves and flowers of a darker purple. Both are natives of South Island, New Zealand, and are altogether admirable for the rock garden or for the front of a choice shrub bed. They are beautiful in leaf and in flower, and the two contrast charmingly with one another.

H. propuinqua resembles H. cupressoides, but is more dwarf, has white flowers, and a pleasant, golden-green color. It is an attractive rock garden shrub.

The Willow-Leaved Hebe, H. salicifolia, is a very variable evergreen shrub, growing as tall as 10 ft. when wild, but often less tall in gardens. It is of erect, bushy habit, with narrow leaves, 2-5 in. long, and slender racemes, 4-10 in. long, of white, lilac or purple in varying shades. It hybridizes freely; the popular Hebe Andersonii is a hybrid between H. salicifolia and H. speciosa.

H. speciosa is a shrub up to 5 ft. high, with glossy leaves, 2-4 in. long and racemes up to 3 in. long of reddish-purple flowers. It is native of North Island, New Zealand, and sparingly of South Island, where it was discovered as long ago as 1833. The typical plant is perhaps not in cultivation at the present time, but it has produced many strikingly handsome hybrids when crossed with various other shrubby kinds. Some of these have fine spikes of crimson, pink, blue, violet and purple flowers, and the influence of H. speciosa is usually betrayed by the reddish or purplish young leaves.

These plants are not very hardy and are best for really mild localities and for growing as pot plants in cool greenhouses.

H. Traversii (brachysiphon) makes a fine bush up to 6 ft. high, and is of shapely rounded outline. The stems are covered with wedge-shaped leaves arranged in four even rows up the stems. The flowers are white and borne in 2-in.-long racemes in great profusion in July. This fine shrub should be grown in every garden where climate permits its cultivation.

HEBENSTRETIA (Hebenstret'ia). Tender perennial plants of minor garden value that are ordinarily grown as annuals. They are wild in South Africa and belong to the Figwort family, Scrophulariaceae. They grow about 2 ft. in height, have small lanceolate leaves and terminal spikes of small, mignonette-like yellow or white flowers with an orange-red spot on the petals. Hebenstretia commemorates John E. Hebenstreit.

Plants are raised in a greenhouse in spring and planted in the garden in May or seed may be sown directly outdoors after danger from frost has passed.

The chief kind is H. comosa, 18 in., which bears white flowers in summer.

HEDERA—*Ivy* (Hed'era). Evergreen climbing or trailing plants that attach themselves to supports and usually ascend to a considerable height by means of aerial roots. They are found wild in Europe, Asia, northern Africa and the Canary Islands, and are characterized by thick, leathery, often long-stalked, glossy leaves. Hedera belongs to the family Araliaceae. The name is the ancient Latin name for Ivy.

The Ivies vary considerably between their juvenile and mature states. The climbing and trailing condition is the juvenile state and at this stage the plants do not flower. When they reach the top of tall supports, however, they undergo a change. The climbing habit gives place to a

Hedera helix variety hibernica makes a handsome and effective evergreen ground cover.

The English Ivy, Hedera Helix, is a great favorite. It is self-clinging, attaching itself to masonry by means of small rootlets.

bushy form and the aerial roots cease to appear. Moreover, the shape of the leaves changes; it is this state which is sometimes known as the Tree Ivy. The flowers are yellow or greenish yellow, a number being produced together in round clusters in autumn; they have a great attraction for some insects.

The fruits develop during winter and, when ripe, are the size of small Peas, usually dark purple or black, sometimes yellow, very occasionally reddish.

The Ivies vary a good deal in shape and color of leaves, and many have been given varietal names. It is possible to perpetuate some mature forms of Tree Ivies by grafting, and to cultivate them as bushes. Some of them have been given horticultural names very different from those of the juvenile forms from which they spring.

Ivies grow well in ordinary garden soil. They thrive in full sun, provided they receive adequate supplies of moisture, and in semishade, but in cold climates they are liable to suffer severely from winter burn in sunny, exposed locations. They succeed in towns, but the leaves get very dirty in winter.

Not Suitable for Hot, Sunny Walls. It is not advisable to plant Ivies against a wall exposed to hot sun. They thrive better on northern and western exposures. The Ivies are well suited for carpeting ground beneath trees where grass will not grow and in other shaded places. They should be planted in spring and, if it is intended that they should climb, they should be cut back to a length not exceeding 6 in. at planting time, and should be set as close as possible to the wall or other support to which they are to cling.

When to Clip Ivy. When Ivies are grown against a wall they should be cut back as close as possible to the wall and well below the eaves, when on the walls of buildings, in spring. Later in the year it may be necessary to remove long, straying shoots. An annual hard clipping in spring gets rid of much of the dirt collected during the winter, and keeps the stems close to the wall.

Easily Increased by Cuttings. No plant is more easily propagated by cuttings than the trailing and climbing Ivies. Make the cuttings 6-9 in. long (shorter in some of the short-jointed, tiny-leaved varieties), remove the leaves from the lower part of the stem and plant the cuttings in a propagating bed in a greenhouse or cold frame that is kept close. In mild climates the cuttings may be planted directly out of doors in a shaded place that is sheltered from sweeping winds.

When grown as house plants, Ivy cuttings root readily if planted in a pot of moist sand or ver-

The English Ivy climbs vigorously. At Williamsburg, Virginia, it ascends trees and, several feet above the ground, produces its flowering and fruiting branches.

miculite and if they are kept covered with a bell jar or mason jar, so that the atmosphere about them is kept moist until they have rooted. They also may be rooted by merely placing their lower parts in jars or other containers of water. The variegated-leaved Ivies usually root better indoors than in the open garden.

In the garden, where Ivy is used as a ground cover, the stems will naturally layer themselves and root into the soil. When that occurs, rooted pieces may be taken off in spring and be planted elsewhere. This is a very simple and a very sure means of obtaining increase.

The mature type of Tree Ivy may be grafted on vigorous rooted cuttings of the trailing kinds. Stocks for this purpose should be established in pots and grafting should be carried out in a greenhouse in spring. Plants of Hedera can also be raised from seeds.

As Pot Plants. English Ivy, Hedera Helix, and particularly some of the more ornamental, smaller-leaved varieties of it, make attractive house plants when grown in pots of leafy compost; they are also useful for shady window boxes, especially on town houses.

Kinds of Ivy. Hedera Helix is the typical English Ivy. Even in a wild state it is very variable in habit and in the size, shape and marking of the leaves. Under cultivation this variation is intensified and numerous varieties have originated as sports. These varieties may have large or small leaves; the margins may be divided into a varying number of blunt or pointed lobes; they may be green, purple, or gold or silver-variegated, and a few are so dwarf and stunted that they form admirable subjects for the rock garden. There is also the difference in habit and appearance to consider between varieties named from the juvenile or climbing and the mature type or Tree Ivy.

In the United States the large-leaved variety, H. Helix hibernica, is most commonly grown as English Ivy. H. Helix baltica is a very hardy variety; at Boston, Massachusetts, tall-growing specimens on walls winter without serious damage. Another variety that is extremely hardy to winter cold is named 238th Street. A characteristic of this distinct kind is that it produces trailing, vining shoots directly from mature flowering and fruiting branches.

All kinds live as ground covers under severer winter conditions than they will tolerate as tall-growing vines. The nomenclature of varieties of English Ivy is much confused, varieties having been described and sold under the names listed in the following three paragraphs, but it is not possible to be sure that the names given are botanically valid. Some may be synonyms of others.

The flowers of the English Ivy are greenish and are produced in clusters late in the year.

In winter, clusters of pealike berries follow the flowers of the English Ivy.

Climbing Ivies with Colored Leaves. Useful varieties of the climbing type are aurea elegantissima, with small golden variegated leaves; Cavendishii, with small, cream-margined leaves; aurea maculata, large leaves mottled with gold; palmato-aurea and flavescens, with gold and green leaves; and scutifolia spectabilis aurea with golden leaves. Ivies with silver-variegated leaves are tricolor Crippsii, marginata major, marginata media, minor variegata and lacteola.

Many varieties of Hedera Helix, English Ivy, make attractive pot plants for house and greenhouse cultivation. Being evergreen, they continue attractive throughout the year.

Ivies having small leaves with deeply lobed margins are digitata, digitata nana, minima. Purpurea has purple leaves, nigra, dark purple leaves, and Emerald Green has small, bright green leaves; this is an excellent variety for covering low fences. Other useful free-growing sorts are ovata, pedata, rugosa, lucida and venosa. Two dwarf stunted forms suitable for the rock garden are conglomerata and minima, both forms of the common Ivy, but quite unlike the wild plant.

In recent years a number of handsome small-leaved, freely branching varieties that are especially adaptable for pot culture have been raised in the United States; noteworthy among these are Pittsburgh, Hahn's Self-branching, Hahn's Variegated, Manda's Crested, Maple Queen, Silver Garland, Merion Beauty, Pin Oak, Silver Emblem, Silver King, Sylvanian Beauty, and Weber's California.

Irish Ivy. Hedera Helix hibernica is the Irish Ivy, a vigorous plant with large, leathery, long-stalked leaves. This is the Ivy that is often planted against high walls by reason of its vigor and generally known in North America as English Ivy. Aureo-maculata with gold-mottled leaves, maculata with white- or gray-mottled leaves, and folliis argenteis, silver variegated, are useful varieties.

A pot-grown specimen of the variegated Canary Island Ivy, Hedera canariensis, a tender species with large green and cream leaves. It is a good quick-growing climbing house plant.

Hedera canariensis, the Canary Island Ivy, is a rather tender, quick-growing, large-leaved kind, and H. colchica, the Persian Ivy, found wild in north Persia and the Caucasus, has very large, green, leathery leaves which are sometimes 9-10 in. long and 5-7 in. across. Its varieties, amurensis and dentata, are specially worthy of note. The Himalayan Ivy, H. nepalensis (cinerea), is a neat-growing, distinct kind, as is H. rhombea, the Japanese Ivy.

A curious bigeneric hybrid has been raised between the Ivy and Fatsia japonica, named Fatshedera, which see.

HEDGEHOG BROOM. See Erinacea.
HEDGEHOG CACTUS. See Echinocactus.

HEDGES: FOR PRIVACY AND SHELTER
How to Use Them to the Best Advantage

A hedge may be desirable for various reasons. In some places a tall hedge serves as a windbreak for protection of house and garden. It may also serve the purpose of a screen or fence, to give privacy and prevent intrusion. Very often it is used to define limited areas within the garden. A well-kept hedge, properly placed, can be a most attractive garden feature when made of an appropriate plant. It may be evergreen or deciduous (leaf-losing), dwarf or tall, kept formal by close shearing, or informal by merely trimming straggly shoots.

Before selecting a suitable plant for a particular hedge, you should give consideration to local climatic conditions and to the nature of the soil. A hedge is usually intended to stand in place for a long time. In order to give it a good start, thorough soil preparation should be made. Good drainage is essential as most plants will not long survive where water stands about their roots for any length of time. Sometimes the removal of a foot or so of soggy subsoil 2-3 ft. down and its replacement with cinders or gravel will suffice; if not, then some other drainage method suitable to the situation should be carried out. A strip of earth 2-3 ft. in width and 2 ft. deep should be enriched with leaf mold, peat moss, compost or other well-decayed material and with bone meal in preparation for the planting of a hedge.

Planting and Care. In general it is advisable to set out plants of rather small size. Smaller plants are more easily established and less expensive to buy than larger ones. A single-row hedge serves the purpose in most cases. Space the plants 9 in. apart for the smaller hedge, and up to 2 ft. or so apart for larger deciduous and evergreen plants. Where a very dense hedge is desired, 2 rows may be planted 10 to 12 inches apart, with the plants set in alternate fashion—that is, staggered.

Deciduous plants should be cut back to 6 in. or so at planting time in order to promote dense growth at the base. For solid effect a hedge should be built up gradually to the desired height. Evergreen plants do not require this cutting back at planting time, but a leveling off of the tops is advisable. Plants set for an informal hedge may be more widely spaced. Deciduous shrubs may be cut back one half or more to induce good bushy growth from the base.

Privet hedges need frequent trimming to keep them compact and neat. A string is stretched tightly between two stakes to provide a guide for making the hedge top level.

The sides of hedges should be clipped so that the hedge broadens slightly towards its base.

How to Prune Hedges. *(Top)* A. Formal (clipped). B. Informal (unclipped). *(Center)* Clipping a hedge wider at the base than at the top permits sunlight to reach the lower branches and prevents excessive accumulation of snow. 1. Good. 2. Good. 3. Fair. 4. Poor *(Bottom)* R. Severe cutting back of newly set plants induces dense basal growth. W. Open, leggy bases resulting from improper cutting at planting time.

Trimming and Shearing. When the hedge is established, trimming or shearing is required once or more during the year. To maintain a privet hedge in good form at least 3 shearings should be given, but, except for the most vigorous of the deciduous shrubs, one trimming a year will do. A good time to trim is in early summer, or when the year's growth is completed. A hedge of flowering shrubs should be trimmed as soon as the flowers fade. Trimming at midsummer is usually sufficient to keep evergreen hedges in good form, but a pine hedge may be trimmed while the new growth is still soft, before the needles have fully unfolded.

A hedge remains in better condition when the sides are somewhat sloping in from the bottom up. The top may be left flat, but in areas where heavy snows are usual, damage from breakage is less likely if the top is rounded. It is not always possible to knock snow off a hedge before the snow freezes on and breaks or twists it out of shape.

Cultivation. Weeds and trash should promptly be cleared from the base of a hedge to prevent possible weakening of the lower branches as well as maintain the desirable neat appearance. Thorough waterings in dry times should be given if possible, especially to evergreens. These may be greatly helped under dry conditions by forceful mistlike spraying of the foliage to keep down spider mites. If growth is not thrifty a mulch of leaf mold and decayed manure or rich compost applied in late fall, followed by an application of a complete fertilizer in spring will prove beneficial.

Overgrown deciduous hedges, if healthy, may

California Privet, Ligustrum ovalifolium, is a popular hedge. It stands shearing well.

The evergreen glossy-leaved Privet, Ligustrum lucidum, is a favorite in the South.

The Canadian Hemlock, Tsuga canadensis, forms a dense evergreen hedge when well cared for.

be renovated by cutting them back almost to the ground in early spring. New growth is helped if the soil is loosened with a fork and a mulch applied. Yew responds well to hard cutting back if need be, but evergreens such as Pine, Hemlock, and Spruce do not.

Hardy Shrubs Suitable for Hedges. The following groups are generally hardy in the North; heights will be variable, according to location and conditions.

Deciduous: Up to 2 ft. Berberis Thunbergii erecta, and B. Thunbergii minor, Chaenomeles japonica, Deutzia gracilis, Spiraea Bumalda, Anthony Waterer, S. japonica ovalifolia, Viburnum Opulus nanum.

Deciduous: Up to 5 ft. Acanthopanax Sieboldianus, Berberis mentorensis, B. Thunbergii, Chaenomeles lagenaria, Deutzia Lemoinei, Euonymus alatus compactus, Ligustrum amurense, L. obtusifolium Regelianum, L. ovalifolium, Physocarpus monogynous, Rhamnus Frangula, Spiraea Thunbergii, Stephanandra incisa.

Deciduous: 5 ft. and over. Caragana arborescens, Carpinus Betulus, Crataegus Crus-galli, Euonymus alatus, Fagus sylvatica, Hibiscus syriacus, Myrica pensylvanica, Quercus imbricaria, Spiraea Vanhouttei, Syringa Josikaea, Viburnum Lantana.

Evergreen: Up to 2 ft. Buxus microphylla koreana, B. sempervirens suffruticosa, Euonymus

Hardiest of evergreen hedges is the American Arborvitae, Thuja occidentalis.

The White Pine, Pinus Strobus, forms a rather unusual hedge of light and feathery appearance.

The American Holly, Ilex opaca, forms a splendid evergreen hedge. This example is in Virginia.

Square-topped hedges such as this example of Ilex crenata are more likely to be damaged by snow than hedges cut to a rounded or pointed top.

A hedge of the hardy Black Hills Spruce, Picea glauca variety densata.

Ilex crenata microphylla forms a neat hedge of medium height.

Fortunei Carrierei, and Taxus cuspidata densa.

Evergreen: Up to 5 ft. Berberis Julianae, Chamaecyparis obtusa compacta, C. pisifera filifera, Ilex crenata microphylla, Juniperus virginiana Canaertii, Pinus Cembra, Taxus cuspidata, T. cuspidata columnaris, T. media varieties, Thuja occidentalis robusta, T. occidentalis compacta.

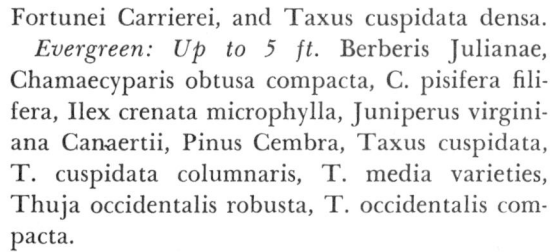

Evergreen: 5 ft. and over. Chamaecyparis pisifera, Ilex crenata, I. opaca, Juniperus scopulorum viridifolia, Picea Abies, P. glauca, Pinus Strobus, Pseudotsuga taxifolia, Thuja orientalis, T. occidentalis, Tsuga canadensis.

Tender Shrubs Suitable for Hedges. The following evergreens may be used for hedges in parts of the country where conditions are suitable and winters are not severe.

Dwarf to Medium Height. Abelia grandiflora, Buxus sempervirens, Carissa grandiflora, Euonymus japonicus microphyllus, Ligustrum japonicum rotundifolium, L. lucidum, Lonicera nitida, Myrtus communis minima, Pittosporum Tobira, Raphiolepis indica.

For Evergreen Hedges 5 ft. or over. Acacia longifolia, Camellia japonica, Camellia Sasanqua, Casuarina equisetifolia, Chamaecyparis Lawsoni-

The Bayberry, Myrica pensylvanica, may be used effectively to provide a somewhat informal hedge.

ana, Eugenia paniculata australis, Euonymus japonicus varieties, Ilex Aquifolium, I. vomitoria, Murraea paniculata, Myrica cerifera, Prunus Laurocerasus, Severinia buxifolia, Viburnum Tinus.

HEDYCHIUM—*Garland Flower, Ginger Lily* (Hedy'chium). Tropical, evergreen herbaceous plants with sweet-scented flowers in summer. They are natives of India and China and belong to the Ginger plant family, Zingiberaceae. They have thick, fleshy rhizomes (underground stems) from which rise long, slender stems 4 ft. in length, bearing oval glossy leaves, 6 in. in length and 2½ in. in diameter. At the top of each stem a raceme of white, yellow or red flowers is produced in summer. The name is derived from *hedys,* sweet, and *chion,* snow, and refers to the white, sweet-scented flowers of some kinds.

Moisture-loving Plants. They may be grown outdoors in southern Florida; elsewhere in greenhouses. When grown indoors, they require a minimum winter temperature of 50 degrees. The best potting compost consists of equal parts of loam and leaf mold with a small amount of sand. Repotting is done in March, when all the old soil is removed and the plants are placed in fresh soil. Water is applied freely in summer, and well-rooted plants do best when standing in saucers of water. After flowering, the water supply is gradually reduced and the soil is kept dry throughout the winter. Propagation is by division of the rhizomes in spring.

Flower spike of the Ginger Lily, Hedychium Gardnerianum, a handsome plant for warm climates and tropical greenhouses.

The chief kinds are H. Gardnerianum, 4 ft., lemon yellow, fragrant, summer; H. coccineum, 6 ft., red, summer; H. flavum, 5 ft., yellow blotched with orange, summer; H. Greenei, 6 ft., orange-red with red lip, summer; and H. coronarium, 4 ft., white, fragrant, summer.

HEDYSARUM—*French Honeysuckle* (Hedys'-arum). Perennial herbs, or subshrubs, found wild in Europe, North Africa, temperate Asia and temperate America. A few are useful in gardens, but, generally, they are more attractive in a wild state than cultivated. The herbaceous kinds succeed in deep, loamy soil and can be increased by division in autumn.

The most decorative for general cultivation is H. coronarium, the French Honeysuckle, a plant from southwestern Europe, which grows 2-4 ft. high, bearing dense heads of red or crimson flowers in summer. H. sibiricum, 3-4 ft., with yellowish or purple flowers, is also attractive, as are H. flavescens, yellow, a native of Turkestan, and H. grandiflorum, from the Caucasus.

H. multijugum is a very attractive shrubby plant from Mongolia; it grows 2-3 ft. high and has rather soft shoots bearing elegant gray-green leaves made up of numerous tiny leaflets, and during summer produces long racemes of rosy magenta flowers. It requires a light, warm, loamy soil, and is propagated by seeds and cuttings; the dead ends of the previous year's shoots must be cut off in spring. These plants belong to the Pea family, Leguminosae. Hedysarum is the ancient Greek name for the common European kind.

HEDYSCEPE CANTERBURYANA — Umbrella Palm (Hedysce′pe; Hedys′cepe). A Palm, belonging to the family Palmaceae, which grows wild on Lord Howe Island, where it reaches a height of 30 ft. It is spineless, with a thick trunk and large recurving leaves, with broad leaflets. The name Hedyscepe is from *hedys,* sweet, and *skepe,* covering. It may be grown outdoors in southern Florida and southern California; elsewhere in greenhouses.

A Hothouse Palm. Plants in small pots are very ornamental, although they are not widely cultivated, as the Howea, which Hedyscepe resembles, is much quicker in growth and easier to propagate. This Palm requires a minimum winter temperature of 55 degrees, and is repotted in March in a compost of equal parts of peat, loam and sand. Propagation is by seeds sown in pots of sandy soil plunged in a propagating case in a hothouse in spring. The only kind is H. Canterburyana.

HEEL. A term used by gardeners in describing cuttings which are removed from the plant with a piece or "heel" of the old branch or shoot attached at the base. Such cuttings are said to be "taken" with a "heel" or with a "heel of old wood." They often form roots more quickly than others which are prepared in the usual way—i.e., by cutting through the shoot beneath a joint to form the base of the cutting.

HEELING IN. A term used by gardeners to describe the practice of dealing with trees, shrubs or plants which cannot at once be planted permanently, by placing them temporarily in a trench dug in an out-of-the-way place and covering the roots with soil.

Unpack trees and shrubs received from nurseries as promptly after their arrival as possible.

Place the roots in a hole and cover them with soil to keep them from drying.

So that no air pockets remain about the roots, press the soil firmly against them with the foot.

When trees or shrubs are heeled in, it is usual to slope them at an angle of about forty-five degrees.

HEERIA. See Heterocentron and Schizocentron.

HE-HUCKLEBERRY. See Lyonia ligustrina.

HEIMIA (Heim′ia). Shrubs or subshrubs from the warmer parts of the Americas and Africa. They belong to the Loosestrife family, Lythraceae and are named in honor of a Dr. Heim of Berlin, Germany.

Heimia myrtifolia and H. salicifolia are sometimes planted in California and in other mild climates. The former attains a height of about three feet, the latter grows 10 ft. tall. Both have yellow flowers. They grow without trouble in any ordinary soil in sunny locations and are easily increased by seeds and cuttings.

HELENIUM—*Sneezeweed* (Helen′ium). Mostly herbaceous perennials, 1½-5 ft. high, which are of great value for the herbaceous border. They bloom during the summer and early autumn months and bear large, somewhat daisy-like flowers of various colors. They are natives of North America and belong to the Daisy family, Compositae. Helenium is derived from *helenion*, a Greek name of which the origin is obscure.

The annual Helenium tenuifolium grows 2 ft. high, has yellow flowers and is easily raised from seeds.

A dwarf yellow Helenium.

Flourish in Ordinary Soil. Heleniums thrive in ordinary loamy soil, where they grow more vigorously and bloom more freely than in light, poor land. The latter, however, can be made suitable by adding leaf mold, decayed garden refuse, peat moss or manure when the ground is being prepared for planting. A mulch or soil covering of decayed manure or compost placed on the soil above the roots in May is beneficial to these plants when they are grown on light land. The best time to plant is in fall, but the work may be done during spring also.

Propagation. The tall Heleniums are vigorous plants which soon develop into large clumps; the best way to propagate these is to lift them in fall in alternate years and separate them into small clusters for replanting separately 12 in. apart. Only the strong outside pieces should be chosen for replanting; the inner, older portions should be thrown away. Three or five clusters should be grouped together when replanting.

If a large number of plants is needed, the clumps can be separated into single rooted shoots in March–April, these being planted 6 in. apart in nursery rows. By autumn they will each have made clumps of ideal planting size. Perennial species (wild types), but not improved garden varieties, can be raised from seeds; annual kinds, such as H. tenuifolium, are always raised from seeds.

If the dead blooms of Heleniums are trimmed off, they produce a second crop without harm to the plants.

Showy Kinds. Helenium autumnale, 4-6 ft., bears light yellow flowers in August–September, but its many showy varieties are superior to it for garden decoration. Some of the best of these are

The Heleniums are among the most profusely flowering of hardy perennial plants that bloom in late summer and autumn. They thrive in any average garden soil and are easily increased by division. Of the dwarfer kinds, which bloom from early July onwards, one of the showiest is Helenium Bigelovii aurantiacum, here seen in full bloom.

Baron Linden, light orange red, 4 ft., June–August; Chipperfield Orange, orange yellow and red, 5-6 ft., August–September; Riverton Beauty, yellow, 5 ft.; Riverton Gem, yellow and red, 5 ft.; Old Gold Giant, petals dull gold above, mahogany shaded bronze beneath, 3-4 ft., August.

Helenium Moerheim Beauty, rich crimson-red, 3-4 ft., July–September, is one of the showiest of all plants for the herbaceous border; and for the front of the border invaluable kinds are autumnale pumilum, 2 ft., light golden-yellow; Butterpat, pale yellow, 2 ft., Crimson Beauty, orange-crimson, 2 ft.; and H. Bigelovii aurantiacum, orange-gold. All of these more dwarf kinds bloom from early July onwards.

The only annual kind likely to be cultivated is H. tenuifolium, a native of the southeastern United States which has yellow flowers, slender leaves and grows about 2 ft. high.

HELIANTHELLA (Helianthel'la; Helian'thella). A small genus of herbaceous perennials, natives of western North America, belonging to the Daisy family, Compositae. The chief kind is H. quinquenervis, 3 ft. or more, with finely cut foliage and small, yellow Sunflowers. It thrives in ordinary soil and is increased by division.

HELIANTHEMUM — *Sun Rose* (Helianth'emum). A large group of evergreen, or partly evergreen, subshrubby and herbaceous perennials, and a few annuals. About 110 kinds grow in Europe, northern Africa, western Asia, and North and South America. Numerous named varieties and hybrids are cultivated in gardens. The Helianthemums are allied to the Rock Rose (Cistus) and belong to the family Cistaceae. The name is from the Greek, *helios,* sun, and *anthemom,* flower.

One of the many fine varieties of Helianthemum nummularium.

Must Be Planted in a Sunny Place. The Sun Roses are essentially sun-loving plants, and are suitable for the rock garden or sunny banks; they bloom from May to July and thrive in ordinary, well-drained garden ground including limestone soil. Most kinds are not long-lived, or after a few years become so straggling and untidy that it is better to replace them by young plants rather than subject them to continual hard pruning.

Helianthemum apenninum roseum has grayish leaves and rosy-red flowers.

[5–10]
*Yellow Daylilies
(Hemerocallis)*

[5–11, 5–11a, 5–11b, 5–11c]
Daylily
(Hemerocallis varieties)

Need Protection in the North. In the North, Sun Roses need some winter protection. A light, loose layer of salt hay, evergreen branches, or similar material that permits a free circulation of air about the plants is satisfactory. H. nummulariaum and its varieties are among the most satisfactory Sun Roses for gardens in the North. In California and places favored with similar climates Sun Roses flourish.

Planting and Pruning. The Sun Roses do not transplant very well, and for this reason the young plants are usually grown in pots until large enough to plant out finally. Planting is best done in April. Most do not benefit by hard pruning, but exceptions are found in the large number of named varieties of H. nummularium (vulgare), which benefit by being trimmed or clipped rather hard each year after flowering; young shoots will then grow freely from the rootstocks. The individual flowers only last one day, but the plants produce an abundance of blossoms from May to July or August.

Propagation is by cuttings of young shoots, about 3 in. long, inserted in a cold frame or under a bell jar during August. When rooted they should be placed singly in 3-in. pots, and wintered in a cold frame for planting permanently the following spring. They can also be raised from seed sown under glass in spring, although named varieties will not, of course, come true to color.

Beautiful Sun Roses. These are some of the best of the named varieties of Helianthemum nummularium: The Bride, white, silvery foliage; Fireball, scarlet-red; Mrs. C. W. Earle, double, crimson; rubens, orange; album plenum, double, white; Butter and Eggs, double, soft orange; Croceum, yellow; Tangerine, White Queen, and Wisley Primrose.

The Tighanagarh strain of Sun Roses is particularly fine. A few of the most distinct are Ben Alder, terra cotta; Ben Dearg, deep red, orange center; Ben Mare, flame, crimson center; Ben Rhada, yellow with orange zone; Ben Lawers, pale orange; Ben Lomond, rose madder, orange center; Ben More, flame, crimson center; Ben Nevis, chrome-yellow, with crimson ring. These attain a height of about 10 in.

For the Rock Garden. H. alpestre is a small, tufted alpine, from the mountains of central Europe, which has tiny green leaves and yellow flowers. H. apenninum is a spreading plant, 1-1½ ft. high, with gray leaves and pure white flowers. It grows freely from seeds and is not long-lived. H. appeninum variety roseum has rose-red flowers. The varieties of the common Sun Rose, H. nummularium, already named, are also suitable for planting in the rock garden.

H. Tuberaria is a herbaceous kind, suitable for a sunny position in the rock garden. It forms tufts of brown leaves, from among which rise clusters of golden-yellow flowers, on 6- to 8-in. stems in June–July.

HELIANTHUS — *Sunflower* (Helianth'us). Hardy herbaceous perennial or annual plants, chiefly found in North America, which bear large yellow flowers in late summer and autumn. They belong to the Daisy family, Compositae. The name Helianthus is derived from *helios,* the sun, and *anthos,* a flower.

The perennial Sunflowers are tall, vigorous plants which thrive in ordinary soil in a sunny, or partially shaded place, and spread quickly.

Flowers of the miniature Sunflower, the modern seedsmen's strains of which have been derived from Helianthus debilis. The flowers are of varied coloring, often with contrasting zones, and are good for cutting.

HELICHRYSUM

Most of them soon become a nuisance by crowding out neighboring plants unless they are lifted and separated into single rooted pieces for replanting in alternate years.

The easiest method of propagation is by lifting and dividing the plants in the fall.

The best kinds for general planting are Helianthus decapetalus (multiflorus) and its double variety named Soleil d'Or: they grow only 4-5 ft. high and are very attractive.

The giant Sunflower, Helianthus annuus.

The most handsome of all is one called Monarch: it is a variety of H. atrorubens (sparsifolius), grows 6-7 ft. high, and bears large blooms of rich golden-yellow. Other showy tall kinds include H. laetiflorus Miss Mellish, semidouble, orange yellow; H. decapetalus Capenoch Star, single, rich yellow; and Loddon Gold, double, yellow. H. salicifolius (orgyalis), 6-7 ft., has narrow ornamental leaves. All the perennial Sunflowers have yellow blooms.

The Annual Sunflowers. Helianthus annuus, is a familiar plant. It bears huge, rounded, black-centered blooms on stems 6-10 ft. high. There are varieties of this common annual Sunflower with blooms of different colors—reddish, pale yellow and deep yellow. The largest of all is the variety Russian Giant.

H. argyrophyllus, the Silverleaf Sunflower, is an annual kind that grows about 6 ft. high and is a most attractive plant for flower borders. Its leaves are covered with soft, silky hairs which give them a distinctly silvery appearance, and it bears large numbers of yellow flower heads which have dark brown-purple centers. The flower heads measure about 3 in. in diameter.

Another attractive annual Sunflower is H. debilis (cucumerifolius), $3\frac{1}{2}$ ft., from which have been derived the garden strains known as Miniature Sunflowers. The plants reach a height of 2-4 ft., and bear flowers of moderate size which are of attractive and varied coloring.

A double-flowered Sunflower.

Favorites are Stella, golden-yellow; Primrose Stella; Dazzler, chestnut-red, tipped orange; Excelsior, yellow, with red and crimson markings; and Orion, deep yellow. All grow 2-3 ft. tall.

Seeds of all annual Sunflowers may be sown out of doors in spring, where the plants are to bloom, or in boxes of soil in a greenhouse in March, the seedlings being planted out in May.

Economic Uses. The seeds of the annual Sunflower are rich in oil, the best forms containing up to 28 or 30 per cent. When cold pressed, this oil is very useful as a salad oil, for cookery and for the manufacture of margarine. The seeds are also used for poultry food and as food for parrots and other large cage birds, and are an excellent crop for poultry keepers and bird fanciers to grow.

HELICHRYSUM — *Everlasting Flower, Immortelle* (Helichry'sum). In this large genus of

Flowers of a good seedsmen's strain of Helichrysum bracteatum. The showiest of the "Everlasting Flowers", it is available in a wide range of colors and is valuable for dried flower arrangements.

plants are included annuals, herbaceous perennials and shrubs. They belong to the Daisy family, Compositae. The annuals are the most popular kinds; they are grown for their flowers, which are cut and dried for winter decoration. The shrubby kinds are hardy in mild climates, such as that of California. The name Helichrysum is derived from *helios,* sun, and *chrysos,* gold.

The Annuals. These are natives of Australia. They grow 2-3 ft. tall and have daisy-like flowers 1-2 in. in diameter. They have been bred from the species named H. bracteatum, and the flower colors range from white and cream, through shades of pink, yellow and orange to scarlet, blood-red and crimson. Seeds are sown in pots or flats of light soil in March in a greenhouse, temperature 50-55 degrees. The seedlings are pricked out, 2 in. apart, in boxes, and when established are planted in light, well-drained soil in a sunny position in April or May. When the flower heads are fully developed they are cut with long stalks, and hung in a dry, cool place to dry. Seeds may also be sown outdoors where the plants are to grow.

For Summer Bedding. A pretty subshrubby kind that is sometimes grown for inclusion in summer bedding schemes is H. lanatum, which grows 12 in. in height and has small leaves covered with silvery down of flannel-like appearance. Propagation is by division of the clumps in spring.

The Principal Hardy Perennial. H. arenarium, a native of Europe, grows about 10 in. in height, has oval leaves for the most part, and bright-yellow flowers. It should be planted in rich, loamy soil in April, and it requires a sunny position. Propagation is by division in spring. The flowers may be dried for winter decoration.

A Shrubby Kind. H. rosmarinifolium (Ozothamnus rosmarinifolius), a native of Australia, grows 8 ft. high, has ribbed branches, and narrow leaves, 1 in. long; both branches and leaves are sticky. The flowers, which are small and white, are produced in great profusion in summer. This tender shrub must be planted in a well-drained sandy soil.

For the Rock Garden. H. bellidioides and H. frigidum, both with small white flowers in summer, are attractive mat-forming plants for the rock garden. They need sunny, well-drained positions, and are not likely to be hardy, even with protection, north of Philadelphia.

HELICONIA — *False Plantain* (Helico'nia). Tropical ornamental foliage plants which are closely allied to the Banana, and belong to the Banana family, Musaceae. They are natives of tropical America, and have banana-like flowers and leaves, the latter being striped with red, green or yellow. The name Heliconia is derived from Helicon, the mountain of the Muses.

Hothouse Plants with Ornamental Leaves. They need a minimum winter temperature of 55 degrees and a compost of equal parts of loam and leaf mold, half a part of thoroughly decayed manure and a sprinkling of sand. They are repotted in February, when they are set in slightly larger pots. A warm, moist atmosphere is essential. Propagation is by division.

The chief kinds include several varieties of H. illustris, notably aureo-striata with green leaves with ivory and pink veins, Edwardus Rex with coppery red foliage, rubricaulis with green leaves with pink veins, and spectabilis with green leaves with a brown midrib and wine-red on their under surfaces. Other kinds are H. humilis (Lobster's Claw), green leaves, salmon-red and green bracts, yellowish flowers; H. psittacorum (Parrot Flower), green leaves, orange and red bracts, flowers greenish yellow with black spots; H. Bihai, leaves green, bracts scarlet and yellow, flowers greenish yellow; H. caribaea, leaves green, bracts crimson and yellow.

HELIOCEREUS—*Sun Cereus.* A small group of bushy Cacti from Mexico and Central America, previously included in the genus Cereus. Their branches, which usually need support, have up to seven well-defined, spiny ribs, and bear large, red, fragrant flowers. For details of cultivation see Cacti.

Two of the showiest kinds are H. elegantissimus and H. speciosus. The latter hybridizes freely and has been crossed with Epiphyllum to produce some very showy hybrids.

HELIOPHILA (Helioph'ila). Beautiful plants, chiefly annuals, natives of South Africa and belonging to the Mustard family, Cruciferae. Heliophila is derived from *helios,* the sun, and *phileo,* to love.

The annual kinds thrive best in rather light or well-drained soil in a sunny place, but do not thrive in very hot weather. The seeds may be sown out of doors in early spring where the plants are to bloom, though it is usual to sow the seeds in a flat of light sifted soil in a greenhouse in March, the seedlings being planted out of doors in May. The seedlings should be thinned out from 4-6 in. apart.

The chief kinds are H. leptophylla, 18 in., blue and white, and H. linearifolia, 12-18 in., blue, a subshrubby plant usually treated as an annual. Both make attractive pot plants for the greenhouse; the seedlings are raised in September and, when large enough, are placed singly in 5-in. pots or 3 in a 6-in. pot to bloom in spring.

HELIOPSIS—*Orange Sunflower* (Heliop'sis). Hardy herbaceous perennial plants, natives of North America, which bear yellow or orange-yellow sunflower-like blooms in July and August. They belong to the Daisy family, Compositae. Heliopsis is from *helios,* and sun, and *opsis,* like.

These plants are grand subjects for the herbaceous border, and excellent for cutting for home decoration. They flourish in ordinary soil

The dainty blue-flowered Heliophila linearifolia, 12-18 in. tall, is best grown as an annual, though technically a tender perennial.

An old-fashioned plant, Heliotrope (Heliotropium) is much valued for its fragrant flowers.

in a sunny or slightly shaded place, and are increased by lifting and dividing the clumps in fall. Among the showiest kinds, all first-rate hardy border plants, are Heliopsis scabra varieties incomparabilis, 3 ft., orange-yellow, semi-double; Gold-Greenheart, 3-4 ft., buttercup yellow with green centers in partly opened flowers; Light of Loddon, 3-4 ft., bright yellow; patula, 4 ft., golden-orange; and zinnaeflora, 2½ ft., orange, double, zinnia-like flowers. All bloom from July onwards, as does H. helianthoides (laevis), 3-6 ft., rich yellow.

HELIOTROPE. See Heliotropium.

HELIOTROPE, GARDEN. Valeriana officinalis, which see.

HELIOTROPE, WINTER. Petasites fragrans, which see.

HELIOTROPISM. The action of plants in growing towards the light (positive), or away from the light (negative). It is most marked in those plants which change the position of their leaves according to the intensity of sunlight, as, for instance, the String Bean and Sensitive Plant.

HELIOTROPIUM — *Heliotrope, Cherry Pie* (Heliotro'pium). Tender subshrubs with attractive sweet-scented flowers. They are natives of Peru and belong to the Borage family, Boraginaceae. The principal kinds are H. arborescens, which forms a woody-stemmed shrub up to 6 ft. in height, has ovate, hairy green leaves and flat terminal clusters of lavender-blue sweet-scented flowers; and H. corymbosum, which has much larger flowers than the first named. From these have been raised the popular garden Heliotropes. They are favorite plants for the greenhouse and for summer bedding. The name Heliotropium is derived from *helios,* sun and *trope,* turning; the flowers are said to turn towards the sun.

Summer and Winter Treatment. Heliotrope requires a minimum winter temperature of 45 degrees and a compost of loam, two parts, and leaf mold, one part, with sand freely added. Repotting is done in March or April. Plants in large pots or tubs do not need repotting every year as they can be kept growing vigorously by top-dressing them in spring. Pruning of large plants consists of cutting back the shoots of the past summer's growth to within 2 or 3 in. of the base in February.

Seeds are also sown in pots of sandy soil in a greenhouse in early spring, and excellent strains are offered by the leading seedsmen. The seedlings are potted separately in 3-in. pots and treated as outlined for cuttings.

When to Take Cuttings. Plants in 4-in. or 5-in. pots for window decoration or for summer bedding are obtained by taking cuttings annually in autumn or spring. Autumn-rooted cuttings make the largest plants. Flowerless side shoots, 2-3 in. in length, are taken off, carefully trimmed with a sharp knife and inserted in a sand bed in a greenhouse, temperature 50-55 degrees, where they are shaded from strong sunlight; they must not be kept in a close moist atmosphere, as this causes them to damp-off. When rooted, they are potted in 3-in. pots and, in early spring, in 5-in. pots, in which they form good-sized plants for greenhouse decoration or for filling the summer flower beds. To ensure bushy plants the top of the main shoot is pinched when the plants are 5 or 6 in. high and the side shoots similarly treated.

Standard or Tree Heliotropes are obtained by growing the plants without "stopping" until the desired height is reached. The tip of the plant is then pinched out and the subsequent side shoots which develop are treated similarly until the "head" is formed. All shoots lower down the stem are rubbed out. During the summer months Heliotropes require an abundance of water and occasional applications of liquid fertilizer, but throughout the winter water must only be applied when the soil is fairly dry.

HELIPTERUM — *Immortelle* (Helip'terum). Shrubs, perennials and annuals, natives of South Africa, Australia and Tasmania. The annuals bear "everlasting" flowers that are useful to cut and dry for winter decoration indoors and are dyed and used in large numbers for making wreaths and other floral devices. They belong to the Daisy family, Compositae. Helipterum is derived from *helios,* the sun, and *pteron,* a wing.

Helipterum is generally raised by sowing seeds in fine soil in a cool greenhouse in March, the seedlings being planted out of doors 6 in. apart, in May.

Seeds may be also sown out of doors in April where the plants are to bloom in July and August. Well-drained, rather light soil is most suitable for these plants, and a sunny place must be chosen. The seeds are scattered thinly, and lightly covered with fine soil; the seedlings, which will ultimately grow about 18 in. high, should be thinned to 6 in. apart.

The chief kinds are Helipterum Humboldtianum, 18 in., which has yellow flowers; H. Manglesii, often listed as Rhodanthe, 1-2 ft., pink, red to purple, with golden discs; and H. roseum (Acroclinium), 1-2 ft., pink, of which there are white, large-flowered and double forms.

HELLEBORE. See Helleborus.

HELLEBORE, FALSE. See Veratrum.

HELLEBORUS — *Christmas Rose, Lenten Rose, Hellebore* (Hellebor'us). Hardy, erect, evergreen or leaf-losing perennials, from southern Europe and Asia, which belong to the Buttercup family, Ranunculaceae. They grow 12-18 in. high, have large leaves, and showy single flowers during winter and early spring. Helleborus is an ancient Greek name for Helleborus orientalis.

For a Partly Shaded Border. The Hellebores are attractive, both in leaf and flower, and are suitable for a partly shaded border or for naturalizing in the wild garden, or they may be grown as pot plants in a very cool greenhouse. They thrive best in moist, well-drained soil en-

A vigorous stand of self-sown seedlings have sprung up under these Christmas Roses in a New York garden.

riched with leaf mold and decayed manure, in a semishaded place. The best time for planting is in early spring. The flowers of the earliest kinds should be protected with a hand light or frame, or moss placed round the plants will keep the blooms from being spoiled by soil splashed in wet weather.

The plants should be set 12 in. apart, mulched with equal parts of rotted manure and peat moss or leaf mold in April, and watered with liquid fertilizer in April–May. They should not be lifted for replanting more often than every 6-7 years.

For a Cool Greenhouse. In October, plants may be potted separately in 6-in. or 8-in. pots filled with equal parts fibrous loam, leaf mold and rotted manure with a little coarse sand added; they should be placed in a cold frame or greenhouse. After flowering, they may be planted out of doors during April, or the pots plunged to the rims in the ground in a semishady place.

Another method of cultivation is to grow the plants in a frame filled to within 15-18 in. of the glass with a similar compost to that used for pots; the Hellebores are planted 9-12 in. apart in October. Water is given moderately during the winter and air is admitted freely on all favorable occasions. The plants should be kept permanently in the frame to provide early blooms; they must be lightly shaded from sunlight during the summer and kept as cool as possible.

Propagation is by lifting the old clumps dur-

A group of the lovely Christmas Rose, Helleborus niger, in full bloom. The flowers are pure white and are produced on stems about 15 in. tall from November to March. This is one of the loveliest of winter flowers.

The light green flowers of Helleborus viridus are attractive in early spring.

ing April and separating them into pieces for replanting; each piece should have four or five growth buds.

Seed sowing is a very slow method of propagation and is not worth while unless new varieties are desired. Sometimes, in favorable locations, self-sown seedlings appear. These may be transplanted to a bed of woodsy soil in a cold frame to grow on to flowering size.

The Christmas Rose. The Christmas Rose, Helleborus niger, a native of Europe, grows about 15 in. high and bears single white flowers 3 in. or more across from November to March; this and its variety altifolius are ideal for cultivation in pots and frames.

The Lenten Rose, Helleborus orientalis, native of Greece, bears large flowers of various shades of purple, pink and green on erect stems, 12-18 in. high, from February to April; many named varieties are given in catalogues. A few of the best are Alcyone, blush; Isolde, pale rose; Larissa, deep rose; and Snowdrift, white.

Other species worthy of note are H. foetidus, 2 ft., a native of western Europe, bearing green and purple flowers during late winter; H. lividus from Corsica, with clusters of pale-green flowers on stems 12-18 in. high during March; and the Green Hellebore, H. viridus, a European plant naturalized in eastern North America, bearing yellow-green flowers in clusters on stems 1½ ft. high during early spring. All these are suitable for naturalizing in the wild garden.

HELONIAS—*Swamp Pink or Studpink, Studflower* (Helo'nias). Hardy tuberous plants of North America, which belong to the Lily family, Liliaceae. They grow about 18 in. tall and have stout stems at the base of which is a cluster of narrow leaves 6-12 in. in length. The stems bear racemes of pink, six-lobed flowers, ½ in. in diameter, with purple stamens. The name Helonias is derived from *helos*, a marsh, and refers to the habitat of the plants.

The Swamp Pink, Helonias bullata, is an American native. It is attractive for planting in moist, slightly shaded locations.

For a Moist, Shady Border. Helonias should be planted in April in a moist, shady border, or by the waterside, in a compost of loam and peat or leaf mold. Propagation is by division of the roots in April, or by seeds sown in sandy peat in a cold frame in early summer.

The chief kind is H. bullata, 18 in., rose and purple, summer.

HELXINE SOLEIROLII — *Baby Tears* (Helxi'ne). A tender, perennial rapid-spreading plant from Corsica which belongs to the Nettle family, Urticaceae. It is of creeping growth with threadlike stems covered with tiny, roundish, bright-green leaves. The flowers are inconspicuous. The name Helxine is from the Greek *helko*, to tear, because the seeds cling to the clothes.

For Planting in Paved Paths. In mild sections this pretty plant is used for planting between paving, flagstones, in dry walls, and for making carpets of foliage in the rockery. Small clumps are planted in April, or at any time during summer, and well watered until established, when no more attention is required. This plant spreads very rapidly.

If grown in pots, the plant is suitable for a cool greenhouse or sun room; it eventually covers the pots with a mass of bright-green foliage. A few small clumps should be set in pots filled with sandy and loamy soil, and kept moist throughout the year. This plant forms a neat edging to the greenhouse benches, but must be kept under control. A layer of soil is placed near the edge of the bench, and small clumps are planted a few inches apart; if kept moist they quickly form a continuous edging of greenery.

HEMEROCALLIS—*Day Lily* (Hemerocall'is). Hardy herbaceous plants which grow from 12 in. to 3-4 ft. high, have long, strap-shaped leaves and in summer bear lily-like flowers chiefly of orange, yellow and mahogany shades. The individual flowers are short-lived but they are borne over a period of several weeks. They belong to the Lily family, Liliaceae. Hemerocallis is found wild in Japan, and other eastern countries, and southern Europe; some kinds are naturalized in eastern North America. The word is derived from *hemera,* a day, and *kallos,* beauty, an allusion to the short life of the bloom.

Hemerocallis variety Royal Ensign has excellent evergreen foliage and flower stalks nearly 3 ft. tall. The flowers are large and full. The throat is golden orange, and this color extends in a stripe along the midveins of the petals. The blades of the petals are a rich maroon red, but the sepals are somewhat lighter in color. The plants are low-growing.

Hemerocallis variety Copperpiece is sturdy and has much-branched flower stems which rise above a mound of attractive evergreen foliage. The flowers have rich golden-orange throats and there is a delicate blend of coppery bronze in the blades of petals and sepals that is somewhat more intense in the midzone of the petals.

Handsome Garden Flowers. The Day Lilies are easily grown in ordinary loamy garden soil, which has been dug and manured. They thrive best in a sunny place, but do not mind light shade. If they are planted in light soil, it is an advantage to set them in a slightly shady position; compost, peat moss or old manure should be mixed with light soil, and it is beneficial to mulch the soil with compost or decayed manure in May. These plants are in full beauty from May to September.

If an increased stock of plants is required, the clumps may be dug in spring or fall and separated into pieces for replanting at 18-24 in. apart.

Day Lilies withstand heat and drought better

Hemerocallis variety Sun Dust has evergreen foliage. The stiff erect scapes reach a height of 42 in. The flowers are large. The general color is golden yellow; the blades of petals and sepals are delicately sprinkled with brownish red that is somewhat stronger on the sepals.

Although the individual flowers of Day Lilies last only a short time many flower buds are produced and these open and provide a good display over a long period.

than most garden flowers and for this reason are especially valuable in many parts of the United States and Canada. They are excellent for grouping in perennial borders and for planting naturalistically in less formal parts of the garden; low growing varieties can be used effectively in rock gardens. Although they do not thrive in waterlogged soils they grow well when planted on high banks besides streams and ponds and when they are so located look very handsome and appropriate.

American and Canadian plant breeders have

Day Lilies are among the most reliable of summer-flowering hardy perennials. They succeed well in gardens in the Middle West as well as in more humid and cooler climates.

been and are very active in raising new varieties. The American Hemerocallis Society records data regarding Daylilies, registers new varieties, publishes a journal and generally promotes interest in these flowers.

The Best Kinds. Several of the species or wild types are beautiful flowering plants, though the handsome named varieties have largely supplanted them in gardens. The best of the former are H. aurantiaca, and its variety major, 2½-3 ft., orange-colored; H. Dumortieri, 12 in., yellow inside, brownish-red outside; H. flava, 2½ ft., yellow; H. luteola, 3 ft., yellow; and H. fulva, 3-3½ ft., reddish-buff, and its double-flowered variety, flore-pleno, 2-2½ ft.

Modern Varieties. Dealers' catalogues list numerous fine varieties and new ones are added each year. Consult these before planting.

HEMIONITIS — *Strawberry Fern.* Easily grown Ferns from tropical Asia and the West Indies, specially recommended for cultivation in terrariums. They thrive in a mixture of fibrous peat and sand, and are easily raised from spores (see Ferns), and by removing the plantlets formed in the angles of the frond segments, or at the base of the plant.

The most distinct kind is H. arifolia, which produces barren and spore-bearing fronds up to 12 in. tall. Other species worth growing are H. palmata and H. Smithii.

HEMIPTELEA (Hemiptel'ea). A hardy, leaf-losing tree that is a native of China and that is sometimes used for hedges. It is a member of the Elm family, Ulmaceae. Its name is derived from *hemi,* half, and *ptelea,* a wing, and refers to the winged fruits.

Hemiptelea Davidii (Zelkova Davidii) forms a small, spiny, shrubby tree that grows without difficulty in any ordinary soil. It is propagated by seeds, layers, and by grafting on the elm.

HEMLOCK. See Tsuga.
HEMLOCK, POISON. See Conium.
HEMLOCK SPRUCE. See Tsuga.
HEMLOCK, WATER. See Cicuta.
HEMP. See Cannabis.
HEMP, AFRICAN. See Sparmannia.
HEMP AGRIMONY. See Eupatorium cannabinum.
HEMP, EAST INDIAN. See Crotalaria.
HEMP, SISAL. See Agave.
HEMP, SUNN. See Crotalaria.
HEN AND CHICKENS. See Sempervivum tectorum.

HEPATICA (Hepat'ica). A small genus of early spring-flowering anemone-like plants which grow wild in open woodland throughout the North Temperate Zone. They form dense tufts of 3- to 5-lobed leaves of leathery texture which appear after the flowers have faded and remain green throughout winter. They are ideal for

Hepatica triloba, 4–6 in. tall, produces its lavender-blue flowers abundantly in early spring. There are also white, blue, rose-red and double-flowered forms of it. It is closely related to Anemone.

shady nooks in the rock garden, or for planting in open woodland, in leafy or peaty loam. Increase is by division, or by seeds sown in light soil in a frame in fall. The name is from *hepar,* the liver, for which it was thought to have curative value. These plants belong to the Buttercup family, Ranunculaceae.

Favorite Kinds. H. acutiloba, blue, white, pink, 4 to 8 in., March–April; H. nobilis, lavender-blue, 4 to 6 in., with notable varieties in alba (white), caerulea (blue), rubra (rose-red), and double-flowered forms of each, all blooming in early spring; H. americana, identical with H. nobilis except that it is less hairy; and H. angulosa, pale blue or pinkish, 8 to 12 in., larger than H. nobilis.

HERACLEUM — *Cow Parsnip* (Heracle'um). Vigorous hardy herbaceous perennials. They are

Heracleum lanatum, a Cow Parsnip that occurs wild in North America, is suitable for naturalizing in wild gardens.

of little value from the horticultural point of view, though one or two are suitable for the wild or woodland garden, particularly in moist or wet soils. They belong to the family Umbelliferae and are natives of southern Europe and central Asia chiefly; H. lanatum occurs wild over most of the United States. The name is from *Heracleon,* and the plant is said to have been named after Hercules.

The kind chiefly worth garden room is H. villosum (giganteum) which reaches a height of from 8 to 10 ft., has large leaves and bears an immense inflorescence in the form of an umbel or flattish bunch which consists of numerous small, dull-white or whitish flowers. It thrives in ordinary soil but attains its largest proportions in deeply dug and manured ground. A stock of plants can be raised by sowing seeds out of doors in a reserve border in April.

HERB. Botanically, all plants without persistent, woody stems are herbs. Tulips, Lilies and Narcissi are included, as are Delphiniums, Sunflowers and Dandelions. This botanical use of the word "herb" is in contradistinction to tree and shrub.

Herb is also used in another sense to denote plants that are, or have been, employed as flavorings, perfumes and medicines. Most such plants are aromatic and not all are herbs in the botanists' sense; some, such as Rosemary, Sage, and Bay are woody plants—trees or shrubs.

HERBACEOUS. A word which means of herblike growth. It is applied to plants which bear soft stems in contradistinction to those of trees and shrubs which are woody.

HERBACEOUS BORDER. See Perennial Border.

HERBACEOUS PERENNIAL. This term is used very frequently in gardening books and catalogues. It means a plant which has a perennial or long-lived rootstock and stems, if any are produced, which die down annually and do not become woody.

HERB GARDEN. The formation of herb gardens was one of the first attempts towards making collections of plants in the vicinity of houses or institutions, and herb gardens were certainly the forerunners of botanical gardens. Early herb gardens were formed by apothecaries and by the inmates of religious institutions with a view to the study of medicinal plants and potherbs, and for the convenient collection and study of drug plants. They were gradually extended until they became a necessary adjunct to every house of importance; even the poorer people cultivated certain plants in the vicinity of their houses for

In a small patch near the kitchen door a variety of herbs can be grown.

A knot or medicinal garden may be created easily by combining, in formal pattern, herbs of different foliage textures and shades. Such a planting should be charted first, so that the pattern can be maintained with a minimum of effort. Careful trimming and weeding will keep the garden neat.

use in the preparation of simple medicines.

At one period a recognized duty of the women of a household was to collect and dry the shoots and leaves of these herbs for winter use, either for medicinal purposes or for use in the kitchen. Numerous modifications of the original herb gardens, where as many medicinal herbs as possible were gathered together, came about, and in some places only potherbs or herbs that could be used for culinary purposes were encouraged. In others, sweet-smelling herbs only were cultivated; or a mixture of useful and decorative herbs was made, and so on. Moreover, these gardens were not always devoted strictly to herbs, for fragrant-leaved shrubs were admitted. Eventually the herb garden proper almost disappeared from large estates, and the few culinary herbs in demand were grouped in a corner of the vegetable garden.

Of late years there has been a tendency to set aside a definite area of a garden for the cultivation of herbs, and it is a good idea, for such a place is full of interest, more particularly when it is possible to study the plants that are grown with the aid of old herbals or modern books devoted to the subject.

For utilitarian purposes, rectangular beds, about 4 ft. wide, with paths between are most appropriate. The soil in an herb garden should be of good quality, such as may be expected to produce well-developed vegetables. The plants must be lifted occasionally, the ground being dug, and the position of the different kinds changed. When herbs are grown for commercial

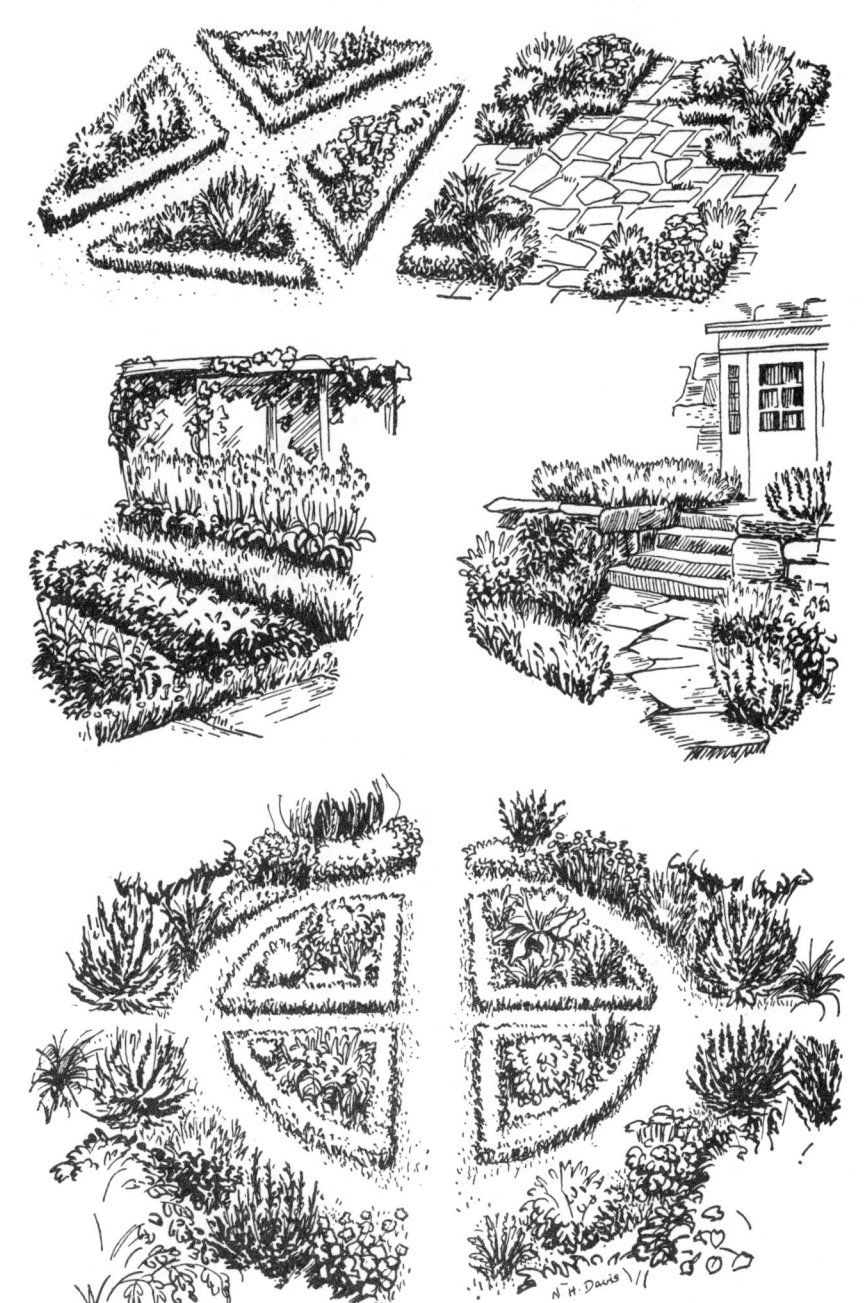

Various interesting ways of growing herbs to create pleasing landscape effects.

purposes the ground should be placed under an entirely different crop when the yield of the herbs begins to decrease.

Culinary herbs that should be given a place in an herb garden are Sage, Thyme, Lemon-scented Thyme, Mint, Marjoram, Tarragon, Parsley, Mustard, Garden Cress, Endive, Fennel, Chicory, Dandelion, Chervil, Caraway, Basil, Chives, Angelica, Borage, Horse-radish, Savory, Celery and Watercress.

Plants with aromatic foliage, in addition to those included above, which are planted in herb gardens, are Bay, Myrtle, Rosemary, Lavender, Lavender Cotton, Rue, Lad's-love, Scented Verbena in the milder parts of the country, Sweet Briar, Balm, Bergamot and Sweet Cicely.

Herbs of medicinal value are Linseed, Peppermint, Hellebore, Henbane, Belladonna, Houseleek, Chamomile, Lungwort, Foxglove, Red Poppy, Mustard, Pennyroyal, Licorice, Evening Primrose, Feverfew, Wormwood, St. John's Wort, Hyssop, Aconite, Alkanet, Tansy, Castor Oil Plant, Dill, Thorn Apple, Saffron, Male Fern, Cowslip, Woodruff, etc. In addition to these, many culinary herbs are also of medicinal value.

HERB PATIENCE. Rumex Patientia, which see.

HERCULES'-CLUB. Deciduous trees with very prickly branches, natives of North America. See Aralia spinosa and Zanthoxylum Clava-Herculis.

HEREROA (Herero'a). A group of South African succulent plants allied to Mesembryanthemum and requiring the same cultural treatment. See Mesembryanthemum.

HERMAPHRODITE. A botanical term used to describe flowers in which both stamens (male organs) and pistil (female) are present.

HERMODACTYLUS — *Snake's-Head Iris* (Hermodac'tylus). A genus consisting of one species, H. tuberosus, which was previously included in the genus Iris. It is quaint rather than attractive, with a curious, handlike bulb, and is easy to grow in any average well-drained soil. The flowers are blackish-purplish, marked with green, carried singly on 12-in. stems in April–May. The bulb is hardy in the North in protected places only.

HERNIARIA GLABRA—*Rupturewort* (Hernia'ria). Herniaria glabra grows wild in Europe and northern and western Asia. It is a creeping perennial, forming a low, close carpet of almost mosslike appearance, and of pleasing fresh green color. It belongs to the family Caryophyllaceae. Herniaria is derived from *hernia,* a rupture, because of its supposed cure for this trouble.

For Planting in Paved Paths. Herniaria is planted in the rock garden as a ground cover for bulb flowers, Crocus, etc., for mingling with Thymes and other carpet plants in the formation of an alpine lawn; it is also useful for planting in the crevices of paved paths. The flowers are small, greenish, and of no importance. Herniaria is of the easiest possible cultivation, content with almost any soil and situation. It is propagated by division at any time.

HERON'S-BILL. See Erodium.

HERREANTHUS (Herreanth'us). A South African succulent plant related to Mesembryanthemum and needing the same cultural care. See Mesembryanthemum.

HESPERALOE (Hesperal'oe). Desert plants that are natives of Texas and Mexico and are not generally hardy in the North. They are adapted for growing in dry climates and in greenhouses. Hesperaloe belongs to the Lily family, Liliaceae. It name is derived from *hesperos,* western, and Aloe, a genus of succulent plants.

These plants require a well-drained soil and a sunny location. They are propagated by seeds. The only kinds likely to be cultivated are H. parviflora and its variety Engelmannii. Both grow to a height of about 4 ft.; their flowers are pink; those of the variety somewhat smaller than those of H. parviflora.

HESPERANTHA — *Evening Flower* (Hesperanth'a). Tender bulbs from South Africa, which belong to the Iris family, Iridaceae. They are closely related to Ixias which they resemble. The flowers, which are sweet-scented and open in the evening, are borne in loose spikes at the ends of stems 6-12 in. in length; they are tubular and chiefly red or white. The name Hesperantha is derived from *hesperos,* evening, and *anthos,* a

Hermodactylus tuberosus, the Snake's Head Iris.

flower—the flowers will open in the evening.

Outdoor Culture. These plants are not generally hardy north of Washington D. C., although with winter covering they may persist in sheltered places somewhat further north. They are well adapted for outdoor cultivation in climates such as that of California. They need a light, well-drained soil and a sunny location. The corms are planted in the fall, 2 in. deep and 2-3 in. apart.

For a Cool Greenhouse. The best soil consists of two parts sandy loam, one part decayed leaf mold, and a small quantity of sand. The bulbs are potted in October, five in a 5-in. pot, and covered with an inch of soil. They are kept in a cold frame until growth commences, when they are placed in a greenhouse in a temperature of 45 degrees minimum. Water must be given sparingly until the flowers are forming; then it is applied liberally. When they have finished blooming, water is gradually withheld, and the soil is kept dry until October, when the bulbs are shaken out and repotted. Propagation is chiefly by offsets. The small corms are potted in October and "grown on" until flowering size is reached.

The chief kinds are H. cinnamomea, 6 in., white, May; H. pilosa, 6 in., white, spotted with red, May; and H. falcata, 10 in., brown and white, May.

HESPERIS — *Sweet Rocket, Dame's Violet* (Hes'peris). Perennial and biennial hardy flowering plants, belonging to the Mustard family, Cruciferae. They are natives of Japan, Asia Minor and Europe. H. matronalis (Sweet Rocket) is an old-fashioned plant which is grown in gardens and is naturalized in eastern North America. The various kinds grow from 12 in. to 3 ft. in height, have pointed ovate leaves and terminal spikes of four-petaled white, purple, or violet flowers. The name Hesperis is derived from *hesperos*, the evening, and refers to the flowers of some kinds which are scented in the evening.

For a Sunny or Lightly Shaded Border. The perennial kind, H. matronalis (Sweet Rocket), is planted in fall or spring, in ordinary garden soil, which has been deeply dug and well manured. A sunny or lightly shaded position is required and the soil is kept moist in summer by mulching and by watering when needed. The stems are cut down in autumn, but the plants are not disturbed until they show signs of deterioration, when they are lifted, divided and replanted in fresh soil.

The Sweet Rocket, Hesperis matronalis, grows well in partial shade. Flowers of individual plants vary from deep lilac to pure white.

Sowing Seeds and Taking Cuttings. They are propagated by sowing seeds ½ in. deep in light soil out of doors in June. The seedlings are transplanted 6 in. apart, in a nursery bed, and subsequently planted out in their final positions. They may also be divided in spring or autumn. The double Rocket, now rare, is raised from cuttings of shoots, 3 in. in length, which are inserted in sandy soil in a cold frame in August. The biennial kinds are raised from seeds in the same manner as the perennials, but as they die after flowering, a fresh stock is raised each year.

The chief kinds are H. matronalis (Sweet Rocket), 3 ft., white to lilac, perennial; H. matronalis flore-pleno, double, perennial; H. violacea, 12 in., violet, biennial; and H. tristis, 18 in., white to purple. The last named, which is sometimes called the Night-scented Stock (though that name is correctly applied to Mathiola tristis), thrives best on poor, light soil; it is biennial and must be raised from seeds sown annually in early summer.

HESPEROYUCCA (Hesperoyuc'ca). One southern California desert plant belonging to the

Lily family, Liliaceae. Its name is derived from *hesperos,* western, and Yucca, a genus of plants.

This plant requires the same general culture as Agave, which see. Hesperoyucca Whipplei bears flower scapes up to 12 ft. tall; the flowers are creamy-white.

HESSEA (Hes'sea). Tender bulbous plants from S. Africa which belong to the Amaryllis family, Amaryllidaceae. They grow about 12 in. in height, have long, strap-shaped leaves and stout flower stalks, bearing terminal clusters of tubular, pale yellow or red flowers. The genus is named after Paul Hesse, a botanist and plant collector.

Bulbs for the Greenhouse. The bulbs are potted in February in a compost of two parts loam and one part leaf mold, sand being added freely. They are placed 2 in. deep in 6-in. pots, which are set in a greenhouse with a minimum temperature of 45 degrees. They must be watered carefully until the pots are filled with roots, after which the soil is kept moist until the flowers have faded. Then the water supply is gradually reduced, and is discontinued when the foliage dies down. During the winter the pots are stored on their sides under the greenhouse benches. Propagation is by offsets, which are removed and set in small pots in February.

The chief kinds are H. gemmata, 12 in., yellow, August; and H. stellaris, 6 in., pink, October.

HETEROCENTRON (Heterocen'tron). A small genus of herbaceous and subshrubby plants belonging to the family Melastomaceae, suitable for greenhouse cultivation in the North, and for cultivation outdoors in southern California and in similar climates. The name is from *heteros,* variable, and *kentron,* spur.

The principal kind is Heterocentron roseum, previously called Heeria rosea. It grows 2-3 ft. tall and bears clusters of bright rose-pink flowers almost continuously. H. roseum variety album has white flowers. Plants raised from cuttings of young shoots in early spring, and potted on in a compost of equal parts of sandy loam and peat, bloom the following winter.

HETEROMELES ARBUTIFOLIA — *Toyon, Christmasberry* (Heterome'les; Hetero'meles). A tender evergreen tree, closely allied to Photinia, and included by some botanists in that genus. It is a native of California, where it reaches a height of 15 ft. The stems of the young shoots are covered with fine hair; the leaves are lance-shaped, 2 in. or more in length, and 1 in. in width.

The plant bears large white flowers in terminal clusters; these are followed by red berries like those of the Holly. So abundantly are these produced in California that they are used for Christmas decoration.

Heteromeles belongs to the Rose family, Rosaceae. Its name is derived from *heteros,* variable, and *mele,* an Apple tree, and refers to the fact that Heteromeles is related to the Apple although it differs in appearance.

For Mild Climates. This plant is hardy only in warm parts of the United States. It is planted in spring in deep, well-drained, loamy soil.

Propagation is by inserting firm, well-matured shoots as cuttings in a cold frame or greenhouse in summer, by layering in summer, and by seeds in spring.

HEUCHERA — *Alumroot* (Heucher'a; Heu'chera). Hardy plants which grow wild chiefly in North America and belong to the Saxifrage fam-

The small-leaved plant in flower is Heuchera sanguinea. The large-leaved plant behind is Rodgersia podophyllum.

ily, Saxifragaceae. They form tufts of lobed leaves, and in May and June bear small flowers on stems 18-30 in. high; the flowers are white, blush, crimson, or rose, and are useful for cutting. Heuchera commemorates a German professor, Johann H. Heucher.

These charming hardy plants thrive in ordinary, well-tilled garden soil, preferring that which is well drained; light, loamy ground suits them. Garden varieties should be planted in a sunny place towards the front of the perennial border, in fall, or in spring. Native woodland kinds prefer part shade.

Propagation is by separating the plants into rooted pieces in October or spring; or seeds may be sown in very sandy soil in a cold frame in March–April. The seeds often germinate slowly. Heuchera thrives best when undisturbed, the plants should not be moved unnecessarily.

Few of the species or wild types are now grown in gardens, for many beautiful named varieties have been raised which yield a profusion of long, graceful flower stems with blooms in attractive colors.

H. sanguinea (Coral-Bells), 12-15 in., bears scarlet flowers; and H. micrantha, 2 ft., pale greenish-white flowers. These are wild types or simple hybrids.

Among native kinds suitable for growing in wild and woodland gardens, primarily for the beauty of their foliage, are H. americana, to 3 ft. high, a native of dry woods, and H. villosa, to 3 ft. high, a native of moist, shaded places.

Of the modern named varieties, which deserve to be widely grown in gardens, these are some of the most beautiful: Bressingham Hybrids, in a wide range of colors from white through pink to red; Pluie de Feu, a delightful coral-red; Rosamondi, coral-pink, a strong grower; Matin Bells, a fine coral-red-flowered variety; Snow Clouds, a good white.

HEUCHERELLA (Heucherel'la). The plant commonly known as Heuchera tiarelloides is correctly named Heucherella tiarelloides, the generic name being a combination of Heuchera and Tiarella, of which it is a hybrid.

It is a hardy herbaceous perennial, forming compact tufts of rounded, shallowly lobed leaves that are attractively mottled with bronze when young. The small, bell-shaped, pink-tinted flow-

Heucherella tiarelloides, a hybrid between Heuchera and Tiarella. It produces dainty panicles of blush-tinted flowers 12 in. or so tall. There is also a white variety.

ers are produced in early summer, in loose panicles about 16 in. tall. There is also an attractive white-flowered variety, alba. Neither kind produces seeds.

Heucherella is of easy cultivation, in sun or light shade, and is an attractive subject for the rock garden. It spreads by means of short underground stolons and is increased by division in autumn or early spring.

HEVEA—*Para Rubber* (He'vea; Heve'a). Trees of great size found wild in the moist tropical forests of South America. The most important kind is H. brasiliensis, the tree from which the rubber of commerce is obtained.

Hevea belongs to the Spurge family, Euphorbiaceae. The name is a native Brazilian one.

Hevea is sometimes grown in tropical greenhouses as a plant of interest because of its economic importance. It thrives in any good soil that is well drained and needs an abundance of moisture from spring through fall; less during the winter. A minimum night temperature of 60 degrees is needed, with a daytime rise of 5-15 degrees permitted in winter, and more in summer. The atmosphere should be humid. Shade from strong sunshine is required.

Established plants should be repotted or top-dressed in late winter or early spring. At that time, too, any pruning that may be needed should be done. Specimens that have filled their pots with healthy roots benefit from weekly applications of dilute liquid fertilizer during the summer and fall.

Propagation for greenhouse purposes is effected by means of seeds sown in porous soil in a temperature of 70-80 degrees. The seeds must be fresh; they soon lose their power to germinate. In the tropics, where H. brasiliensis is grown as a plantation crop, trees that yield high proportions of rubber in their latex are propagated by budding on seedlings.

HIBBERTIA (Hibber'tia). Tender evergreen climbing plants with attractive flowers. They come from Australia and belong to the family Dilleniaceae. The woody, twining stems grow 10-30 ft. in height, and have very dark green, oblong, ovate or lanceolate leaves, 2 in. in length. The large, yellow, buttercup-like flowers are formed in clusters during the spring and summer. The name Hibbertia commemorates George Hibbert, an English botanist.

Attractive Climbing Plants. These plants may be grown outdoors in southern California and southern Florida and in greenhouses. When grown indoors they require a minimum winter temperature of 45 degrees and a compost of equal parts of peat and loam, with sand added. They are potted in large pots or tubs or planted in a border in the greenhouse in March. The shoots are trained to stakes or wires, and pruning consists of shortening some of the longest shoots in February. During the summer months water is applied liberally to established plants, but throughout the winter the compost is only moistened when it becomes dry.

Propagation is by inserting young shoots in sandy peat in June. The pots of cuttings are set under a bell jar or propagating frame in the greenhouse until roots are formed. They are then potted separately in 3-in. pots and subsequently in 5-in. pots. When well rooted, they are planted in their permanent positions.

The chief kinds are H. dentata and H. volubilis; both bear yellow flowers in summer.

HIBISCUS (Hibis'cus). A large group of flowering plants, including tender and hardy shrubs, and hardy annual and perennial herbaceous plants. They belong to the Mallow family, Malvaceae. The origin of the name Hibiscus is uncertain; it may be derived from *ibis*, a stork; these birds are said to feed on some kinds.

Tropical Kinds. These are planted in most warm countries. They form shrubs up to 30 ft. in height, have evergreen leaves, sometimes variegated with rose or cream, and produce large, trumpet-shaped, pink, scarlet, yellow, or crimson flowers in spring and summer.

The best-known are varieties of H. Rosa-sinensis (Rose of China), which is a native of tropical Asia. These are the Hibiscus that are so common in Hawaii and that are planted freely in southern Florida and southern California. They thrive only in frostless or practically frostless regions. They grow in any fairly good soil in sunny locations and form good hedges.

Other tropical kinds that are planted in the United States include H. cannabinus, from the tropics of the Old World, which has yellow and red flowers, is a source of fiber, and yields edible seeds; H. Eetveldeanus, a South African plant with red stems and leaves and magenta-red flowers; H. mutabilis (Cotton Rose, Confederate Rose), a Chinese species with flowers that are white or pink in the morning and turn red in the evening; H. schizopetalus, from eastern Africa, with drooping flowers that have much-divided petals and are white, pink or red and have long-protruding pistils and stamens; and H. tiliaceus, a native of the Old World tropics, with yellow flowers that change later in the day to a pinkish hue.

Indoor Culture. The tropical Hibiscus are suitable for growing in greenhouses. When so

Hibiscus Coeleste, a blue, single-flowered form of H. syriacus.

The Rose of Sharon, Hibiscus syriacus, thrives in a sunny location in light, well-drained soil, forming a compact bush up to 10 ft. tall, smothered in bloom in late summer. There are numerous varieties, both single and double-flowered. Here they are planted as an informal screen.

grown, they need a sunny location and a winter temperature of 45-50 degrees. A temperature of 55-65 degrees should be maintained after the plants are started into new growth, following their annual spring pruning.

Large specimen plants can be obtained in large pots or tubs, or they may be planted in a bed in the greenhouse and either grown as bushes or trained to wires or a trellis on a wall.

Pruning and Propagation. Pruning consists of shortening the side shoots by two thirds in spring. Propagation is by inserting cuttings 3 in. long in sand and peat moss in March–April in a propagating case in the hothouse and kept there until roots are formed; the rooted cuttings are potted separately in 3-in. pots and, later, in larger pots. The main shoots are pinched when the young plants are 6 in. in height, and the side branches are similarly treated to ensure bushy plants. The variegated kinds are very decorative foliage plants.

Hardy Herbaceous Perennials. These kinds grow about 6 ft. in height, have ovate or hastate (spear-shaped) hairy leaves and bear large, trumpet-shaped, pink or white flowers in summer. They are planted in ordinary garden soil that is not too dry in October or spring, and the flowering stems are cut down in autumn. A sunny position suits them best.

Propagation is by seeds sown in drills 1 in. deep in light soil in May or June. The seedlings are transplanted 6 in. apart in a nursery bed and set in their final positions in autumn. The clumps may also be divided.

The Best Herbaceous Perennial Kinds. The Rose Mallow, H. Moscheutos, grows natively throughout eastern North America in brackish marshes; related kinds are H. grandiflorus, which grows in similar locations from Georgia southwards, and H. oculiroseus, which is distinguished by its prominent red flower centers. From these are derived the magnificent hybrids and named varieties that are offered by dealers as Rose Mallows. They are useful for seaside planting and for planting in raised parts of bogs as well as for setting in ordinary soils, not excessively dry. Among the best of the hybrids, the flowers of which may measure 10-12 ins. across, are: Clown, white and pink with crimson center; Crimson

Hibiscus Manihot is a tall plant suitable for growing as an annual. Its yellow flowers have dark brown centers.

The Rose of China, Hibiscus Rosa-sinensis, bears gorgeous flowers in a variety of colors. It is a tropical species, suitable for cultivation outdoors only in warm climates.

Wonder, crimson-red; Fresno, silvery pink; Satan, velvety crimson; Snow White, pure white; Poinsettia, red; Silver Rose, pink; White Giant, white.

The Annual Kinds. H. Tritonum (Flower of an Hour) is grown in flower gardens by sowing seeds in a sunny location and well-drained soil in spring. The short-lived flowers are pale yellow or white with dark centers. H. esculenta is an annual kind that is grown for its edible pods under the name Okra. For its cultivation see Okra. H. Sabdariffa, the Roselle or Jamaica Sorrel, is an annual that is grown in the warmest part of the South for its immature calyces, which are used in making acid jellies, in drinks, and as a substitute for cranberries. Seeds are sown in spring in rows 4-6 ft. apart, in fertile soil in a sunny location. The plants attain a height of 6-8 ft. H. Manihot is an annual or is grown as such. It grows 8-9 ft. tall and has large yellow flowers with dark brown centers.

Hardy Flowering Shrubs. These deciduous (leaf-losing) shrubs grow 10-15 ft. in height, have ovate, deeply notched, deep green leaves and bell-shaped, single or double, red, blue, rose or white flowers in late summer. They are planted in early fall or spring in well-drained soil and a sunny position. Very little pruning is necessary but the shoots of overcrowded bushes should be thinned out in spring.

Propagation is by cuttings inserted in summer in a sand bed. They are set in a cold frame·or greenhouse which is kept close until roots are formed, then planted in a nursery bed and finally transplanted to their permanent positions. The named varieties may be grafted on the common kind in March.

These plants can also be propagated by hardwood cuttings taken in fall.

The Best Kinds. H. syriacus (Althaea frutex), pink, 10-15 ft., from Syria, has numerous garden varieties, of which good single-flowered kinds are: coelestis, light blue; Hamabo, blush, with crimson zone; Mauve Queen, mauve; totus albus, white; Woodbridge, ruby-red, and ruber, rose-pink. Some of the best double-flowered varieties are ardens, pale blue; Jeanne d'Arc, white; coeruleus plenus, lavender; Leopoldii plenus, blush-pink; and paeoniflorus, pink.

H. syriacus is the Rose of Sharon or Shrub Althaea, one of the best flowering shrubs of late summer. When well developed, it blooms very freely and provides a display at a time when few other shrubs are in flower.

HICKORY. See Carya.

HIDALGOA WERCKLEI—*Climbing Dahlia* (Hidalgo′a; Hidal′goa). A tender climbing plant with attractive flowers, which comes from Costa Rica and belongs to the Daisy family, Compositae. This plant, which climbs by twisting its leafstalks around the support, has pinnate leaves and orange-scarlet, dahlia-like flowers. The name Hidalgoa commemorates a Mexican botanist, Hidalgo.

A Greenhouse Climbing Plant. When grown under glass, this plant requires a minimum winter temperature of 40 degrees, and a compost of equal parts of loam and leaf mold with sand freely added. The plants are set in a large tub or prepared bed in spring and the shoots are trained to wires or a trellis. During the summer, abundance of water is required, but throughout the winter very little is needed, the soil only being moistened when it becomes quite dry.

Propagation is by inserting shoots in a propagating case in the greenhouse in spring, or by seeds sown at the same time. Young plants may be planted out of doors in May to flower in late summer. They require a sunny position and light, rich soil.

The roots are lifted, placed in a deep box and stored in a greenhouse for the winter in the same manner as are Dahlias. H. Wercklei, 12 ft., orange-scarlet, is the only species.

HIERACIUM — *Hawkweed* (Hiera'cium). Comparatively few of the plants belonging to this large group of herbaceous perennials are worthy of cultivation in gardens, and some are troublesome weeds. The name Hieracium is from the Greek *hierax*, a hawk, because it was supposed that hawks used the plant to strengthen their powers of vision. About 400 kinds are known; they are natives chiefly of Europe and northern Africa, and a few are wild in America. They belong to the Daisy family, Compositae.

The Hieraciums are propagated by lifting and dividing the clumps in fall or spring; or seeds may be sown in a nursery border out of doors from May–July; the seedling plants will flower a year later. The Hawkweeds thrive in almost any soil in sunny or partly shady places, but they respond well to good cultivation. They are suitable for the front of the mixed flower border, for the outlying portions of the rock garden, dry walls and garden banks.

The Shaggy Hawkweed, H. villosum, averages 12-in. high, but may grow taller in rich soil; it has silvery leaves and bears golden-yellow flowers 2 in. across in summer. It is suitable for planting on dry, sunny slopes. Also worthy of attention is H. bombycinum, a distinct plant with silvery foliage and yellow flowers.

HIEROCHLOË — *Holy Grass* (Hier'ochloë). Hardy perennial Grasses, with fragrant flowers. The North American Indians weave the inflorescences into mats which retain their fragrance for years. These plants, which belong to the Grass family, Gramineae, are natives of North Temperate Regions, including North America. They grow about 2 ft. high, have narrow grass-like leaves and panicles (loosely branched spikes) of brownish flowers. The name Hierochloë is derived from *hieros,* holy, and *chloe,* Grass, and refers to the plants having been used for strewing on church floors.

For Moist Soil. The plants are set out in a moist position near the bog garden, waterside or rock garden, in spring. They require a semi-shaded position and thrive in ordinary garden soil. Propagation is by division of the roots in spring, or by sowing seeds where the plants are to grow, at that same season.

Notable kinds are H. odorata, or Sweet Grass, 2 ft., and H. redolens, from Tasmania, both strongly scented.

HIGH-BUSH BLUEBERRY. Vaccinium corymbosum, which see.

HIGH-BUSH CRANBERRY. The native American shrub, Viburnum trilobum, is known as High-Bush Cranberry and as Cranberry Bush. It is a vigorous, handsome shrub that produces bright red berries which bear a superficial resemblance to Cranberries; hence the common name that is applied to it. It is very hardy and drought-resistant and is grown to some extent for its fruit in the Great Plains Region where few other fruits can be grown because of the harsh climate. The fruits make a good jelly and preserve.

Propagation is by seeds, hardwood cuttings, mound layering and tip layering. See also Viburnum.

HIGH-BUSH HUCKLEBERRY. Gaylussacia baccata, which see.

HILLS. Gardeners speak of sowing in hills when small clusters of seeds are planted on mounds of soil spaced at fairly wide intervals, and when similarly spaced seed clusters are sown at surface level and soil is mounded around the bases of the growing plants later. Each hill is a station where a few seeds are sown and is at a comparatively great distance from the next hill. Sowing in hills is thus quite different from sowing in drills or sowing broadcast. When seeds are sown in drills they are spaced as evenly as possible along a row; when they are broadcast, they are scattered as evenly as possible over the entire seed bed.

The term hill is also sometimes used to describe a single plant around the base of which soil has been mounded, as, for instance a hill of Potatoes.

HILLS OF SNOW. Hydrangea arborescens grandiflora, which see.

HILL UP. To mound soil about the base of a plant with a hoe or other suitable tool. This is done with Corn and other plants that produce roots from the lower parts of their stems, both to encourage these roots by providing earth for them to grow into, and also to help to support the stems. Other plants, such as Roses, are hilled up in fall to protect the lower parts of their

Using a hoe to mound soil around the bases of Pole Beans in the technique known as hilling up.

stems from being killed or severely damaged by winter cold.

HIMALAYA BERRY. See Rubus procerus.

HINDSIA (Hind'sia). Tropical evergreen flowering shrubs from Brazil which belong to the family Rubiaceae. They grow about 3 ft. high, have woody stems, narrow ovate leaves, and axillary trusses of tubular blue or white flowers in summer. The name Hindsia commemorates R. B. Hinds, a naturalist.

Hothouse Flowering Shrubs. These shrubs require a minimum winter temperature of 55 degrees and should be potted in a compost of equal parts of peat and loam, with a sprinkling of sand and charcoal. Repotting is done in February. Pruning consists of shortening the longest shoots after flowering. Water is applied moderately to the soil in winter, freely in summer.

Propagation is by inserting shoots 3 in. in length in sand and peat moss in April. They are kept in a propagating case until rooted; then potted separately in small pots and subsequently in larger ones. The shoots are pruned to ensure bushy plants which will flower in the second year.

The principal kinds are H. longiflora, 3 ft., blue, and its varieties, alba, white, and violacea, blue; and H. violacea, 3 ft., ultramarine, May.

HIP. The fruit of the Rose.

HIPPEASTRUM—*Amaryllis* (Hippeas'trum). Tender bulbous plants of great beauty, from tropical America, which belong to the family Amaryllidaceae. They are commonly known as Amaryllis. Hippeastrum is derived from *hippeus,* a knight, and *astron,* a star.

Culture. In Florida and similar mild climates Hippeastrums can be grown outdoors throughout the year; a considerable industry exists in Florida in raising bulbs for market. They grow well in fertile soil in light shade. In most parts of North America Hippeastrums must be grown indoors, and they are popular subjects as pot plants, both in greenhouses and in window gardens.

Hippeastrum can be grown successfully in a greenhouse with a minimum temperature of 55-60 degrees. The modern varieties bear handsome flowers, larger than those of the species or wild types, and of brilliant colors. The deep green leaves average about 1½ in. wide and 18 in. in length, and the stout flower stalks, carrying from 2-4 six-petaled blooms, rise well above the foliage. By potting successive lots of bulbs the flowering period may be extended from January–May.

Potting the Bulbs. The pots are prepared by thorough cleaning and draining. For each large

Bulbs of Hippeastrums stored in their pots of soil under a greenhouse bench during their resting season.

Hippeastrums (Amaryllis) have always been popular in subtropical gardens; they are also popular for potting. The pot should be twice the diameter of the bulb, which should be planted with its neck and top above the soil.

bulb a 6-in. pot should be used, whereas the medium-sized bulbs can be potted separately in 5-in. pots. A compost is mixed of fibrous loam, two parts; leaf mold or peat moss, one part; and well-decayed manure, half a part, with coarse sand and a scattering of bone meal added. These ingredients must be well mixed.

When to Pot the Bulbs. The earliest lot of bulbs should be potted in January, and the last in March. The plants are knocked out of their

Repotting of Hippeastrums is done at the end of the resting (dormant) period. After the bulb is removed from its pot, as much of the old soil as can be removed without damaging the roots is picked out with a pointed stick.

The bulb, with some soil still adhering to its roots, is set in a well-drained pot slightly larger than the old root ball.

Rich, porous soil is worked between the roots and is made quite firm with the aid of a potting stick.

When potting is completed, the upper portion of the bulb protrudes from the soil, and the surface of the soil is sufficiently low in the pot to allow for watering.

The newly potted bulbs are watered, and in a warm humid greenhouse they soon push up their flower spikes.

pots, all the old soil being removed and dead roots cut away; they are repotted firmly, the bulbs being half-buried. Offsets or small bulbs should be taken off and potted in 3-in. pots; they will flower in two or three years. After potting is finished the plants are put in the greenhouse and kept moist by damping between them two or three times a day. Only sufficient water must be given to the bulbs until new roots have formed to keep the soil just moist. Excessive watering is harmful.

When the new leaves and flower spikes begin to show, the temperature may be increased to 70-75 degrees if it is desired to force the plants into flower earlier. When they are in bloom, cooler conditions will prolong the flowering period.

Treatment After Flowering. The production of flowers reduces the size of the bulbs considerably and, accordingly, as soon as the flowers have faded, feeding with liquid fertilizer must be commenced. The plants should be kept growing

In just a few weeks after potting, the Amaryllis is in bloom, and shortly thereafter will be in full leaf.

freely in a warm, moist atmosphere. By the end of August, growth will have ceased, and the plants must be exposed to full sunlight to ripen, the supply of water being gradually diminished as the leaves fade and finally discontinued. During the winter the pots should be laid on their sides in a temperature of about 50 degrees, and kept dry, but not so dry that the bulbs shrivel. Propagation is effected by removing and potting the offsets in the way explained, by bulb cuttings in August, and by sowing seeds.

When to Sow Seeds. Seeds are sown in April or May in well-drained pots of sandy loam, and the pots are plunged in a warm propagating case. In about four weeks the seedlings will be ready for pricking off into deep seed pans; they are set 1 in. apart, watered and replaced in the glass case for a few weeks, subsequently being placed in the greenhouse benches. They should not be dried off until the winter following their first blooming. In the following spring they are repotted separately in 3-in. pots and treated as advised for the old plants. Seedlings take two or four years to reach flowering size.

The chief kinds are Hippeastrum Leopoldii, crimson and white; H. vittatum, crimson; H. reticulatum, rose; H. pardinum, green, yellow and scarlet; H. puniceum, orange-red or salmon-red; and H. psittacinum, orange and scarlet. These species or wild types, however, are rarely grown, preference being given to the large, brightly colored modern varieties, which are very numerous.

For the plant sometimes named H. procerum (Blue Amaryllis), see Griffinia.

HIPPOCREPIS—*Horseshoe Vetch* (Hippocre′pis). Evergreen, trailing herbaceous plants with yellow flowers; they are wild mostly in southern Europe. They have small, pinnate leaves, and bear compact clusters of yellow, pea-shaped

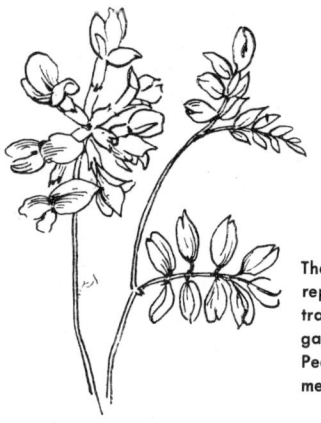

The Horseshoe Vetch, Hippocrepis comosa, a plant of trailing growth for the rock garden, produces yellow Pea-shaped flowers in summer.

flowers in summer. The name Hippocrepis is derived from *hippos,* a horse, and *krepis,* a shoe, and refers to the shape of the seed pods.

These plants belong to the Pea family, Leguminosae.

For Sunny Banks. H. comosa is useful for covering dry places in the rock garden or sunny banks. It thrives in limey soil.

HIPPOPHAË — *Sea Buckthorn* (Hippo′phaë; Hippopha′ë). Leaf-losing shrubs or small trees with spiny branches and willow-like leaves; the female plants bear attractive orange berries in autumn and winter. Two species are known, one of which, H. rhamnoides, is hardy in the North. They are natives of Europe and Asia. They belong to the Oleaster family, Elaeagnaceae. The name *Hippophaë* is the ancient Greek name for a spiny plant; the branches are clothed with spine-tipped twigs.

The Sea Buckthorns thrive in ordinary soil. They are useful for planting by the waterside, and suitable also for exposed seaside banks and hedges. Planting may be done in fall or spring, when the ground is not sodden.

Sowing Seeds and Layering. The Sea Buckthorns are propagated by seeds sown in sandy soil in a cold frame early in the year, and by layering in autumn. When fruiting trees or bushes are particularly required, the Sea Buckthorn should be propagated by layering the branches of known male and female bushes, for, until they fruit, the sex of the seedlings cannot be determined.

Orange-colored Fruits Which Birds Dislike. Hippophaë rhamnoides, the common Sea Buckthorn, forms a dense thorny bush or small tree about 30 ft. high. It has linear leaves, grayish-green above, silvery on the underside. The very small yellowish flowers appear before the leaves in spring, borne on the twiggy branches in short, axillary clusters. The orange-colored fruits, about the size of Holly berries, ripen in autumn and hang all through the winter for, having a very acrid taste, they are not taken by birds.

To ensure good crops of berries a male bush should be planted in each group of five or six berry-bearing ones. H. rhamnoides grows wild over a wide area in Europe and temperate Asia.

The second kind, H. salicifolia, is found only in the Himalaya region. It is taller than the common Sea Buckthorn, a large bush or tree which may reach a height of 50 ft.; it has less spiny branches than H. rhamnoides, broader, dull green leaves and yellow fruits. It is suitable for planting in the South.

HIPPURIS — *Mare's-Tail* (Hippur′is). Hardy aquatic plants with ornamental foliage. They grow wild in North America and in many other parts of the world and belong to the family Haloragidaceae. They have upright, unbranched, soft, pithy stems faintly tinged with pink, and narrow green leaves, ½ in. in length, in rings (whorls). The submerged leaves are twice the length of those above the water. The flowers are inconspicuous. The name Hippuris is derived from *hippos,* a horse, and *oura,* a tail, and refers to the appearance of the plants.

A Hardy Aquatic Plant. Hippuris is planted in ornamental pools in early spring, the roots being set in soil at the bottom of the pool. As this plant spreads rapidly, it is best to confine its roots in separate compartments built of cement. The feathery, green foliage appearing above the water is very ornamental.

Propagation is by division of the roots in spring. The chief kind is H. vulgaris, 2-4 ft. tall.

HIRSUTUS, HIRTUS. Terms used botanically to denote hairiness.

HISPID. A botanical term used in describing stems or leaves which are covered with bristly or stiff hairs.

HOARHOUND. Marrubium vulgare, which see.

HOARHOUND, BLACK. Ballota nigra, which see.

HOBBLEBUSH. Viburnum alnifolium, which see.

HOE. The various kinds of Hoe are invaluable garden tools. The Dutch Hoe or Scuffle Hoe is indispensable during the spring and summer months; it is known also as the Push Hoe, because it is pushed by the cultivator, in contradistinction to the Draw Hoe, which is drawn through the soil towards the cultivator.

The Dutch Hoe is of great service in destroying weeds and aerating the soil.

The Dutch hoe in use.

The Draw Hoe is a useful tool for thinning vegetable seedlings and cutting out weeds between them, for making ridges of soil, and for destroying weeds on paths. It is valuable on rough land for breaking down lumps.

Other types of Hoes include the Warren Hoe, which has a triangular blade; the Potato Hoe or Manure Drag; and special Wheel Hoes or Cultivators that are especially valuable in large gardens.

HOFFMANNIA (Hoffman'nia). Tender shrubs and plants with ornamental foliage, and small yellow, white or red flowers. They are natives of Mexico and Central and South America, and belong to the Rubiaceae, the Madder Family. Most kinds grow about 3 ft. in height; some have stems spotted with red. The leaves are ovate or lance-shaped, green above, and marked with red, purple or yellow. The name Hoffmannia commemorates G. F. Hoffmann, a German botanist.

Tropical Plants with Ornamental Leaves. These plants, which are chiefly grown for their ornamental foliage, require a minimum winter temperature of 55 degrees, and a compost of two parts of loam and one part equal proportions of leaf mold or peat moss and sand. In February the old plants are pruned back hard and syringed frequently until new shoots appear. They are then repotted in slightly larger pots.

Propagation is by cuttings in spring or summer. Shoots 3 in. in length are inserted in a propagating case. When rooted, they are potted separately in 3-in. pots and subsequently in larger ones. Bushy plants are obtained by pinching the tips of the main shoots and side branches.

The chief kinds are H. discolor, red, green and purple; H. Ghiesbreghtii, velvety green above, reddish purple beneath; H. Ghiesbreghtii variety variegata, gray-green blotched with creamy white, yellow and red; and H. refulgens, red and green. These colors refer to the leaves and stems.

HOG PLUM. Ximenia americana, which see.

HOHERIA—*New Zealand Lace Bark* (Hoher'-ia). Evergreen and deciduous (leaf-losing) shrubs or small trees, natives of New Zealand, and belonging to the Mallow family, Malvaceae. Hoheria is from the New Zealand name, *Hoihere*.

The New Zealand Lace Bark, Hoheria populnea, an evergreen shrub which may be grown outdoors in mild climates. It bears white flowers in summer.

Hoheria populnea is evergreen, grows up to 30 ft. tall, and bears clusters of white flowers in late summer. It is only suitable for planting in the open in the warmer parts of the United States. Hoherias thrive in parts of California.

Because of its very variable growth and leaf variation, extreme forms have been given specific names by some botanists, but it is now generally agreed that they are all variations of Hoheria populnea. For purposes of botanical collections the forms or varieties are known by the various names: angustifolia, crataegifolia, obtusifolia, Sinclairii and vulgaris.

This shrub thrives best in a well-drained loamy soil. Planting is best done during spring, the young plants being grown in pots until large enough to set out permanently. Pruning should be done in April, though little is required except to keep the bushes shapely.

Propagation is by cuttings inserted in a glass case in a greenhouse during July; or in a cold frame, or beneath a bell jar or hand light during August and September.

The beautiful leaf-losing shrub known as Gaya Lyallii (Plagianthus Lyallii) is sometimes included in the genus Hoheria, but botanists do not appear to be agreed on this, and in this work the name of Gaya is used.

HOLBOELLIA LATIFOLIA (Holboell'ia). A tender evergreen, climbing plant from the Himalayas, which belongs to the family Lardizabalaceae. The twining stems climb 20 ft. high, have digitate leaves and racemes of greenish-white flowers, which are followed by large, purple, edible fruits. The name Holboellia commemorates F. L. Holboell, a Danish botanist.

A Climbing Plant. The plants are suitable for outdoor cultivation in mild parts of the United States and for growing in greenhouses. When grown indoors, they are planted in large tubs or in a specially prepared bed of soil in the greenhouse in March. The best compost consists of two parts loam, one part leaf mold, and a little sand. The shoots are trained to wires fixed to the greenhouse roof. A minimum winter temperature of 45 degrees is required. Pruning consists of removing the weak shoots in autumn.

Propagation is by cuttings of shoots 3 in. in length inserted in sand and peat moss in a glass-covered case in April.

HOLCUS — *Velvet Grass* (Hol'cus). Holcus lanatus is the name of a hardy perennial grass, 18-24 in. high, with soft, downy leaves, which grows wild in Europe and is naturalized in North America; its variety named albo-variegatus, which has green and white leaves, is sometimes grown in gardens as an edging to flower beds, or in groups towards the front of the perennial border. It reaches a height of 12-15 in., thrives in ordinary soil, and can be propagated by lifting and separating the plants in March.

Holcus belongs to the family Gramineae; the name is derived from *holkos,* an old Greek name for Grass.

HOLLY. See Ilex.

HOLLY FERN. See Cyrtomium falcatum and Polystichum.

HOLLYHOCK. Althaea, which see.

HOLLY, SEA. See Eryngium.

HOLM OAK. See Quercus Ilex.

HOLODISCUS—*Rock Spirea* (Holodis'cus). Western American shrubs hardy as far north as New England. They belong to the Rose family, Rosaceae. The name is derived from *holos,* entire, and *diskos,* disc, and refers to the fact that the disc of this particular flower is entire.

These plants prefer a sandy loam soil, preferably not too dry, and full sun. They are propagated by seeds, layers and by greenwood cuttings under glass in summer.

H. discolor, the best-known kind, has creamy-white flowers in July arranged in 9-in.-long panicles; it grows 10 ft. or more tall. H. dumosus is similar, but is somewhat lower and has leaves that are white-hairy beneath; it grows 8 ft. tall, has flower panicles some 7 in. long in July. H. microphyllus, 3 ft. tall, bears shorter panicles of flowers; its leaves are white-silky beneath.

HOLY GHOST FLOWER. Peristeria elata, which see.

HOMALOCLADIUM—*Ribbon Bush, Centipede Plant* (Homaloclad'ium). This plant belongs to the Knotweed family, Polygonaceae. Its flattened stems are leaflike and decorative. H. platycladum, sometimes called Muehlenbeckia platyclados, bears small, greenish flowers on leafless stems. The leaves appear later. Homalocladium is tender and is grown as a pot plant and in the open in the far South, where it grows 4 ft. high. It is propagated by cuttings in early summer and by division in spring. It is a native of the Solomon Islands.

HOMALOMENA (Homalome'na; Homalo'mena). Decorative foliage plants of the Arum family, Araceae; natives of Asia and tropical Africa. The name derives from *homalos,* flat, and *nema,* thread, and refers to the form of the stamens. There are about 80 species. The plants require essentially the same culture as Dieffenbachia, which see, but they are less adaptable to a dry atmosphere and other difficult conditions, and so do not succeed so well as house plants. H. picturata has leaves some 16 in. long and 8 in. wide, dark green with variegated yellowish-white markings along the centers. H. Wallisii has narrower leaves spotted yellow and white margins.

HOMERIA (Home'ria). Tender bulbous plants which bear handsome flowers in spring; they are natives of South Africa and belong to the Iris family, Iridaceae. The bulbs produce long narrow leaves, about 18 in. in length, and flowering stems which are shorter than the leaves, bearing terminal clusters of funnel-shaped flowers with deeply cut segments. The name Homeria commemorates the poet Homer.

Spring-flowering Bulbs. The bulbs are planted 1 in. apart in deep flower pans in fall. A compost of two parts of loam and one part of leaf mold with sand added is used. After potting, the bulbs are set in a frostproof cold frame and are covered with an inch or two of moss until young shoots appear, when they are taken into a greenhouse with a minimum temperature of 45 degrees. Water is applied carefully until growth becomes active; the soil is then kept moist. After the flowers have faded, the plants are gradually dried off and the pots stored on their sides in a sunny frame until October, when the bulbs are shaken out and repotted. The offsets may be potted separately.

The Homerias may also be planted out of doors in light, well-drained soil in a sunny position in mild climates.

The chief kinds are H. collina, 12 in., red and yellow; H. lineata, red and yellow; and H. elegans, yellow and dull blue or tawny-brown. All bloom in spring or early summer.

HONESTY. See Lunaria.

HONEY BALM. See Melittis.

HONEY BELL. Mahernia verticillata, which see.

HONEY BUSH. Melianthus, which see.

HONEYDEW. An excretion produced in large quantities by aphids and scale insects is known as honeydew. Ants are fond of it, and sooty mold fungi flourish on it.

HONEYFLOWER. See Melianthus.

HONEY LOCUST. See Gleditsia.

HONEYSUCKLE. Lonicera, which see.

HONEYSUCKLE, AUSTRALIAN. See Banksia.

HONEYSUCKLE, BUSH. Diervilla, which see. See also Lonicera.

HONEYSUCKLE, CAPE. Tecomaria capensis, which see.

HONEYSUCKLE, FRENCH. See Hedysarum coronarium.

HONEYSUCKLE, WHITE SWAMP. Rhododendron viscosum, which see.

HOODIA (Hoo'dia). Tender succulent plants allied to the Stapelia, which may be grown outdoors in dry, frostless or nearly frostless, climates. They grow wild in tropical and South Africa, and belong to the Asclepias family, Asclepiadaceae. They are low-growing, branching, leafless plants with spine-tipped tubercules, and bear large flowers in summer. The name Hoodia commemorates a botanist named Hood.

For a Sunny Greenhouse. They are grown in a sunny greenhouse with a minimum temperature of 50 degrees. Repotting, which is only necessary every three or four years, is done in February. A little of the old soil is removed and the plants are set in slightly larger pots. The best compost consists of equal parts loam, sand, and crushed bricks. The pots are half-filled with drainage. Very light shade from the strongest summer sunshine is desirable, and the glasshouse is ventilated freely on all favorable occasions.

Propagation is by inserting pieces of fleshy stems in sand in spring or summer. Water must be carefully applied until roots are formed.

The chief kinds are H. Bainii, yellow; H. Dregei, pale brown; and H. Gordonii, yellow and purple.

HOOF AND HORN FERTILIZER. Waste material of this kind has long been used as a manure or fertilizer in the garden, either alone or in various mixtures. See Fertilizers.

HOOP PETTICOAT DAFFODIL. Narcissus Bulbocodium, which see.

HOOP PINE. See Araucaria.

HOP. See Humulus.

HOP CLOVER. Medicago lupulina, which see.

HOP HORNBEAM. See Ostrya.

HOP TREE. Ptelea, which see.

HORDEUM JUBATUM — *Squirrel's-Tail Grass* (Hord'eum). A hardy annual ornamental grass, native of North America, Europe and Asia, which grows 18-24 in. high and bears inflorescences somewhat similar to those of Barley, to which it is related. It flourishes in ordinary soil and is raised from seeds sown, in early spring, out of doors where the plants are to bloom in summer. It belongs to the family Gramineae. Hordeum is an old Latin name for Barley.

HOREHOUND or HOARHOUND. See Marrubium.

HORIZONTALIS. A botanical term indicating a horizontal habit of growth.

HORMINUM (Hormi'num). A hardy perennial plant of the Mint family, Labiatae. It will grow in any well-drained soil in a sunny location. It is readily increased by seed, or by division in spring or autumn. The name is an old Greek one for a kind of Sage.

H. pyrenaicum grows 1 ft. or less tall and has bluish-purple flowers on leafless spikes in summer. It is suitable for planting in rock gardens.

HORMONES. Plant hormones or auxins are more scientifically and descriptively termed "growth-regulating substances." A number of these substances have been isolated and their chemical structure ascertained, and several have now been synthesized and developed commercially for horticultural use to bring about desired changes in the growth of treated plants. These synthetic chemicals are marketed in powder, liquid or tablet form, and, used at the correct strength and in the proper manner, function as follows.

Root-inducing hormones, such as alpha naphthalene-acetic acid and indole-acetic acid, quicken the formation of roots in cuttings, layers and other vegetatively propagated parts of plants. They are useful in increasing the "strike" with all cuttings, but particularly helpful in inducing softwood cuttings to root quickly and in propagating from plants normally difficult to root.

Fruit-setting hormones, like beta naphthalene-acetic acid and p-chloro phenoxy-acetic acid, induce the rapid development of the flesh and tissues without seeds. They are at present largely used in setting seedless fruits on Tomatoes and Cucumbers, but may also be employed on Melons, Strawberries, Apples and Pears. They are valuable for use when conditions of weather or environment inhibit normal fertilization. Overdosing, however, leads to abnormal development.

Pre-harvest Fruit-drop Preventives. Hormones such as naphthalene-acetic acid, applied to wet the stalks of tree fruits nearing harvest, prevent the formation of the abscission layer of cells between stalk and branch or spear and thus strengthen the bond between the tree and its fruit. They are particularly useful in preventing losses from the pre-harvest fruit-drop in Apples that tend to suffer this. Application is made 1-3 weeks before normal harvesting time, and fruit improves in ripeness, size and quality as a result.

Bud-retarding hormones, notably maleic hydrazide and naphthalene-acetic acid at certain strengths, inhibit the opening of vegetative buds. This effect is useful in preventing the premature sprouting of Potatoes, Carrots and other root vegetables when stored, permitting such vegetables to be kept well into spring without sprouting or loss of food values.

Selective Weed Killers. These hormones, such as 2-methyl-4-chloro-phenoxy-acetic acid (MCP) and 2 : 4 dichloro-phenoxy-acetic acid (2, 4-D) are, broadly speaking, injurious to dicotyledon or broad-leaved plants, killing or injuring them by overstimulating their growth processes, but are noninjurious to monocotyledons. This selective action is valuable for controlling weeds in lawns, since it destroys many, though not all, lawn weeds, without impairing the grasses. The full effect may take 2-3 weeks to show, according to the resisting powers of the weeds treated.

Other hormones have been found, such as naphthalene acetamide, to induce normally sterile or hybrid plants to set seed; to thin newly opened blossoms on fruit trees with a view to preventing overcropping and checking the tendency to biennial bearing; to retard bud development of fruit trees in spring so as to avoid frost damage; to destroy brambles; and to quicken the ripening of tree fruits, but the application of such techniques is limited, and needs further investigation.

HORNBEAM. See Carpinus.

HORNED POPPY. See Glaucium.

HORNED VIOLA. Viola cornuta, which see.

HORNWORT. See Ceratophyllum.

HORSE BALM. Collinsonia canadensis, which see.

HORSE CHESTNUT. See Aesculus.

HORSEMINT. Monarda, which see.

HORSE-RADISH. The botanical name of this root vegetable is Armoracia rusticana. It belongs to the Mustard family, Cruciferae, and is naturalized in North America.

A small bed of Horse-radish is all that is needed in most gardens; as a rule it receives scant attention, and is planted in any odd corner where little else will grow. It is certainly very easily managed and thrives in ordinary garden soil, though the best produce can be obtained only by planting in well-cultivated ground in a sunny or shady place.

Horse-radish is planted in early spring in rows

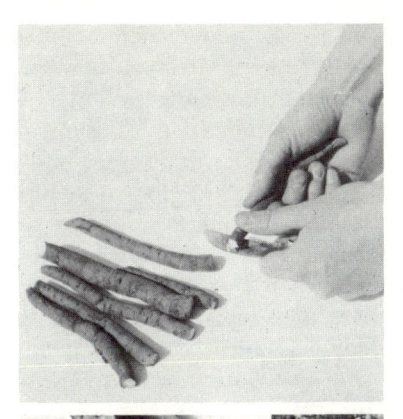

It is worth going to some trouble to produce good straight roots of Horseradish by replanting every second year. For planting, roots of medium thickness are cut into pieces 6—9 in. long and are set 3 in. deep and 9 in. apart.

about 15 in. apart, the roots being set 8 or 9 in. from each other and covered with 3 or 4 in. of soil. Horse-radish is often left undisturbed for years, but it is a better practice to lift the roots in alternate years; throw away those not wanted and replant the bed. For replanting, straight roots 10 in. long should be selected, each with a bud or crown, and planted, crown end upwards, in the way advised. The roots are chiefly valued for use in autumn and winter.

It is very difficult to clear Horse-radish completely from the site it has occupied, owing to the fact that the smallest piece of root will form a plant. One method of keeping it under control is to plant the roots in drainpipes set upright in the prepared ground.

HORSE-RADISH TREE. See Moringa.

HORSETAIL. See Equisetum.

HORSETAIL TREE. Casuarina equisetifolia, which see.

HORTICULTURE. The science and practice of gardening as it relates to the cultivation of plants.

HOSE. During the summer months a hose for purposes of watering must be regarded as an essential part of the equipment of a garden. Its use enables plants and shrubs to be kept moist at the roots during prolonged drought. Water applied through a garden hose is not so beneficial to the plants as rain or soft water and should not be given excessively or except when necessary. Unless, however, the ground is kept moist the growth of plants will be stunted and their blossoming will be poor. The best time of day to water the garden is in the evening, and it is better to soak the soil thoroughly once a week than to moisten it every day. Plants sprayed in bright sunshine may lose their freshness. An occasional light spraying in the evenings is sometimes beneficial.

It is wise to purchase a sound and reliable garden hose: it will prove more economical in the end than a cheap, inferior one which, after a few months, will probably become worn and leaky in places and cause endless trouble. The hose, when not in use, should always be kept on a reel. When the hose is required for use it can be played out from the reel: if it is dragged over paths or coiled up carelessly, it will soon wear thin in places. During the winter the garden hose should be stored under cover.

HOSE IN HOSE POLYANTHUS. The name given to varieties of Polyanthus Primrose which have semidouble blooms in which both calyx and corolla are colored. See Primula.

HOSTA—*Plantain Lily* (Hos'ta). Hardy herbaceous, flowering and foliage plants from eastern Asia which belong to the Lily family, Liliaceae, and were previously grouped under the generic name of Funkia. They grow 18-36 in. in

The Plantain Lilies, now called Hosta but more commonly known as Funkia, are attractive foliage and flowering herbaceous perennials for cool, moist, shady places. Hosta Fortunei has handsome blue-green leaves up to 8 in. long and 6 in. across, and flowers of pale lilac produced in July.

Hosta Sieboldiana is a plant of noble appearance. Its broad leaves are bluish-green, its flowers pale lilac or almost white.

height and have large ovate or lance-shaped green or variegated leaves which form attractive clumps. In summer they produce long spikes of large funnel-shaped lilac-blue or white flowers. The name Hosta commemorates Nicolaus T. Host, an Austrian physician.

For Moist, Shaded Positions. Although Hostas can be grown in the perennial border, they do best in a moist, shady position. They require a soil rich in humus, so if the ground is exceptionally light and sandy or clayey, it must be improved by digging in liberal quantities of compost or well-rotted manure. Planting is done in fall or spring, the tops (crowns) of the plants being set just below the soil.

Propagation is by division of the clumps at planting time. Seeds may also be sown in a shaded frame in light soil in June. The seedlings are pricked out 2 in. apart and kept in the frame until the following spring, or early summer, when they are planted in a nursery bed; there they remain until large enough to set in their permanent positions.

For Cultivation in Pots. The variegated-leaved kinds make pretty pot plants in early spring. They are potted in loamy soil in October, and kept in a frame until February or March, when they are taken into a warm greenhouse or room, where the leaves quickly develop.

Noteworthy kinds for garden planting are H. Fortunei, leaves blue-green, flowers pale lilac; H. Fortunei variety variegata has cream-white variegated leaves; variety gigantea is a vigorous form. H. lancifolia has narrow green leaves, which, in its variety albo-marginata, are white-margined. H. Sieboldiana has bluish-green leaves and whitish, purple-tinted flowers. H. undulata has green leaves splashed with white. H. caerulea has deep-green foliage and lavender-blue flowers, and H. plantaginea is noteworthy for its white, fragrant flowers and light green leaves.

HOST PLANT. A plant or tree which supports a parasite—e.g., Mistletoe and Dodder—or which serves as a host for diseases or insect pests.

HOTBED. A hotbed is a layer of soil, of peat moss and sand or of other mediums in which plants may be grown or in which cuttings may be rooted; it is heated from beneath and covered with a regular cold frame to conserve the heat. Warmth may be supplied by fermenting manure or manure and leaves or by special electric heating cables.

Hotbeds are exceedingly useful in late winter and spring for hastening the development of seedlings and for rooting cuttings. It is possible, too, to secure early supplies of Radishes, Lettuce, Cauliflowers and some other vegetables from a hotbed, but since modern methods of packing and transportation have made such edibles so easily obtainable from distant places that they are offered regularly in food stores at all seasons of the year, their out-of-season home

Hosta undulata has green leaves that are conspicuously variegated with creamy white.

[5–12]
Amaryllis (Hippeastrums)

[5—13]
Rose Mallow
(Hibiscus Moscheutos)

[5—13a]
Plantain Lily
(Hosta)

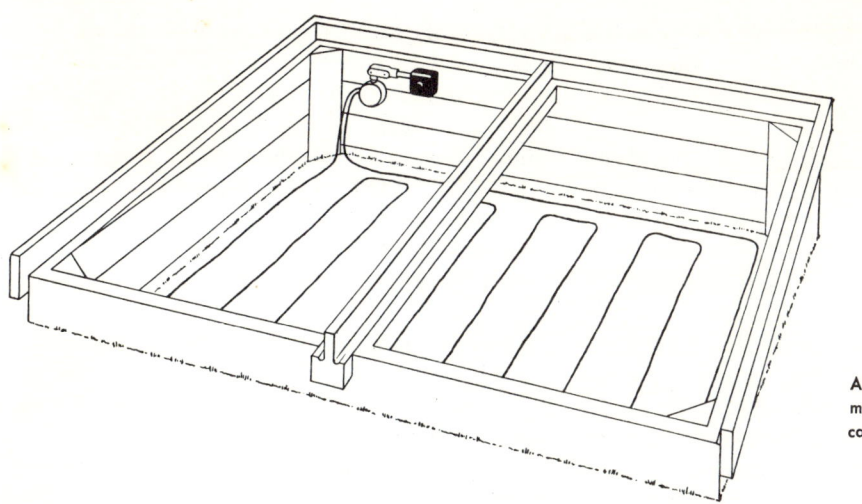

An electric hotbed, showing placement of thermostat and heating cable before soil is added.

production in hotbeds is rarely undertaken.

A hotbed in spring is of especial value to those who do not have a greenhouse available; it enables the gardener to gain a really early start with many of the more tender plants he wants to grow.

Electrically Heated Hotbeds. Because of their cleanliness and simplicity and because suitable manure for making hotbeds is not available in many places, hotbeds heated by electricity have won a well-deserved popularity in recent years.

Units, consisting of a thermostat and a length of lead-sheathed resistance cable, are offered for sale by dealers in horticultural supplies and sometimes by greenhouse manufacturers. The cable is pliable and is buried in the soil or rooting medium at any suitable depth up to about 7 in. The cable is laid in a gridiron pattern with the grids spaced about 1 ft. apart; around the outsides of the frame the two outer rows of wires may be spaced 6 in. apart to counteract the cooling effect that strikes inwards from the outside.

Hotbeds of Fermenting Material. To make a satisfactory hotbed of this type a supply of fresh horse manure is really needed although mild hotbeds are sometimes made of fermenting leaves or other materials.

The manure is heaped as it becomes available

A manure-heated hotbed built entirely above the ground level.

and is turned several times during the course of a week or ten days. If very dry, it should be moistened, but care must be taken not to make it saturated.

A hotbed of fermenting material should be about 3 ft. high, and of such a width and length that it will project about 12 in. beyond the frame to be placed on it. The manure ought to be trodden moderately firm as it is placed in position.

When the frame is in position on the hotbed a layer of soil about 8 in. deep is placed on the manure; the "sash" or top of the frame ought to be left slightly open for a few days to allow of the escape of fumes from the manure. When the heat of the bed has declined to a temperature of 90 degrees, seeds may be sown in the soil.

By mixing dry leaves with the manure in the proportion of one third leaves and two thirds fresh horse manure, more lasting but less intense warmth is assured. Leaves which have been exposed to the rain are useless for this purpose. A hotbed made of leaves alone can be used; it will provide still less heat than one made of manure and leaves in mixture, but the warmth will last longer. The leaves must be trodden down firmly until a bed not less than 2 ft. high is obtained.

Placement and Care of Hotbeds. Hotbeds should always be located in places well protected from cold winds; usually they are faced to the south. At nighttime thick mats or wooden shutters may be placed over the glass sash that forms the tops of the frames to afford additional protection and conserve heat.

Very careful attention must be given to the matter of ventilating the frames. When the sun shines on the glass the temperature inside quickly rises and may soon reach a harmful level. Before this occurs the sash must be opened a little, but in such a way that inrushing cold air does not harm the plants or lower the temperature inside below the desired level. Ventilating should be done gradually and, always, the frame should be closed early enough in the afternoon to trap some of the sun heat. See Ventilation.

Watering should be done with care; choose mild and preferably sunny days to attend to this. The water used should be warmed to the air temperature inside the frame; the use of very cold water is very harmful.

HOTHOUSE. Technically a hothouse is a greenhouse in which the temperatures that are maintained are those satisfactory for the cultivation of tropical plants. The minimum night temperature in a hothouse is 55-65 degrees.

HOTTENTOT FIG. Mesembryanthemum (Carpobrotus) edule, which see.

HOTTENTOT'S BREAD. See Testudinaria.

HOTKAPS AND HOTTENTS. See Protecting Plants.

HOTTONIA — *Water Violet* (Hotto'nia). Hardy aquatic flowering plants, natives of Europe, which belong to the Primula family, Primulaceae. They have creeping rootstocks, finely divided leaves, and a leafless stem which rises out of the water in summer and bears a raceme (loose spike) of pale-purple flowers. The plants are planted on the margins of a pond in shallow water in spring, and are increased by division in September, or by seeds sown in pans of muddy soil in summer. The chief kind is H. palustris, light blue, June.

HOULLETIA (Houllet'ia). Epiphytal Orchids which grow wild in Brazil and Peru chiefly. They have small pseudobulbs each of which bears a single leaf. The flowers, which open in summer, are fragrant. The name commemorates Monsieur Houllet, a French gardener.

Hothouse Orchids. Houlletia requires a warm greenhouse with a tropical atmosphere in summer and a minimum winter temperature of 60 degrees. The compost should consist of three parts osmunda fiber and one part sphagnum moss. Some half-decayed leaves may be added and an addition of finely broken crocks is an advantage, for careful watering is necessary even when growth is vigorous. When the plants are dormant, i.e., when growth is finished, the shading should be removed, and though water must not be altogether withheld, the compost must be watered only occasionally.

The Chief Kinds. H. Brocklehurstiana, from Brazil, has leaves 2-3 ft. high, and the flowers are 3 in. across, dark chocolate tinged with yellow and white on the lip. H. odoratissima resembles it closely; both are fragrant. H. Sanderi, from Peru, has cream-white flowers which are unpleasantly scented.

HOUND'S-TONGUE. See Cynoglossum.

HOUSELEEK. See Sempervivum.

HOUSE PLANTS
Their Selection and Care

House plants are immensely popular and there are many varieties to choose from. Some grow well under the unnatural condition of being indoors; others are distinctly difficult. Intelligent attention is needed if plants are to thrive and, unless they do so, no one wants them. Knowledge of general and of special requirements, proper selection and care, all do much to overcome the handicaps that any house presents to plants that were intended to live outdoors. With good soil, proper drainage, correct watering and suitable light conditions, a high degree of success may be expected.

Arrangement of Plants. There are many ways in which plants can be arranged in the house, such as on shelves, in brackets, on benches, window sills and on tiered stands. The great difficulty with plant stands is that to give the plants maximum light they must be turned toward the window, which means that the back of the stand is toward the room. What is best used to hold plants is largely determined by the surroundings and the space.

Inside window boxes, however, are popular and can be most effective because the plants get sufficient light, can be seen easily and can be

This room is made gay by potted plants which stand in saucers on the wide wooden ledges of the window frame. The spotted-leaved Dieffenbachia at the right is growing in a large planter which stands on the floor.

To furnish this study generous use has been made of trailing plants in hanging pots and specimen plants on the window ledges.

When potting plants for the house, containers should be chosen that will give the roots no more than comfortable space. Containers that are too large are likely to cause the roots to rot.

made to frame a window. If the window is flush with the wall, the plants should be low-growing. A bay window with a box in the center section is very attractive. Bay windows, incidentally, with light from three sides, are excellent places for plants.

Boxes may be of wood, preferably cypress, or of metal. Wooden boxes should have an inside metal tray six inches deep, half-filled with granulated peat moss. The pots are placed in this to conserve moisture. The tallest is placed in the center, with plants of similar appearance to the right and left. A line of three or four low plants along the front edge, with hanging plants between, gives an orderly, well-arranged effect. After they are in position, enough peat moss should be added to come to the brims of the pots, giving the effect of a natural planting. Peat moss has the advantage that, if the plants become too big or straggly, they can be changed more easily than if they are planted in soil.

If plants are to be set in soil, a light, porous mixture of grass-sod loam, peat moss or leaf mold and sand should be used in equal parts. Concave broken pots should be placed on the bottom and covered next with coarse leaves, and finally by the soil.

Cultural Requirements. Light, humidity, water, warmth, sanitation and food are essentials for well-grown plants.

Water and nutrients are easily supplied in amounts and at times most beneficial to the plants; strict sanitation, such as the picking off of faded flowers and dead leaves and the control of insects and diseases, presents no special difficulties but light, atmospheric moisture and temperature are usually less subject to practical manipulation, because other factors, such as the personal comfort of people, largely determine the levels at which these are maintained.

Light. In most cases it is not practicable to do much to change the amount of available light; therefore house-plant growers should usually choose kinds that can thrive under existing light conditions, or under those conditions slightly modified. The modifications may include shading from excessively strong sun and supplementing natural light with artificial light.

During midwinter, house plants benefit from receiving all possible sunshine; none is harmed even by exposure in a south-facing window, but from late winter or early spring until fall or early winter many kinds need protection from strong sun. Such plants should be grown in windows facing north or in other locations that do not receive full sun or they should be shaded during the brightest part of the day. Even a light curtain of muslin or similar material is very effective in cutting down the amount of light. Common symptoms shown by plants exposed to too strong light are a loss of green coloring with a noticeable yellowing of the foliage and, often, a scorching or browning of those parts of the leaves that are most exposed. Removal of affected specimens to a more shaded location usually results in an improvement in their color.

Plants that receive too little light tend to grow thin and spindly, to have their leaves spaced excessively widely on the stems, to bend markedly towards the source of light and to flower sparsely or not at all. Many foliage plants, such as Philodendrons, produce leaves much smaller than normal when grown in excessive shade.

For winter blooms like this, plants must be "timed". They should be purchased or propagated in spring and set outdoors for the summer. Before frost, they should be lifted and put in a cool place to rest for a few days before being brought out into the light and heat of the house.

Most house plants need an even balance of moisture at all times. Watering in the morning allows drainage to take place during the day. This maintains an even soil temperature at night.

By illuminating the plants for several hours each day with either fluorescent or incandescent (Mazda type) electric bulbs, lack of natural light may be compensated for to some extent, but in rooms it is rarely practicable to grow plants without any natural light. It is possible, however, to cultivate African Violets and some other plants that thrive in low light intensities without natural light. This is usually done by arranging an installation that illuminates the plants for about 16 hours a day with 20-watt fluorescent lamps fixed about 12 in. above the plants.

Fluorescent lights have the advantage of not creating as much heat as incandescent lights. If the latter are used it is very important not to place them so close to the plants that the temperature is too high or that the air becomes excessively dry.

Humidity. Lack of sufficient atmospheric humidity is a frequent cause of failure with house plants. It is especially likely to be serious during those seasons when the house is heated. It is largely because of this that plants that have prospered during the summer indoors or that are brought inside from the outdoors in fall begin to fail after the heat is turned on. Common symptoms are the dropping of leaves and the gradual drying up and browning of the foliage. In some cases flower buds dry up or drop before they open. That lack of moisture in the atmosphere is responsible for many failures with house plants is shown by the fact that many kinds will succeed in a terrarium in rooms where the same kinds soon perish or fail to thrive outside the terrarium.

The relative humidity of the atmosphere

The leaves of this shade-loving Maranta are curling because the plant is exposed to strong sun.

varies considerably in different houses and often in different parts of the same house. In some parts of North America the air is naturally much drier than in others. Some types of heating systems result in a drier atmosphere than others. The higher the temperature is raised above that which generally prevails outdoors, the drier it becomes.

Few plants, other than Cacti and similar desert kinds, thrive if the relative humidity of the air is below 50 per cent; for most plants 60-70 per cent is preferable.

It is usually only within modest limits that the atmosphere in a house can be humidified; however, some precautions can be taken and some help given. It is most important to keep plants well away from radiators and other sources of dry heat. Plants grouped together tend to moisten the nearby atmosphere and are more likely to thrive than solitary specimens.

Atmospheric humidity may be increased by making use of humidifiers designed for attachment to hot air furnaces and some other heating units. The type of humidifier that consists of a container of water hung against a radiator is usually not very effective but does add some moisture to the air, and this is better than nothing.

It is a good plan to fill shallow metal or plastic trays with pebbles and then with water and to stand potted plants on the surface of the pebbles. The moisture that rises from the water in the trays will moisten the atmosphere appreciably in the vicinity of the plants. Moss, peat moss, sand or other suitable material may be substituted for the pebbles if preferred.

All plants except those with very hairy foliage, such as African Violets and Peppermint-scented Geranium (Pelargonium tomentosum), benefit from having their foliage misted over regularly with a fine spray of water. This may be done two or three times a day on favorable occasions. Spraying should not be done on very dull days nor so late in the day that the foliage will not dry before nightfall.

Temperature, like light, is often beyond the plant owner's control, but a knowledge of plant needs may be a great help in selection. Tropical plants do well at 68°-72° F. for a daytime temperature. A drop of 10° F. at night is normal. Sharp fluctuations are bad and, where the drop may be much more than 10° F. at night, plants should be covered. The greatest change is next to the window, and that may be controlled easily by slipping a newspaper between the plants and the glass.

The Partridge-breasted Aloe, A. variegata, an excellent subject for growing in pots in a sunny window.

These house plants have been shaded. From left to right, they are Dieffenbachia Seguine, Dracaena sanderiana and Asparagus plumosa.

Examples of tropical plants that thrive in the temperatures mentioned above are Philodendrons, Dracaenas, Palms, Rubber Plants, Bromeliads, Snake Plants and many Ferns.

Many plants need lower temperatures in order to thrive. Cool-temperature kinds, such as Geraniums, Fuchsias, English Ivy, Pick-a-back Plant, Fatshedera, Strawberry Begonia and many Begonias, grow best if the day temperature is 55°-60° and the night temperature a few degrees lower. Some plants get along well with even less warmth than this. Preferred temperatures are mentioned under the directions for the cultivation of the various plants in the articles throughout this Encyclopedia. It must be remembered that even cool-temperature plants are subjected to high temperatures in summer; when temperatures are recommended for plants grown indoors (in houses or greenhouses) they refer generally to those months when the minimum mentioned must be maintained by the use of artificial heating.

Excessively high temperatures, especially if accompanied by inferior light conditions, result in weak, soft growth, poor flowering, pale coloring and a higher susceptibility to pests and diseases. Temperatures that are too low also may have bad effects. They may slow growth, or cause the foliage to turn yellowish, bluish or reddish. They may also cause the leaves and other plant parts to be smaller than normal. Often they cause leaves to drop off and, in extreme cases, may bring about the death of the plant.

In the average house, plants are more likely to be harmed by temperatures that are too high rather than by lack of warmth. When selecting locations for plants, or plants for specific locations, it is well to take into account the fact that temperatures are apt to vary considerably even in different parts of the same room. A few tests with a thermometer may be made to ascertain just what the conditions are.

Watering House Plants. When the plants have been potted in good soil and proper drainage has been provided, the important job of watering is made easier. When in active growth, plants

When house plants need water they should be given enough to saturate the entire body of soil thoroughly.

need ample moisture at their roots. Too much water, however, is bad. A test, which becomes accurate with slight practice, can be made by tapping the pot with the knuckles. If the soil is dry it will sound hollow and emit a clear, ringing sound. A dull, heavy sound suggests that the soil is sufficiently moist.

It is important to try to keep an even balance of moisture at all times. Watering in the morning allows drainage to take place during the day and so maintains an even soil temperature at night. Water temperature is not of great importance except in midwinter when it is better to use water of room temperature.

It is a good plan to place a small, flat stone on the top of the soil, and when watering to let the stream of water strike the stone. This prevents holes being made and roots exposed.

It is not possible to say with accuracy how often a plant should be watered; this should depend upon a number of variable conditions. If the plant is of a kind, such as a Cyperus, Fern or Calla Lily, that is known to prefer moist soil, it will require watering more often than dry-soil plants such as Cacti, Crassulas and Sedums. When a plant is growing actively it will need more frequent watering than when it is partially or entirely dormant (many plants, such as Poinsettias, Calla Lilies and Caladiums, are kept dry and without water during their resting seasons). Specimens that have filled their containers with healthy roots need watering oftener than newly potted ones, the roots of which have not completely permeated the soil. As temperatures increase and as the relative humidity of the atmosphere falls, more frequent applications of water will be needed; the grower of house plants thus should water oftener in sunny, breezy weather than in dull, humid spells.

Although one cannot say how often a plant should be watered, it is quite possible to indicate how much water should be given at each application: enough thoroughly to soak the entire mass of soil. It does not matter whether the water is applied to the top of the soil or allowed to soak upwards through the drainage hole in the bottom of the pot or container; all that is important is that the soil be soaked through at each watering.

The soaking-from-below method is accomplished by immersing the container partway in a receptacle of water and leaving it there until the surface soil is moistened by seepage from below. This is a convenient way of making sure that all the soil is soaked in cases where the surface soil is high in the pot or the contents of the pot consist chiefly of a tight mass of roots, as is often the case with Palms, Aspidistras, Dracaenas and other strong-rooting kinds. This method is also often favored for watering plants, such as African Violets, that thrive better if their foliage is kept dry.

Feeding or Fertilizing. The soil in which plants are newly potted should contain sufficient nutrients to sustain them for some considerable time and so, until the plants have filled their containers with healthy roots, they normally need no supplementary fertilizing. Once the pots or other containers are filled with healthy roots a program of fertilizing regularly should be followed.

A fertilizer that is complete (contains nitrogen, phosphorus and potassium) and soluble is usually the best and most convenient kind to use, and many brand-name kinds are on the market prepared especially for house plants. It is important not to use such preparations in greater amounts or stronger solutions than recommended by the manufacturers; often, superior results are obtained by using them in lesser amounts or weaker solutions at more frequent intervals than the manufacturer suggests. An application of dilute liquid fertilizer applied at weekly intervals is usually satisfactory for house plants in need of feeding.

Plants that are resting or that are approaching dormancy should not be fertilized nor should any that have poor, undeveloped root systems. Fertilizing is not necessarily a cure for a sick plant; it is recommended only if lack of nutrients ordinarily shows itself by a yellowing of the foliage (particularly the lower leaves), by a reduction of the size of the leaves and by general lack of vigor.

During the dull dark days of winter less fertilizing is required than at other times and it is better not to feed at all from the end of November to early January. Plants grown in poor light need less fertilizing than those that receive adequate illumination.

Sanitation, Disease and Pest Control. To maintain plants in good condition it is necessary to keep them free of pests and diseases. Under house conditions the number of diseases that affect

As a sanitary measure it is important to pick all dead leaves off house plants.

plants is not great, because, usually, the air is too dry to favor their development. One of the commonest troubles is rotting of the roots, a condition generally brought about by poor soil drainage or overwatering. Leaf spots are sometimes troublesome and mildews also affect certain house plants, such as Tuberous Begonias. For such troubles see Pests and Diseases.

The number of pests that commonly affect house plants is greater than the number of diseases and they are more frequent. Among the commonest and most serious are aphids; scale insects; mites, including red spider mites; whiteflies and mealybugs. Nematodes can be destructive and, although not really harmful, springtails are common. For methods of control see Pests and Diseases.

The grower of house plants should always be alert to pick off dead leaves and faded blooms, not only for the sake of appearance, but because they are apt to serve as hide-outs for insects and sources of disease infection.

Plants that are kept clean usually are healthy. Dust and dirt settle on their leaves and should be washed off. A weekly trip to the kitchen sink for a fine spraying not only keeps them clean, but provides needed moisture. Clean plants are apt to be pest free. All dead leaves and flowers should be removed promptly.

Soil. Plants get their food from good, well-drained, adequately moist soil. When plants are bought the soil usually is excellent, but when they are potted or repotted at home a special mixture should be used. Sometimes this may be bought from a florist, but it also can be made at home. Generally speaking, all flowering pot plants with a woody stem structure require a porous soil containing nitrogen, phosphorus, potash and (except for definitely acid-soil plants) lime. The proper balancing of these elements is important because the nitrogen produces strong, healthy leaves, the phosphates build up the plant's structural tissue, the potash makes a stronger rooting system and the lime acts as a soil conditioner and corrective.

The formula for a soil for flowering pot plants containing all the elements necessary for growth is:

1 bushel good loam (topsoil)
3 gallons leaf mold or 3 gallons peat moss
1 four-inch pot of sheep manure
1 three-inch pot of bone meal
1 three-inch pot of hydrated lime
1 gallon of sand

Most house plants benefit from having their foliage forcefully sprayed with water at least once a week. The spraying may be conveniently done in the bathtub or kitchen sink.

To obtain good quality loam, take a long-handled pointed shovel and a bushel basket to any dry place where long grass that has not been cut for several years is growing. Such places can be found on open wasteland or along fence rows. Even in ploughed fields a narrow strip often is left next to the fence.

Cut the grass growth off at the ground level, then dig down no more than six inches. The soil containing the grass roots will be found to be a fertile, friable, mellow loam, loose in texture, free from harmful fungus and rich in humus from previous decayed grass growth. It usually contains enough natural inert potash to make the addition of that element unnecessary. This old sod loam is the base to which other elements are added. Decayed vegetable matter is a potential source of nitrogen. Therefore, nitrogen can be provided by adding three gallons of decayed leaf mold, commercial humus, or granulated peat moss to one bushel of loam. Leaf mold is by far the best to use, as it contains a high bacterial count, which is immediately available to do its work of breaking down and making soluble the insoluble elements in the soil so that the plant can use them. Peat moss, being sterile, has to create its bacterial count by moisture and warmth to make it as valuable as leaf mold, but it improves the porosity of the soil and is a good substitute when no leaf mold is obtainable. It also helps to retain moisture, and provides a base for later development of bacteria, as does commercial humus. The addition of one four-inch pot full of dried sheep manure to each bushel of loam is highly beneficial. It is a nitrogen concentrate quickly available to the plant. The phosphoric element is well supplied by bone meal at the rate of one three-inch pot to one bushel of loam. A three-inch pot of hydrated lime to one bushel of loam brings the soil into a good physical condition. The final addition of one gallon of sand insures proper porosity.

For purely ornamental foliage plants there is a slightly different formula: doubling the amount of leaf mold, commercial humus or granulated peat moss gives more luxuriant texture to the leaves.

The soils can be mixed and stored. When good soil is at hand, the next step is proper potting.

House plants need repotting periodically. A potting stick may be used to make the soil reasonably firm.

Potting. At the beginning of their chief season of growth, which for most plants is late winter or early spring, house plants should be examined to determine whether or not they are in need of potting. At that time they should be removed from their pots if they are of a size that permits this to be done easily, and the drainage checked to make sure it is functioning properly. If potting is not needed, a little of the surface soil should be removed from the top of the root mass, the plant slipped back into its pot and a top-dressing of rich soil applied to replace the surface soil taken off. If the plant is in need of potting this should receive immediate attention.

In addition to this annual inspection and potting if needed, some plants will require additional attention in the matter of repotting during their growing season. Young plants of most kinds and vigorous, strong-growing plants, such as Heliotropes, Geraniums, Fuchsias and Impatiens, belong here. When potting is done at the beginning of the growing season it is usually possible to remove some of the old soil from the roots and, sometimes, even to cut back the roots to some extent, without harming the plant; however, when plants in full growth are repotted, it is better to avoid disturbance of the roots as much as possible.

New pots rapidly absorb an extraordinary amount of water. In order to prevent them from robbing the soil of moisture they should be soaked briefly, then dried before being used. Old pots should be scrubbed until entirely clean. It is particularly important that they should be clean on the inside.

In order to insure rapid drainage, a piece of broken pot should be placed convex side up over the hole in the bottom of the pot. A covering of smaller pieces should be placed over it, and on top of these, coarse material or decayed leaves. Siftings from the soil also are effective in preventing the soil from clogging the broken crocks. A plant with proper drainage develops a healthy root system, which is reflected in rapid growth. When potting, the soil is pressed firmly about the old ball of soil or about the roots. Ample space (one half to one inch) should be left between the soil and the rim of the pot to facilitate watering.

In potting plants, the roots should be given no more than comfortable space. Many plants bloom better if the roots are somewhat pot-bound.

Immediately after potting, the plants should be thoroughly watered with a fine spray. They should be kept out of drafts and out of direct strong sunshine for about two weeks after they are repotted.

Cultivation is important. The soil becomes packed and hard in pots, just as it does in a garden, and should be stirred and loosened from time to time. Probably the best possible instrument for this is an old table fork. Prick the surface soil to loosen it without doing serious damage to the surface roots.

Outdoors in Summer. It is quite practicable to keep house plants indoors through the year but most kinds benefit from being placed outdoors during the summer months; exceptions are hairy-leaved kinds such as African Violets, Gloxinias and Episcias, and even these may improve from being kept on a shaded, covered porch during the warm months. The time to put plants outdoors is after all danger of frost has passed and the weather is warm and settled—about the time it is safe to plant outdoors such tender plants as Geraniums, Fuchsias and Heliotropes.

Before transferring house plants to outdoor

A porch or a shady place beneath a tree is a good place to summer plants that cannot stand strong direct sunshine. The plants shown here have just been moved outdoors. The pots will be spaced further apart and sunk nearly to their rims in soil, sand or cinders.

summer quarters, attend to any potting or top-dressing that needs doing and make sure that the drainage in the pots is functioning satisfactorily. Prune the plants to shape if such attention is needed, and stake and tie the branches, should additional support be desirable. Pick off dead and faded leaves and blooms and make certain that the plants are free of pests and diseases.

The location of the summer home for house plants may vary according to the particular needs of different kinds. A great many foliage plants are best accommodated in a semishaded place, but a few, such as Coleus and Crotons (Codiaeums), prefer full sun. The majority of flowering plants succeed best in a sunny location but a few, such as most Begonias, prefer light shade. It is a good plan to sink the pots almost to their rims in a bed of sand, ashes, peat moss or soil, because this prevents the roots from drying unduly and keeps them reasonably cool. If the pots are sunk in soil, place a piece of slate, tile or flat stone under each to prevent earthworms from gaining access through the drainage holes. The place where the plants are located should be well drained so that

Plants with hairy leaves, like these African Violets at the right, are better kept indoors even during the summer.

Plants summered outdoors should be brought inside well before frost threatens them, and two or three weeks before heat is turned on indoors; this permits the plants to become acclimated to the indoor environment before they are called upon to withstand the hardships of comparatively dry, heated air.

Campanula isophylla is an attractive trailing plant for the window garden.

there is no danger of the pots becoming waterlogged in wet weather.

Pots located as described above should be lifted every 2-3 weeks from the bed in which they are plunged to make sure that the roots are not coming through the bottom of the pot and spreading to such an extent that the plants will be harmed when these are later cut off. If roots are coming through, cut them off and, if necessary, repot the plants in a larger container.

Forcing Bulbs. Bulbs of many kinds may be forced into bloom in the house. Three tender Narcissus: "Paper White," "Chinese Sacred Lily" and "Soleil d'Or," and Hyacinths, both Roman and Dutch varieties, may be grown in water.

Narcissus bloom six to eight weeks after planting. Those started in autumn or early winter take longer to bloom than those started in midwinter and early spring, their normal time of bloom. The container should be deep enough to hold plenty of fiber or pebbles around each bulb. The roots are strong and if cramped will push the bulbs too far out. Water should touch the base of the bulbs, but it should not go much higher or the bulbs will rot.

When first planted the bulbs should be left in a cool, dark place where they cannot freeze. This gives the roots a chance to develop before the tops grow, as they will as soon as they are brought into the light. Bulbs are of different sizes and prices. There is no object in buying the

Chlorophytums are among the most easily grown of house plants.

For sunny windows Echeverias are excellent house plants.

largest or most expensive, but usually it is poor economy to buy bulbs anywhere except at a good seed store. After the bulbs have bloomed they are of no further use for forcing again, but, in many cases, if planted in the outdoor garden, will recover and bloom there in future years.

Hyacinths require a longer time to develop roots: the Roman Hyacinth must be kept in a cool, dark place for about eight weeks and the Dutch from 10 to 12 weeks. These, too, may be grown in pebbles or in specially constructed Hyacinth glasses which have a cup-shaped top to hold the bulb in place just above the water. Single Dutch Hyacinths are more satisfactory than the larger variety.

Lily of the Valley blooms well in the house and may be grown in soil or in a bowl filled with fiber, peat moss, or sand. These delicate, fragrant flowers are very easy to grow if the roots have been thoroughly frozen before they are brought into light and heat. The ones offered for sale by reputable firms have all been in cold storage and will come into bloom in three or four weeks after they are given water and light. It is possible to dig up roots from the garden, but these must be left outside until they have been hard-frozen for five or six days. One trouble about using roots from the garden is that because they differ in size the bloom may not be even and is, therefore, less attractive. Lilies of the Valley may also be grown in soil.

Other Kinds of House Plants. In addition to the plants already mentioned there are a great many more. These are listed under their appropriate entries in other parts of this book. For some of the more important, consult Abutilon, Acalypha, Achimenes, Aglaonema, Ardisia, Asparagus, Aspidistra, Aucuba, Australian Silk Oak, Azalea, Begonia, Beloperone, Bird of Paradise Flower, Bromeliads, Cactus, Caladium, Ceropegia, Chlorophyton, Cissus, Clerodendrum, Clivia, Crassula, Croton, Dieffenbachia, Dracaena, Echeveria, Euphorbia, Fatsia, Ferns, Ficus, Fittonia, Fuchsias, Geranium, Gloriosa, Grevillea, Heliotrope, Hippeastrum, Hoya, Hydrangea, Impatiens, Ivy, Kalanchoë, Lantana, Leopard Plant, Liriope, Mahernia, Maranta, Mesembryanthemum, Monstera, Myrtle, Nephthytis, Oleander, Oxalis, Palm, Pandanus, Pelargonium, Peperomia, Philodendron, Pickaback, Pilea, Plectranthus, Plumbago, Podocarpus, Portulacaria, Pothos, Primrose, Saintpaulia, Sansevieria, Schefflera, Sedum, Schizobasopsis, Scindapsus, Spathiphyllum, Syngonium, Thunbergia, Tibouchina, Ti Plant, Tradescantia, Urginea, Vallota, Veltheimia, and Zebrina.

HOUSTONIA — *Bluets* (Housto'nia). A group of some twenty hardy herbaceous perennials, which belong to the family Rubiaceae; they are natives of North America. Houstonia commemorates Dr. W. Houston, 1695-1733, an American botanical writer.

Dwarf Rock Garden Plants. The Houstonias are low plants, 2-15 in. tall, with small leaves,

Houstonia caerulea, a dainty little pale blue, June-flowering plant for the rock and wild garden.

and four-petaled flowers, produced in profusion. Most are of moderate, creeping habit, and are best grown in light, rich soil containing an abundance of well-decayed leaf mold. They enjoy a rather cool, half-shady position, and the soil should be kept moist. They may be propagated by means of seeds, sown in fine soil in a frame in spring, by division of the plants in spring or fall, or by cuttings, taken in spring, and inserted in sand in a cold frame.

Blue Flowers. Houstonia caerulea has blue to white flowers, about ½ in. across; it grows 2-3 in. high. It is a very pretty plant for a cool position in the rock garden, and flowers profusely in early summer. H. serpyllifolia has blue flowers, on 2- to 5-in. stems, and forms a mat of low foliage.

HOUTTEA (Hout'tea). Brightly flowered shrubby plants from Brazil, closely related to Isoloma and Corytholoma, belonging to the family Gesneriaceae. The genus is named after Louis van Houtte, a famous Belgian nurseryman, and the chief kinds are H. Gardneri, 2 ft., red, July–August; and H. pardina, 18 in., orange-red, August–October. For details of cultivation see Isoloma.

HOUTTUYNIA (Houttuy'nia). A moisture-loving ground cover plant suitable for the margins of ponds. It belongs to the family Saururaceae. Houttuynia commemorates Dr. Martin Houttuyn, of Amsterdam. The chief kind is H. cordata, from Japan; it has blue-green, heart-shaped leaves and cone-shaped inflorescences with white bracts, on stems 18 in. tall in summer. The flower heads look something like miniature ones of the flowering Dogwood.

H. cordata has proved hardy at New York City and grows well there even in soil not especially moist. It is readily propagated by division in spring and early fall, and cuttings taken in summer and early fall root with ease in a bed of moist sand in a cold frame or greenhouse.

HOVEA (Ho'vea). Tender evergreen, flowering shrubs from Australia, which belong to the Pea family, Leguminosae. They grow up to 10 ft. in height, have alternate, long, lanceolate to oval leaves, and bear clusters of blue flowers in spring. The name commemorates A. P. Hove, a Polish botanist.

Flowering Shrubs. They may be grown outdoors in mild climates and in greenhouses. When grown indoors they require a minimum winter temperature of 45 degrees. The best compost consists of equal parts of peat and loam with sand added freely. They are potted in March in well-drained pots, and are placed out of doors from July to September to ripen the growths for flowering in the following year. The shoots are shortened slightly after the flowers have faded. During the winter the soil is only moistened when it becomes quite dry, but throughout the summer it is kept moist.

Propagation is by cutting off young shoots and inserting them in spring in a propagating case until rooted; then they are potted separately in 3-in. pots. The ends of the main shoots and lateral branches are pinched to form bushy plants.

The chief kinds are H. Celsii, 3 ft., blue; and H. longifolia, 5 ft., purple.

HOVENIA—*Japanese Raisin Tree* (Hoven'ia). This is a member of the Buckthorn family, Rhamnaceae. It was named in honor of David Hoven, an Amsterdam senator. H. dulcis is a tree to 30 ft. high with attractive foliage and greenish flowers followed by small fruits, the stalks of which are sometimes eaten. It prefers a sandy

Houttuynia cordata is an interesting ground-cover plant that bears white flowers in summer.

loam soil. The tree is propagated by seeds, root cuttings and cuttings of mature growth under glass. It is hardy in the North.

HOWEA (How'ea). Popular foliage plants which belong to the Palm family, Palmaceae. They grow about 30-60 ft. tall, and have large spreading leaves which are deeply divided. These Palms are commonly known as Kentia, and small specimens are extensively used for indoor decoration. Larger specimens are suitable for decorating the greenhouse and conservatory. They are natives of Lord Howe's Island, from which the name Howea is derived.

Palms for a Greenhouse. They require a moist, shaded position in a greenhouse with a minimum winter temperature of 55 degrees. The best potting compost consists of two parts of loam, one part leaf mold or peat moss and a liberal sprinkling of sand.

Repotting is done in March, when the plants, if they need more root room, are set in slightly larger pots. During the summer months they require an abundance of water, but throughout the winter the soil is only moistened when it becomes dry.

Propagation is by sowing seeds in pots of sandy soil in spring or summer in a propagating case in a temperature of 65-75 degrees. The seedlings are potted in 3-in. and, later, in larger pots.

The kinds are H. Belmoreana and H. Forsteriana.

HOYA—*Wax Plant, Wax Flower* (Hoy'a). Tender evergreen, climbing and shrubby plants with attractive flowers of waxlike texture, belonging to the Milkweed family, Asclepiadaceae. The most popular kind, H. carnosa, climbs by means of its thick succulent stems, clothed with evergreen, ovate-oblong, fleshy leaves, and bears large clusters of pink, star-shaped flowers, half an inch in diameter, in summer. Hoya commemorates Thomas Hoy, onetime gardener to the Duke of Northumberland.

Indoor Climbing Plants. Hoyas are suitable for growing in greenhouses and window gardens. They need a minimum winter temperature of 45 degrees and a compost of equal parts of peat and loam with a small portion of crushed brick and sand. The plants are set in large pots or tubs, or planted in a prepared bed of soil in

The Wax Flower, Hoya carnosa, a lovely climbing plant for the greenhouse and window garden.

the greenhouse, and the shoots are trained to wires fixed to the greenhouse wall or roof. Pruning consists of thinning the shoots when they become crowded, but the old stems must not be cut off, as the flowers are borne on the stumps of the previous year's flowering stalks. Abundance of water is required in summer, but throughout the winter less is needed.

Propagation is by layering the shoots in pots of sandy soil, or by inserting shoots, 3 in. in length, in sand or sand and peat moss in spring or summer. Young plants flower profusely in the second year.

The chief kind is H. carnosa, Wax Plant, summer, 10 ft., pink. H. carnosa exotica has its leaves variegated with two shades of green, yellow and pink. H. carnosa variegata has green and yellow variegated leaves with sometimes a tinge of pink. Other especially notable kinds are H. australis, a climber, 4 ft., white and pink, October; and H. bella, a shrubby kind, 3 ft., white and crimson, summer.

HUCKLEBERRY. See Gaylussacia.

HUDSONIA — *Beach Heather* (Hudso'nia). Dwarf evergreen shrubs of heathlike growth belonging to the Rock Rose family, Cistaceae. They are natives of eastern North America and are not easy to grow in most gardens. Their proper place is the rock garden and in seaside gardens, where they should be set in well-drained acid, sandy soil. H. ericoides grows 6-8 in. high and bears fugitive yellow flowers in May. Two other kinds have been described, H.

[5—14]
Hills of Snow Hydrangea
(Hydrangea grandiflora)

[5—14a]
Peegee Hydrangea
(Hydrangea paniculata grandiflora)

[5-15]
Hydrangea macrophylla variety

[5-15b]
Hypericum patulum Hidcote

[5-15a]
Ismene
(Hymenocallis calathina)

[5-15c]
Winterberry
(Ilex verticillata)

montana and H. tomentosa. Hudsonia was named in commemoration of William Hudson, an English botanist of the eighteenth and early nineteenth centuries.

HUERNIA (Huer′nia). Huernia belongs to the Milkweed family, Asclepiadaceae, and was named in honor of David Justus Huernius, a Dutch missionary. The genus contains several species of small succulent perennials that are suited for desert gardens in warm regions, for greenhouse growing and for window gardens. The blackish-purple flowers grow from the base of the stems, and are usually ill smelling. The plants resemble Stapelias and require the same cultural care. They are natives of Africa, particularly South Africa. Among kinds grown by fanciers of succulents are: H. aspera, dark purple; H. Hystrix, yellow and crimson; H. Pilansii, yellow spotted crimson; and H. transvaalensis, purple.

HUERNIOPSIS (Huerniop′sis). African succulent plants belonging to the Milkweed family, Asclepiadaceae. The plants described resemble Huernia and have malodorous flowers. H. decipiens has brownish-red flowers mottled yellow, about an inch across. H. gibbosa has dark purple flowers with yellowish-white cups.

HUMEA ELEGANS—*Incense Plant* (Hu′mea). An attractive, tender biennial plant which reaches a height of 6 or 8 ft., has large, aromatic leaves, and bears graceful panicles of small, reddish flowers in summer. It is a native of Australia and belongs to the Daisy family, Compositae. The name commemorates Lady Amelia Hume.

When to Sow Seeds. This handsome plant is usually grown for the large greenhouse or conservatory, but is sometimes used in summer flower beds. As the plants are useless after they have flowered, they are raised annually from seeds. These are sown in sifted light soil in a cold frame in June. The frame must be shaded in bright weather and the soil kept moist; the seedlings, when an inch or two high, are potted singly in 3-in. pots in a compost of loam, two thirds, and leaf mold, one third, with a free scattering of sand.

During the remainder of the summer the plants are grown in the frame, the latter being ventilated freely except during heavy rain. When the plants are well rooted in the small pots they

This graceful plant is Humea elegans, the Incense Plant of Australia.

are repotted in 5-in. or 6-in. pots in which they pass the winter. From October onwards they should be placed in a greenhouse having a minimum temperature of 45 degrees.

The Final Potting. In February, the plants should be potted finally in a compost of loam, two thirds, leaf mold and thoroughly decayed manure, one third. Large pots, 8 or 9 in. in diameter, are required to ensure well-developed plants. They need very little warmth but must be kept safe from frost. Some people find that the leaves of Humea cause an irritation of the skin, and gloves should be worn when potting the plants.

HUMULUS—*Hop* (Hum′ulus). Hardy climbing plants that die down in autumn; some have perennial rootstocks; others are of annual duration. The Hops are dioecious, i.e., male and female flowers are borne on different plants. They belong to the Nettle family, Urticaceae. The name Humulus is derived from *humus*, the ground, and refers to the trailing nature of the plants if they are not supported.

Grow Very Quickly. Both annual and perennial Hops thrive in ordinary garden ground, but grow more vigorously in deep soil enriched with manure and wood ash or with fertilizer. The provision of adequate and efficient support is important as the Hop plants grow very quickly. Arches, pillars, porches, verandas, arbors, and horizontal wires supporting perpendicular strings, provide a means of support for the plants, which make excellent screens.

Both annuals and perennials are raised from seeds sown indoors early, or outdoors when danger of frost has passed. The perennial kinds and their varieties can be propagated in spring, by division; or cuttings of young shoots, 3 or 4 in. long, may be inserted in a greenhouse.

The Perennial Hops. Humulus Lupulus is a native of Europe and Asia and is naturalized in North America. In rich soil the shoots will reach a length of 20-30 ft. in one season. The flowers are greenish-yellow; the male flowers are produced in loose axillary panicles, and the female flowers, which produce the fruits known as Hops, are on short-stalked, axillary spikes. The Hops used in brewing are cultivated varieties. The variety aureus has golden-yellow leaves and is an ornamental-leaved climber. H. americanus, a native of North America, is closely related to H. Lupulus and requires the same culture.

The Japanese Hop. Humulus japonicus, the Annual Hop, is a native of China, Japan, and Manchuria. It attains a height of 10-20 ft. in one season and is a popular climbing annual for providing a screen. The variety variegatus is also grown from seeds annually; a large percentage of the seedling plants have leaves which are streaked and splashed with white.

HUMUS. An advanced state of decayed organic matter. It should be the aim of the gardener to keep the soil well supplied with humus, for its fertility depends largely on an adequate quality of this material. Humus retains moisture and keeps the ground from drying out rapidly in hot weather; it is the main indirect source of the food supply of plants. Soil which lacks humus soon becomes impoverished. Humus is supplied chiefly by adding animal manure, leaf mold, decayed garden refuse (see Compost), peat moss, sedge peat, and by turning under crops grown as cover crops or green manures.

HUNNEMANNIA FUMARIAEFOLIA — *Mexican Tulip Poppy* (Hunneman'nia). A Mexican herbaceous perennial plant, which grows 2-3 ft. high, has grayish leaves and bears yellow, poppy-like flowers in summer. It belongs to the Poppy family, Papaveraceae. Hunnemannia commemorates a nineteenth-century botanist, J. Hunnemann.

Hunnemannia is splendid for flower beds and borders and provides useful cut flowers. In frostless and nearly frostless regions this plant may be grown as a perennial outdoors, in a well-drained sandy soil in a sunny location. It is, however, easily grown as an annual, and first-year plants flower profusely over a long season.

The Mexican Tulip Poppy, Hunnemannia fumariaefolia, is a beautiful annual for sunny locations. It blooms from early summer until frost.

Even in the North good results may be had by sowing the seeds out of doors as soon as the weather is warm and settled and all danger of frost has passed. Plants raised from seeds sown in this way will begin to flower in July and continue to the end of summer.

Somewhat earlier bloom may be had by sowing early indoors and transplanting outdoors when the weather is warm. If this is done, the seeds should be sown directly in small pots of sandy soil, and the transplanting done very carefully, for this plant resents root disturbance.

In addition to the common kind, a variety with semidouble flowers is available.

In a sunny greenhouse where the night temperature is maintained at 50 degrees, a succession of blooms may be had over a long period in late winter and spring from plants raised from seeds sown in August or September.

HUNTINGDON ELM. Ulmus hollandica var. vegeta, which see.

HUNTSMAN'S-CUP. See Sarracenia.

HUON PINE TREE. See Dacrydium.

HUSK TOMATO. Physalis, which see.

HUTCHINSIA ALPINA (Hutchin'sia). This plant is a pretty, hardy alpine, abundant in the high Alps of Europe. It belongs to the Mustard family, Cruciferae, and was named after a Miss Hutchins, of Ireland.

The finely divided foliage, of a dark, rich, glossy green, forms dense low cushions bearing, in May and June, countless little heads of small white flowers, which contrast admirably with the deep, lustrous foliage of this alpine plant.

Carpeting Plant for the Rock Garden. Hutchinsia is of the easiest possible cultivation in loamy soil in sun, half shade, or even full shade. It is an excellent ground cover for choice bulbs in a rock garden. Hutchinsia is a good plant, too, for the wall garden. Propagation is easy either from seed or by division. Seeds are sown in April, in a pot filled with fine soil and placed in a cold frame, or the plants may be divided in September.

A rather smaller, more compact kind, Hutchinsia brevicaulis, is found in the High Alps, but is little known in gardens.

HYACINTH. Hyacinthus, which see.

HYACINTH BEAN. Dolichos Lablab, which see.

HYACINTH, CAPE. See Galtonia.

HYACINTH, GRAPE. Muscari, which see.

HYACINTHUS: THE HYACINTH
Fragrant Spring-flowering Bulbs for Home and Garden Decoration

(Hyacin'thus). This is a group of hardy spring-flowering bulbs, many of which are popular for use in flower beds and for cultivation in pots indoors and in the greenhouse. Hyacinthus is the ancient Greek name used by Homer.

About thirty species are known. They are chiefly natives of the Mediterranean Region and the Orient; two or three grow wild in tropical and southern Africa. They belong to the Lily family, Liliaceae.

The most important wild kind is Hyacinthus orientalis, a native of Syria, Greece, Asia Minor and Dalmatia, because from it, and its variety provincialis, from southern France, Switzerland and Italy, the beautiful Hyacinths of our greenhouses and gardens have been raised. The

A glorious bed of fragrant large-flowered Hyacinths. Second-size Hyacinth bulbs are most suitable for spring bedding.

This Hyacinth bulb has been cut in half to show clearly the undeveloped flower spike which at planting time is present in the center of every Hyacinth bulb that will bloom the following spring.

variety albulus from southern France is the parent of the white Roman Hyacinth.

The supply of Hyacinth bulbs for cultivation in pots and in beds and borders comes almost entirely from Holland, and for this reason they are frequently known as Dutch Hyacinths. Many attempts have been made to grow Hyacinth bulbs on a commercial scale elsewhere, but comparatively little success has attended these efforts.

How Hyacinths Are Propagated. Hyacinths can be grown from seeds sown in sandy soil in a cold frame in autumn; the bulbs will reach flowering size in from four to six years. This method of propagation is only adapted for raising new varieties. One method of increasing Hyacinths for commercial purposes is by offsets and by bulbils which develop on old Hyacinth bulbs if deep crosscuts are made through the basal parts of the bulb previous to planting. The following year the bulbils are set out in a nursery bed; by this method flowering bulbs are obtained in three years.

Winter Hyacinths. From November to April it is possible to have Hyacinths in bloom in a greenhouse or window garden. The first to flower in November are the Roman Hyacinths which bear white flowers. These are followed in December and January by the Cynthella or Miniature Hyacinths, which are specially grown and harvested early so that with only a moderate amount of heat the bulbs will develop flowers in midwinter.

Bulbs for Forcing. If very early blooming is desired, specially "prepared" bulbs of Hyacinths of the large-flowered type may be obtained for forcing into bloom.

For early indoor flowers, prepared Hyacinth bulbs should be potted in September, stood in a cold frame, and covered with 6 inches of sifted weathered ashes, sand, or peat moss, care being taken to keep these moist by watering with a fine spray when necessary.

Hyacinths for Christmas. After six weeks they should be removed from the ashes and stood in a dark place, as for instance under the covered benches of the greenhouse, in a temperature of about 65 degrees F. Here they should remain until the flower buds are well clear of the bulbs, keeping them well supplied with tepid water, after which they should be transferred to the benches. A shading of newspaper will be necessary for a time, and will encourage flower stem development, and at the same time the day temperature should be increased to 70 degrees F., with a fall of not more than 5 degrees at night.

Cynthella or Miniature Hyacinths are very graceful and are especially useful for forcing into bloom early.

During the closing days of January, and in February and March, the large-flowered single Hyacinths are indispensable pot plants for the greenhouse and window garden. Some of the best sorts are Enchantress, light blue; Grand

Maitre, deep blue; King of the Blues, dark blue; L'Innocence, white; La Grandesse, white; Lady Derby, rose; Myosotis, light blue; Queen of the Pinks, rose-pink; and City of Haarlem, yellow.

Double Hyacinths. Though little grown in comparison with those having single flowers, the double-flowered Hyacinths are very attractive, and produce large spikes closely packed with small rosette-like flowers.

When to Pot Hyacinth Bulbs. The bulbs that provide the best and earliest flowers are those which are well rooted before top growth begins; early potting is, therefore, necessary. Roman Hyacinths should be potted during late August, the Cynthella Hyacinths in early September, and the large-flowered varieties at the end of September or early in October. A first-rate compost for Hyacinths in pots consists of three parts fibrous loam, one part each of decayed manure, leaf mold or peat moss and coarse grit. When such a compost is not obtainable, the best available garden soil should be used and improved by adding to each bushel a peck of decayed manure and a gallon of coarse grit.

Pots of 5-in. or 6-in. diameter are the most useful sizes for Hyacinth bulbs. Three bulbs of White Roman and Cynthella Hyacinths are set in each 5-in. pot and five bulbs in a 6-in. pot; one good bulb of the large-flowered kinds is sufficient for a 5-in. pot, and three bulbs can be placed in a 6-in. pot. Over the drainage material a little rough fibrous potting compost is placed and the prepared compost is then put in. The bulbs should be pressed into the soil and more of this added to ensure that the bulbs are covered to three-quarters of their depth. The Hyacinth bulbs produce roots only from the bottom, so that there is no object in entirely covering them for greenhouse and room cultivation.

Details of Management. The pots of bulbs are placed outside in a sheltered position, watered and covered to a depth of 6-7 in. with peat moss, sand or old coal ashes. In six to eight weeks the bulbs will be well rooted and top growth will begin to push through; they should be placed in a cool, frostproof frame or greenhouse and shaded for a few days until the growths assume their normal green color. They should then be exposed to the light.

After ten days or a fortnight in the cold frame

Part of the pot containing this Hyacinth bulb has been broken away to show the healthy roots that develop during the period in which the bulbs are kept outside covered with peat moss, sand or coal cinders. No attempt should be made to bring Hyacinths into a warm greenhouse or room until they are well rooted.

a number of the pots of bulbs should be placed in a greenhouse or window garden, beginning with the Roman Hyacinths. If at intervals of ten days or two weeks others are brought into the heat there will be a continuous supply of bloom. When the plants are growing freely liberal supplies of water will be required.

In containers which have no drainage holes Hyacinths may be grown in bulb fiber or vermiculite. If kept in a cool place for eight or ten weeks to encourage root formation, they will soon bloom when brought into a sunny window in a moderately warm room.

Hyacinths in Bowls of Fiber. The varieties of Hyacinths named as suitable for pots can also be grown in bowls of fiber. It is usual to place the bowls and vases in a dark, or moderately dark, airy room, keeping the fiber (a mixture of peat moss, charcoal and chopped oyster shells) moist for six to ten weeks until the bulbs are well rooted and top growth is beginning. The bulbs must not be placed in a close, dry closet or they will not be successful.

Treatment After Flowering. Hyacinth bulbs that have been grown in bowls of fiber need not be discarded after flowering. If they are planted outdoors when danger of frost has passed, allowed to die down naturally, and then left undisturbed, they will thrive and bloom freely for many years.

Hyacinths in Glasses of Water. Hyacinth bulbs are frequently grown in glasses specially made for the purpose. The treatment they require is simple. The glasses are filled with water (rain water, preferably) and a few pieces of charcoal are put in to keep the water sweet. The base of the bulb must be just above the water. The bulbs are set in a cool, dark place until the roots are growing freely, and are then gradually brought into a light position. A little water should be added from time to time as may be required. The large-flowered single varieties recommended for pots are suitable to grow in glasses.

Fragrant Dutch Hyacinths are among the most admired of spring bulbs.

A Hyacinth grown in a glass of water with a few pieces of charcoal in the bottom.

Hyacinths for Beds and Borders. To provide groups of brilliant color in flower beds and borders during early spring, the named varieties of bedding Hyacinths have few, if any, rivals. Firm bulbs of moderate size are preferable to large bulbs which are loose, and will probably produce small side shoots in addition to the main flower spike.

When to Plant. Hyacinths succeed best in well-drained, loamy soil and in a sunny position. October is the best month for planting. Before the bulbs are put in, very decayed manure and compost should be added to the soil. The bulbs are set 9 in. apart and covered with 5-6 in. of soil. To ensure an effective display of color in spring and to cover the ground in winter, suitable spring-flowering plants are used to "carpet" the beds, these being planted before the Hyacinths where climate permits, in spring where winters are severe. If a carpeting plant is used, the Hyacinth bulbs should be placed about 12 in. apart. Suitable carpeting plants are single- and double-

Planting Hyacinth bulbs in fall. They are set with their tops 5 to 6 in. beneath the surface.

In early spring the fall-planted Hyacinths produce a fine show of scented blooms.

flowered Arabis, pink, white and red English Daisies, Pansies, and Polyanthus Primroses.

When the flower spikes push up in early spring they should be supported with neat stakes, or the stems may be broken during heavy rain and wind.

Lifting the Bulbs. Hyacinth bulbs may be lifted and dried off each year. If left in the soil to ripen, or if carefully lifted after flowering and planted in an out-of-the-way place to dry off slowly, the bulbs may be used for bedding for two or three years; but however carefully this is done, they gradually deteriorate, and it is necessary from time to time to replace them by purchasing new bulbs.

Beautiful Varieties. Unlike most florists' flowers, the varieties of Hyacinths do not change much, and most of the named varieties grown twenty-five to forty years ago are the favorite varieties today. These form a selection of the best: City of Haarlem, yellow; Grand Maitre, blue; Jan Bos, red; King of the Blues, rich blue; Lady Derby, rose-pink; L'Innocence, white; Queen of the Blues, Queen of the Pinks, and Winston S. Churchill, blue.

For the Rock Garden or Spring Border. Hyacinthus amethystinus, the Spanish Hyacinth, has bright blue, drooping flowers, loosely arranged on 6-in.-high stems. It is suitable for the rock garden or the front of a flower border; it blooms in spring, and there is also a white-flowered form (albus). The bulbs are planted 1½ in. apart in September or October. Hyacinthus ciliatus (azureus), from Asia Minor, has spikes of light- and dark-blue flowers on stems 4 in. or 5 in. high, in February and March. H. lineatus, also from Asia Minor, bears blue flowers in April, six to twelve on a stem 3 or 4 in. high.

Hyacinthus ciliatus, a dainty little light-blue-flowered species from Asia Minor—a gem for the rock garden, or for growing in small pots indoors for early bloom.

HYACINTHUS CANDICANS. Another name for Galtonia candicans or Cape Hyacinth. See Galtonia.

HYBRID. A term which is correctly used in defining the progeny which results from crossbreeding between two species or wild types. It is often used loosely to describe plants which have been raised by crossbreeding between varieties.

HYBRIDIZATION. The practice of crossbreeding between two species or wild types; this term is now used to indicate crossbreeding generally, whether between species or varieties.

HYDRANGEA

Good Flowering Shrubs for Greenhouse, Tub, and Outdoor Cultivation

(Hydran'gea). The Hydrangeas are an important group of hardy and tender shrubs and several woody climbers. Nearly all are leaf-losing, but a few of the tender kinds are evergreen. About thirty-five species are known; these are natives of the Himalayas, central and eastern Asia and North and South America. The name Hydrangea is from the Greek *hydor*, water, and *aggeion*, a vessel, alluding to the cup-shaped fruits. Though these shrubs are quite unlike the Saxifrage family in growth, the botanical characters of the flowers place them with the Philadelphus, Ribes and Deutzias in the Saxifrage family, Saxifragaceae.

Macrophylla (Hortensia) Varieties

Among the best-known and most popular of Hydrangeas are the numerous varieties of H. macrophylla (H. hortensis) that are often called Hortensias. These are grown in vast numbers by commercial florists for use as pot plants in late winter, spring and early summer and are equally as suitable for growing and flowering in the amateur's small greenhouse. They are also adaptable for cultivating in tubs as subjects for the decoration of terraces and patios in summer. In cold climates the tubs may be stored in a cool, frostproof or nearly frostproof cellar or similar place over winter.

The macrophylla Hydrangeas are hardy outdoors from about New York City southwards and in favored locations even further north, if they are well protected over winter. They are especially well suited for planting near the sea.

Why Hortensias Fail to Flower. Hydrangeas of the macrophylla varieties produce their main flower clusters from the tips of shoots formed the previous season. If anything destroys the terminal buds of these shoots the plants usually fail to bloom, although a few varieties will develop side growths that bloom the first season from some little distance beneath the terminal buds should the latter be destroyed.

The chief causes of destruction of the terminal buds are excessive winter cold and unintelligent pruning. In cold localities the former can be guarded against to some extent by selecting sheltered locations for the bushes and by wrapping them in tar paper and burlap over winter or by protecting them in some other suitable way.

Pruning should be done in summer as soon as

Varieties of Hydrangea macrophylla, blue, pink and white flowered, are popular plants for growing in pots.

Varieties of Hydrangea hortensis bloom freely in late summer. They are especially suitable for planting in gardens near the sea.

Hydrangea macrophylla is pruned immediately after flowering by cutting out old shoots. The new young shoots that arise from near the base of the plant are left uncut.

the flowering season is over. In pruning, remove all old flowering shoots down to a point on the stem from which strong new growths are developing, as well as very weak growths and those that are obviously crowded. Retain the strong new shoots that appear from the base of the plant and from the lower parts of the old stems, and which are the shoots that may be expected to bloom the following year. Under no circumstances should macrophylla Hydrangeas be pruned in late fall, winter or spring if flowers are desired.

How to Propagate Hortensias. Cuttings afford an easy and practical means of propagating these popular Hydrangeas. The best time to insert them is from April to August. The best cuttings are obtained from the ends of nonflowering shoots; each should have two or three pairs of

The flowers of Hydrangea macrophylla are produced from the termination of the previous year's shoots. These should not be cut off in pruning.

Here are shown cuttings taken from a budding Hydrangea macrophylla. To prepare the stems for cutting, their lower leaves and portions of their upper leaves are cut off; then the stems are sliced clean across just below a node.

leaves. The cuttings are prepared by removing the bottom pair of leaves and cutting the stem across just below a joint. They are then inserted in a well-packed bed of sand in a greenhouse propagating case or, in summer, in a cold frame that is kept close until rooting has taken place. The cuttings should be kept shaded from bright sunshine, and on sunny days they should be sprayed lightly with water.

The Best Soil. When the cuttings are rooted a little air must be admitted to the frame or glass case. In a few days the young plants will be ready for potting separately in small pots. The compost used should consist of equal parts of peat, leaf mold, sandy, lime-free loam and coarse grit. Fibrous loam containing lime can be used for the pink and white-flowered Hydrangeas, but for blue-flowered Hydrangeas, loam containing lime must not be used: if suitable loam is not available only peat and leaf mold with plenty of coarse grit should be employed. In autumn or early spring the young plants must be repotted, the strongest in 6-in. pots, and the smaller ones in 5-in. pots.

Treatment in Winter. These Hydrangeas are leaf-losing plants and should have a period of rest in winter: a suitable minimum temperature at that time is 45 degrees and the soil should be watered only when it becomes really dry. In early spring the Hydrangea plants will begin to grow apace. This is the time to water them freely with weak liquid fertilizer. Hydrangeas two, three or four years old, or older plants are grown in large pots and tubs. They may be wintered safely in a cold greenhouse, a frostproof shed or cellar; in mild districts they may be placed in a sheltered corner out of doors.

When the plants are large and do not require repotting they should have a top-dressing of rich soil each year in spring, and be given weak liquid fertilizer freely.

How to Make Pink Hydrangeas Blue. Only Hydrangeas which naturally have pink flowers will bear blue ones in districts where the soil is acid or when treated with substances designed to make the flowers change color. White-flowered Hydrangeas only change to a starchy white or slate color. The deeper pink the flower is normally, the richer and more intense will be the blue of the blooms following the use of a blueing preparation. The simplest method of treatment is to purchase one of the chemical blueing powders sold by garden supply dealers and nurserymen for the purpose and use it according to the manufacturer's directions.

Other means of obtaining blue Hydrangeas are mixing iron filings in the potting soil, watering with alum at the rate of one teaspoonful dissolved in a gallon of rain water, or with 3 oz. of aluminium sulphate dissolved in a gallon of water; they are not, however, so certain in results as the blueing powder.

Attractive Varieties. Many fine varieties of macrophylla Hydrangeas exist and the list is constantly being added to by specialists who breed new varieties. Among the best of those favored for forcing purposes by florists (these plants are useful too for outdoor planting) are Benelux, rose-pink; Charm, carmine-red; Engel's White, white; Gertrude Glahn, dark rose-pink; Jean Merritt, pink; Joan Merritt, white; Kunhert, rose-pink; Merveille, light red; President Eisenhower, carmine; Rose Supreme, rose-pink; Rosabelle, rose-pink; Strafford, dark pink.

No mention is made in the above listing of blue-flowered varieties because all the pink, carmine and red shades assume blue tints when they are grown in acid soils or when treated

Hydrangea macrophylla variety maculata is a handsome foliage plant with beautifully variegated leaves.

appropriately by the use of "blueing" powder or other suitable materials, as explained earlier. Of the varieties mentioned above, those that blue most satisfactorily are Benelux, Gertrude Glahn, Kunhert, Merveille and Rose Supreme.

Especially for Planting Outdoors. In addition to the varieties already mentioned, which have all been raised in American gardens, there are a few varieties and forms of Hydrangea macrophylla of oriental origin that are suitable for planting outdoors. These include caerulea, which has tiny bright blue fertile flowers in the center of the head and sterile flowers, with white or blue, petal-like bracts around the circumference; mandshurica, with pink flowers and black-purple stems; Mariesii, with small fertile flowers in the center of the head and sterile pink flowers around the circumference; and maculata (variegata), which has its leaves beautifully variegated with white and gray and bears fertile flowers that are blue and sterile flowers of paler color.

Other Kinds of Hydrangeas

In addition to the varieties of Hydrangea macrophylla, or Hortensias, there are a number of other kinds of Hydrangea that are very worthwhile planting in gardens. These are shrubs or, in the case of H. paniculata and its varieties, small trees, and two, H. petiolaris and H. anomola, are self-clinging, tall-growing vines.

Hydrangeas grow without difficulty in a fairly wide variety of soils but they prefer those that are fairly rich and not lacking in moisture. Provided they receive ample moisture they thrive in full sun and bloom more freely than when they are subjected to partial shade. However, most Hydrangeas will succeed where they receive some shade and will bloom; indeed, if the soil tends to be dry they succeed better when they are partially shaded than when exposed to full sunshine all day.

The propagation of Hydrangeas is effected without difficulty in several ways. The first is by means of leafy cuttings of half-ripened shoots taken in summer and treated as advised earlier for Hydrangea macrophylla varieties. The second is by means of hardwood cuttings made of leafless shoots in fall; these are kept buried outdoors all winter under several inches of sand, and are planted in nursery rows in spring, vertically, with only their tips showing above the surface.

Seeds, sown in sandy, peaty soil in spring in a greenhouse or cold frame, also afford a good means of securing increase from the wild species, but garden varieties of wild species do not, of course, come true to type from seeds.

Layering provides a convenient means of increasing Hydrangeas and is particularly useful in the case of those having very large leaves such as H. Sargentiana and H. quercifolia.

Hydrangeas may be transplanted without difficulty. Early spring and early fall are the seasons best suited for this work.

Hydrangeas Recommended for Garden Planting. Following are listed some of the best Hydrangeas for garden planting. These are in addition to the varieties of H. macrophylla already discussed.

Hydrangea paniculata, and its varieties grandiflora, the Peegee Hydrangea, and praecox, are very attractive white-flowered shrubs that eventually become small trees, 20-30 ft. in height. Annually, in early spring, the shoots of the past year's growth may be pruned to within an inch or two of their bases; when the new shoots develop in spring they should be reduced in number to ensure the development of fine heads of

The Peegee Hydrangea, Hydrangea paniculata grandiflora, is a popular shrub for garden planting.

The Peegee Hydrangea is pruned by cutting back old flowering shoots close to their bases. This should be done before growth starts in spring.

bloom on the others. The large flower heads of H. paniculata grandiflora, which are in full beauty in August–September, are composed entirely of white sterile florets. The variety praecox flowers in July and the head of bloom consists of a central mass of fertile flowers surrounded by a ring of white florets.

Hydrangea arborescens of the eastern United States is a shrub 4-5 ft. high which bears cream-white flowers in summer; the variety grandiflora, bearing heads of large, cream-white sterile flowers, is more attractive than the type and flowers freely from July–September. It is called the Hills of Snow Hydrangea. H. quercifolia, a native of North America, has oaklike leaves which assume rich autumnal tints of golden-orange and red before falling; it grows 4-6 ft. high and bears white heads of bloom in July. It is well suited for light shade. H. Bretschneideri is a vigorous leaf-losing bush, 7-10 ft. high, with flat bunches, 5-6 in. across, of fertile flowers surrounded by white sterile flowers, in June and July.

H. xanthoneura Wilsonii forms a large bush, 8-12 ft. high, and in June and July bears flattish inflorescences, 5-6 in. across, of white flowers. H. strigosa macrophylla is a large-leaved shrub, 6-8 ft. high; in June and July it bears large heads of pale porcelain-blue fertile flowers and lilac-pink sterile flowers. H. villosa is similar.

Hydrangea quercifolia is especially suitable for planting in light shade.

This is the Climbing Hydrangea, Hydrangea petiolaris. Note the sterile flowers—each with four broad oval white sepals—and the tiny, fuzzy fertile flowers in the center of each cluster.

H. Sargentiana, 6-7 ft., has unusually large leaves, 12 in. long and 6 in. wide, and the young shoots and leaves are covered with a dense purplish pubescence when young; the large, flattish corymbs consist of pale lilac fertile flowers in the center, the outer ring of sterile flowers being pinkish-white. This Hydrangea should be planted in half shade for it is not very hardy and the large leaves are liable to be damaged by wind in an exposed position.

H. cinerea is a native from North Carolina to Georgia and Alabama. It grows about 6 ft. tall and bears heads of white flowers in June and July. In the typical form most of the flowers are small and fertile but in the variety sterilis the flowers are all sterile.

H. radiata somewhat resembles H. cinerea but the leaves are whiter beneath. It produces its white flowers in June and July. It occurs as a native in North Carolina and South Carolina but is hardy much further north.

Climbing Hydrangeas. One of the most distinct Hydrangeas is H. petiolaris (scandens). It is a leaf-losing climber from Japan, and very useful for covering a wall or tree trunks. It climbs by means of aerial roots, clinging firmly to walls and trees and bears corymbs (flat bunches) of white flowers in June and July. H. anomala is another leaf-losing climber, not quite so robust or so hardy, and the flower heads, smaller than those of H. petiolaris, are two weeks earlier.

HYDRANGEA, CLIMBING. See Climbing Hydrangeas above under Hydrangea. Schizophragma is also sometimes referred to as the Climbing Hydrangea. See Schizophragma.

HYDRASTIS—*Goldenseal* (Hydras'tis). Low, hardy, perennial herbaceous plants, one of which is a native of Japan, the other of eastern North America. Only the latter appears to be in cultivation. Hydrastis belongs to the Buttercup family, the Ranunculaceae. The derivation of its name is presumably from the Greek word *hydor,* meaning water.

Hydrastis canadensis is a native of deep, rich woods. It may be planted in wild gardens and rock gardens but is rather difficult to establish. It needs a soil that contains liberal amounts of leaf mold or other well-decayed organic material, and that is uniformly moist but not waterlogged. It is propagated by seeds sown in a shaded cold frame as soon as they are ripe, or in the fall or early spring, and by division in early spring. This plant attains a height of about 1 ft. and has greenish-white flowers. Its roots are used medicinally.

HYDROCHARIS — *Frogbit* (Hydroch'aris). Hardy floating water plants, which grow wild in eastern Asia and Europe, and belong to the family Hydrocharitaceae. These plants have small green leaves which float on the surface of the water. Small white flowers are produced in summer. In the autumn the leaves die and decay, and the stems of the plants form small green buds which sink to the bottom of the pond. These rise in May and form new plants. The name Hydrocharis is derived from *hydor,* water, and *charis,* grace, and refers to its graceful appearance.

No particular cultivation is required as the plants are simply laid on the surface of the water. They are sometimes used in indoor aquaria, but they spread very rapidly. Propagation is by division in summer. The chief kind is H. Morsus-ranae.

HYDROCLEYS—*Water Poppy* (Hydroc'leys). Tender perennial aquatic plants from South America which belong to the family Butomaceae. They have thick, heart-shaped floating leaves and bear yellow, three-petaled flowers 2 in. in diameter, in summer. The name Hydrocleys means Water Key.

Except in frostfree and nearly frostfree climates the plants must be carried over winter in tubs or tanks of water in a greenhouse or other suitable sunny location indoors. They may be planted outdoors after all danger of frost has passed and the weather is warm and settled, about the time it is safe to set out Tomato plants.

Water Poppies may be planted in soil covered with shallow water at the margins of natural ponds, or in tubs or pots of fertile, loamy soil with the soil surface submerged 6-9 in. beneath the water of natural or artificial pools. Another

The Goldenseal, Hydrastis canadensis, is a native American species suitable for shady places. It prefers moist soil that is rich in organic matter.

The Water Poppy, Hydrocleys nymphoides, has glossy green leaves and yellow flowers. It is easily grown in a small pool or water garden.

method of cultivating these plants is to place a few inches of soil in a tub 12-18 in. deep, set the plants in this, cover the soil with an inch of clean sand and then fill the tub with water. Tubs planted in this way may be kept outdoors during the summer, either sunk in the ground nearly to their rims or standing on a terrace or other suitable level surface, and may be moved indoors for the winter.

Propagation of Water Poppies is affected by means of division in spring. The chief kind is H. nymphoides, which flowers over a very long period in summer and fall.

HYDROPHYLLUM—*Waterleaf* (Hydrophyl'-lum; Hydroph'yllum). Hardy perennial plants which are natives of North America; they reach a height of 12-15 in., and bear blue or white flowers in summer. They belong to the family Hydrophyllaceae; the name is derived from *hydor,* water, and *phyllon,* a leaf.

These plants thrive in ordinary garden soil which is moist and in slight shade; they are not suitable for a hot or dry position. An increased stock is obtained by lifting and separating the plants into rooted pieces in spring, and by seeds. Kinds sometimes grown in wild gardens are H. virginianum, which bears blue flowers; and H. canadense, white.

HYDROPONICS: SOILLESS GARDENING
How to Grow Plants with Nutrient Solutions

Hydroponics is the art and science of growing plants without soil by means of nutrient chemical solutions. The principles are not new, but their practical application dates from 1929, following experiments in California by Dr. W. F. Gericke, to whom the new culture owes its name.

The practice consists of growing plants in a suitable rooting medium which gives the roots access to balanced and aerated nutrient solutions, in the presence of adequate sunlight. While commercially most successful in sunny climes, on barren lands where fresh produce has scarcity value, and for out-of-season or highly priced flowers or vegetables, the technique is adaptable for gardening pleasure, profit and experiment. The hydroponic system can be used where soil culture is impossible—in towns and apartments, on flat house roofs, etc.

The advantages claimed are much higher yields and uniformity of growth, virtual freedom from weeds, greater resistance to disease, and savings in time and labor in looking after the plants during growth. Incidentally, there is no discernible difference between the hydroponic-grown produce and the naturally grown in flavor and vitamin or nutrient content.

In earlier experiments, plants grew in a seedbed consisting of litter (excelsior, peat, straw, etc.) laid on a wire mesh, suspended over a tank containing a nutrient solution, with an air space between the seedbed and the solution. The roots of the plants grew down and drew nutriment from the solution. Later, the technique of circulating nutrient solutions through inert rooting substances—sand, gravel, vermiculite—was found to give better results, and is now more generally employed.

Suitable Containers. In most parts of North America, hydroponics is best adapted for greenhouse use. Tanks or troughs can be made from a variety of materials—metal, wood, concrete, etc.; or window boxes and plant pots can be used. Zinc or galvanized metals, however, should be avoided, unless painted with bitumen, as zinc in excess is often toxic to plants. Tanks can be built for permanence, *in situ,* or be portable. Dimensions should be about those used for growing plants in soil.

The tanks must be constructed to drain easily. This is simply arranged with small tanks by sloping them slightly to one end with a drainage outlet. Larger tanks are usually made with a slight arch or camber at the bottom, with drainage holes at every 15 inches at the sides, outletting to drainage channels which collect the surplus solution.

The Rooting Medium. Various aggregates are used for the rooting medium. A depth of at least 6 inches is desirable with the container filled to within 1 or 1½ inches of the top. Fine gravel, ⅛ to ⅜ inch, crushed stone, cinders, broken brick, or granite chips, with a proportion of sand, may be used. Sand alone is good; preferably a neutral, lime-free sand, coarse in texture and washed. For the gardener, one of the most useful materials is vermiculite, a micaceous mineral, which holds moisture well and is sterile and light. Special grades are sold for horticultural purposes.

Two methods of feeding are practiced—surface watering, and subirrigation. Simple surface watering, using a sand culture, consists of regular watering with a watering can or hose, using an appropriate nutrient solution. This system works satisfactorily with pots or small containers. For sustained feeding, automatic overhead spraying of the sand beds with a dilute nutrient solution is used commercially. An alternative is to allow the dilute solution to drip-feed continuously from a tank through a feed line, the surplus solution being collected in a sump and pumped back to the reservoir. Another modification is to apply dry mixed nutrient salts periodically and water them in.

In subirrigation, the tank is periodically flooded with dilute solution from below, then allowed to drain. The drained solution is collected and re-used. By means of a pump, the system can be made automatic, but the solution needs periodical renewal. The solution enters the beds through short lengths of plastic tubing when the bed is extensive.

Nutrient Solutions. Ideally, the composition of the nutrient solution should be calculated to suit the plant species to be grown and the conditions under which it is grown. The following formulae have proved suitable for a wide range of plants:

8.1 oz. nitrate of soda (15.5 per cent N).
1.3 oz. monammonium phosphate (12 per cent N, 56 per cent P_2O_5).
5.9 oz. potassium sulphate (48 per cent K_2O).
1.0 oz. nitrate of lime (13 per cent N).
3.9 oz. magnesium sulphate (Epsom salts).
5/6 pt. minor elements concentrate.
   All dissolved in 100 gals. of water.

10.5 oz. nitrate of soda (15.5 per cent N).
5.6 oz. superphosphate (14 per cent P_2O_5).
4.9 oz. potassium sulphate (48 per cent K_2O).
3.8 oz. magnesium sulphate (Epsom salts).
5/6 pt. minor elements concentrate.
   All dissolved in 100 gals. of water.

A minor elements concentrate solution consists of:

21.5 oz. boric acid.
31.3 oz. manganese sulphate.
205.5 oz. ferric citrate.
   Dissolved in 200 gals. of water.

Another formula, recommended by the New Jersey Agricultural Experimental Station, is:

60 gr. ammonium sulphate.
114 gr. potassium monobasic phosphate.
280 gr. magnesium sulphate.
972 gr. calcium nitrate.
   Dissolved in 100 gals. of water.

Alternatively, balanced nutrients can be bought already prepared for dilution.

The acid-alkaline balance or *p*H of these solutions is important. For most plants, the solution should have a *p*H of 6.0. If it is greater than this, it should be adjusted by adding dilute sulphuric acid (3 parts acid, 7 parts water). For Roses, a *p*H of 6.0 to 7.0 is in order. For Carnations, the *p*H may be 5.0 to 6.5. Rain or soft spring water is best for these solutions, but where a hard water, containing lime, must be used, particular care must be taken to correct the *p*H to the desired value.

In theory, any plant that can be grown by

ordinary methods and soil culture can also be reared by hydroponics. In practice, however, the gardener will probably find it best to grow those plants which best repay him for his trouble. Most vegetables can be grown, including salad vegetables such as Lettuce, Radish, young Onions, Celery, Endive; and produce such as Tomatoes, Sweet Corn, Potatoes, Carrots, Leeks, etc., yield excellently. Peas, Beans and other legumes mature satisfactorily. Most flowers, particularly annuals, grow well, and the system is admirable for Carnations, Roses, Gardenias, etc. Out-of-season produce needs atmospheric heat and the same general care as when grown in soil culture.

Small seeds are best raised separately in pans or boxes, using vermiculite or sand, and the seedlings transplanted to the beds with as little disturbance of the roots as possible. Large seeds such as those of Peas, Beans, Sweet Corn, etc., are best placed direct in the aggregate. Bulbs should be inserted up to their shoulders.

Seeds germinate quite readily, under hydroponic conditions, and plant growth is often more rapid and sustained than in soil culture. Plant tissues do tend to be softer and less hardened, and therefore supports, in the form of canes, wires or trellis, will be needed for the taller-growing plants. Otherwise, cultivation should follow normal horticultural practice.

HYDROSME (Hydros'me). Tender, tuberous-rooted plants resembling Amorphophallus from which they differ in technical characters only. They belong to the Arum family, Araceae. They are natives of Africa and Asia. The name probably refers to the wet locations these plants favor in their native habitats.

The only one in cultivation is H. Rivieri, the Devil's-Tongue or Snake Palm. This plant is easily cultivated and requires treatment similar to that recommended for Amorphophallus, which see. During the summer it may be placed outdoors, either planted in the open ground or buried almost to the rim of its pot or tub in soil, cinders or sand, in a partly shaded place. Plenty of water and liberal feeding with dilute liquid fertilizers are needed throughout the whole season of growth; during its winter period of rest the tuber should be stored, quite dry, in a tem-

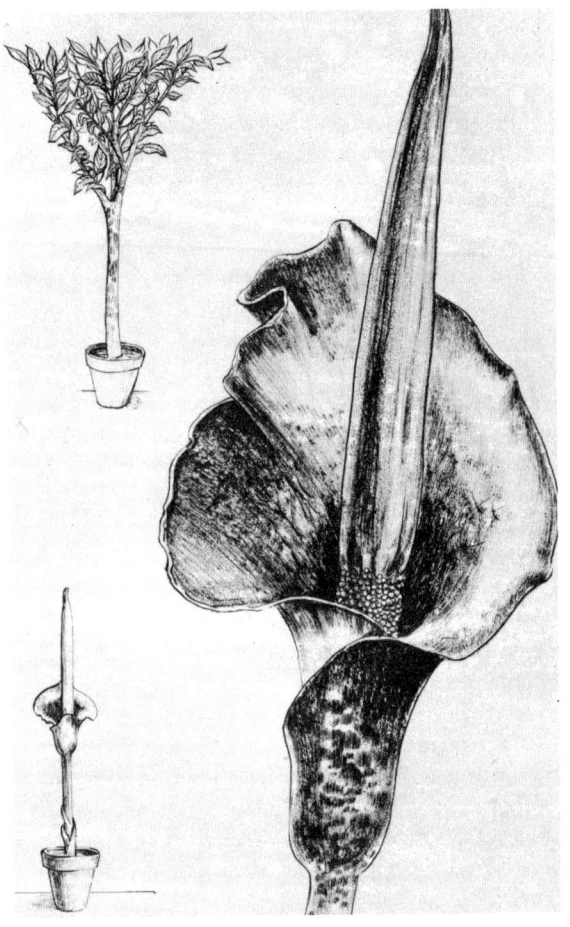

The calla-like inflorescence ("flower") of Hydrosme Rivieri. Of the small drawings the upper one represents a plant in leaf, the lower one a plant in bloom.

perature of 50-60 degrees. Propagation is rapidly effected by means of the freely produced offsets.

Hydrosme Rivieri attains a height of 3-4 ft. Its huge calla-like inflorescence ("bloom") appears in late winter or spring before the foliage. It is succeeded by a single, immense, much-divided umbrella-like leaf. The inflorescence is predominantly brownish-purple; at maturity it emits a disgusting, carrion odor.

HYEMALIS. A term used in describing plants which bloom in winter, and derived from the Latin *hiems,* winter. Eranthis hyemalis is an example.

HYLOCEREUS (Hyloce'reus). Epiphytic Cacti with climbing winged stems furnished with aerial roots and bearing large white or pink flowers which open at night. They appreciate semishade in a warm greenhouse and may be grown permanently outdoors in the far South. The chief kinds are H. Purpusii, pink, from Mexico; H. triangularis, white, Jamaica; and H. undatus, white, from the West Indies, the most commonly cultivated species.

HYMENANTHERA (Hymenan'thera). Evergreen or semievergreen shrubs from New Zealand and Australia, one of which, H. crassifolia, is hardy in protected places at New York City; the others, H. chathamica and H. dentata, are only hardy in mild climates. H. crassifolia forms a slow-growing, wide-spreading, compact bush 3-6 ft. high, bearing small leaves usually less than 1 in. long, inconspicuous brownish flowers and small white fruits. Except as an interesting evergreen it has little value.

In mild winters it retains most of its leaves throughout winter but severe frost causes the leaves to fall. It should be planted in a sunny position in well-drained, light, loamy soil and can be increased by seeds or cuttings. Hymenanthera belongs to the Violet family, Violaceae, and the name is taken from the Greek *hymen*, membrane, and *anther*, and refers to the membranous appendage of the anthers.

HYMENOCALLIS (Hymenocal'lis; Hymenoc'allis). Tender bulb plants, natives of Peru, tropical America, the United States and Africa, which are closely related to Pancratium and belong to the Amaryllis family, Amaryllidaceae. They have lance-shaped leaves, averaging 18 in. in length, and bear flowers on a stout stem 18 in. in length. The flowers are white, salver-shaped, tubular at the base, about 1½ in. in diameter, and produced in clusters of from three to six, in summer or winter, according to the kind. The filaments (stamen stalks) are united by a fine web of tissue into a cup. Hence the name Hymenocallis, which is derived from *hymen*, a membrane, and *kallos*, beauty, referring to the webbed filament.

Outdoor Culture. In the warmer parts of the United States, Hymenocallis, which are also known as Spider Lilies, may be grown outdoors in the open garden. They stand light shade and need soil that is well supplied with decayed organic matter. They should be planted in spring and be kept mulched with compost or leaf mold. The bulbs should be lifted and transplanted only when the plants or the blooms show signs of deterioration.

Culture of Ismene. Hymenocallis calathina is commonly known as Ismene or Basket Flower. It may be grown permanently outdoors in mild climates and in the North as a summer-flowering bulb in the open garden. When required for this use, plant the bulbs, after the weather is warm and settled, with their tips at a distance beneath the surface equal to three times the depth of bulb, and 8-12 in. apart. Water freely in dry weather. After frost dig the bulbs without damaging roots more than necessary, pack soil around roots and store them over winter dry, in a temperature of 60 degrees.

As Greenhouse Plants. The tropical kinds require a minimum winter temperature of 55 degrees and the temperate greenhouse kinds one of 45 degrees. The most suitable soil for both types consists of two parts sandy loam, one part leaf mold and one part well-decayed manure to which sand has been added freely. The times of repotting vary, as the plants flower at different times of the year. This work is best done as soon as there are signs of new growth; repotting is not necessary oftener than every 3 or 4 years, because they bloom best when pot-bound.

They require a sunny position and abundance of water during the growing season. After flowering, the water supply is gradually reduced and the soil is only moistened during the resting

The Ismene or Basket Flower, Hymenocallis calathina.

period when it is noticed to become dust-dry.

Propagation is by removing the offsets and setting them in small pots at potting time; also, by seeds and by bulb cuttings.

Kinds To Grow. *Tropical Kinds:* caribaea, 8-12 in. white; Horsmannii, 24 in., white; littoralis, 12-24 in., white; macrostephana, 24 in., white; speciosa, 18-24 in., white. *Temperate Kinds:* Amancaes, 18-24 in., yellow and green; calathina, 24 in., white (varieties are Advance, white, more vigorous growth; Olympia, cream to light yellow); galvestonensis, 24 in., white; Harrisiana, 12 in., white; Macleana, 12-18 in., yellowish and green; occidentalis, 18 in. *Hybrids and Varieties* (the names in parentheses indicate the parent plants): festalis (Elisena longipetala x calathina); white; Sulphur Queen (calathina x Amancaes), pale yellow.

HYMENOPHYLLUM — Tunbridge Fern, Filmy Fern (Hymenoph'yllum). Hothouse, greenhouse, and hardy Ferns which are found wild in tropical America, tropical Africa, New Zealand, Australia and Europe. They have slender, creeping rhizomes (underground stems), and delicate, semitransparent, feathery fronds, from which the popular name Filmy Fern is derived. They belong to the family Polypodiaceae. The name Hymenophyllum is derived from *hymen,* a membrane, and *phyllon,* a leaf, and refers to the appearance of the leaves.

Need Shade and Moisture. They require a very moist atmosphere, and a compost of equal parts of peat, loam and leaf mold and one part of sand, crushed sandstone and charcoal. They should be grown in shallow pans which are set under a bell jar or hand light, in a closed case, or a damp corner of the greenhouse. A shaded position and a very moist atmosphere are essential. The fronds must not be syringed. Repotting is done in February or March, or as soon as new growth commences. The minimum winter temperature is 55 degrees for the hothouse kinds and 45 degrees for the greenhouse kinds.

The hardy kinds can only be grown out of doors in favorable localities; they are planted in shaded positions where the atmosphere is always moist; rock crevices by a waterfall on the rockery provide suitable positions. More often they are grown in a shady frame and kept moist.

Propagation is principally by division of the rhizomes in spring.

The chief kinds are—for the hothouse: H. caudiculatum and H. dichotomum; for the greenhouse: H. demissum, H. australe (javanicum), and H. pulcherrimum. H. tunbridgense is hardy in sheltered places only.

HYOPHORBE—Pignut Palm (Hyophorb'e). Tender Palms which grow wild in Mauritius and belong to the Palm family, Palmaceae. In their native habitat they grow 30 ft. in height, have stout, treelike, smooth trunks and terminal clusters of pinnate leaves. Small plants in pots are decorative and they may be grown outdoors in southern Florida. The name Hyophorbe is from the Greek *hyos,* pig, and *phorbe,* food.

The plants are repotted in February in a compost of equal parts of peat, loam and leaf mold to which sand is added freely. After repotting, they are watered carefully until established, then during the remainder of the summer the soil is kept moist. During winter less water is required. They must be shaded from bright sunlight. The chief kinds are H. Verschaffeltii and H. amaricaulis. The former is the Spindle Palm, the latter the Bottle Palm.

HYPERICUM—St.-John's-wort, Aaron's-Beard (Hyper'icum). A very large group of hardy and tender shrubs, subshrubs and herbaceous plants, all of which bear yellow flowers in summer, many of them of considerable beauty. They are widely distributed in Europe, Asia and North America, and at least one kind introduced into New Zealand has become a serious pest on farm land. The kinds cultivated are suitable for the shrubbery, herbaceous border and rock gardens, the rock garden kinds being choice and beautiful plants. Hypericum gives its name to the family Hypericaceae and the name is an old Greek one used by Dioscorides.

Details of Cultivation. The herbaceous kinds thrive in ordinary garden soil, in sun or in semishade. The shrubby sorts require light loamy soil and a fairly sunny position. In most instances the flowers are borne in late summer and autumn on the current year's growth; the plants are improved by severe pruning in spring. Old, weak shoots should be cut out and the remainder shortened to from 9-12 in. A surface

Hypericum patulum Forrestii, an attractive summer-flowering shrub, 3—4 ft. tall. The golden, saucer-shaped flowers are followed by conspicuous bronze-brown seed pods.

dressing of decayed manure or compost placed above the roots every second or third year will do good.

Many of the shrubby Hypericums are not long-lived plants and when they show serious signs of deterioration it is wise to dig them up and begin again with young plants. Some of the best kinds such as H. Moserianum, H. patulum var. Henryi and H. Hookerianum are very good plants for beds or large groups; others are suitable for the shrubbery, and H. calycinum, sometimes called Aaron's-Beard, is suitable for covering sunny banks or banks in semishade. It should

The hybrid Hypericum Moserianum is one of the hardiest kinds suitable for garden planting.

be cut over with shears each spring to within a few inches of the ground.

When to Take Cuttings. The shrubby kinds can be increased by seeds or cuttings; as cuttings of short soft shoots, taken in June and July, and dibbled in sandy soil in a frame kept close, root very quickly and soon grow into good plants, seeds are not often used. The herbaceous kinds and H. calycinum, a subshrub, are easily increased by division; in fact, some of the herbaceous sorts spread too rapidly and need keeping strictly within bounds; otherwise they may become a nuisance.

The large golden-flowered Rose of Sharon, Hypericum calycinum, a dwarf subshrub ideal for clothing dry banks in sun or semishade.

For the Rock Garden. H. aegypticum is a dwarf compact shrub with small, blue-green leaves and attractive flowers; it is a native of the Mediterranean region and not very hardy. H. balearicum, a shapely bush 1-2½ ft. high, is conspicuous on sun-baked hillsides in the Balearic Islands; it has small, wrinkled leaves and small, yellow flowers, and should be planted in a very sunny and warm position in mild climates. H. olympicum from Asia Minor, H. quadrangulum from Europe, H. Buckleii from the eastern United States, H. polyphyllum from Cilicia, H. Coris from southern Europe, and H. empetrifolium from Greece and Asia Minor, are all neat dwarf kinds suitable for the rock garden. As H. Coris is liable to perish in cold or wet winters it is not suitable for northern gardens. These dwarf Hypericums flourish in well-drained, light or sandy loamy soil.

Vigorous Shrubby Kinds. H. Androsaemum, the Tutsan of Europe, 2 ft. high, has large leaves and clusters of small flowers followed by conspicuous fruits which are black when ripe. H. frondosum (aureum), a graceful bush, 2-3 ft. high, from the southern United States, flowers during summer. H. calycinum, previously referred to, 1-1½ ft. high, an excellent ground cover for West Coast gardens, bears golden flowers 3 in. across with great freedom. H. densiflorum, H. Kalmianum, H. galioides, and H. prolificum, four native American kinds of compact growth, form short annual shoots and flower freely in summer. They require little pruning. H. Hookerianum, a Himalayan shrub, 2-3 ft. high, has large shapely flowers in late summer, but is adaptable to gardens in the far South only.

One of the Most Attractive. H. Moserianum, a hybrid between H. calycinum and H. patulum, is a spreading free-flowering plant, 12-15 in. high; it is one of the most beautiful, and is well worth planting in a bed in a conspicuous place. H. patalum, a widely distributed shrub in India, China, etc., of graceful habit, 1½-2½ ft. high, is attractive when in flower, but not very hardy. Its varieties Henryi and Forrestii are hardier, more vigorous, and bloom more freely. Two specially good forms are H. patulum varieties Gold Cup and Hidcote, both with large, golden, saucer-shaped flowers. They should be chosen for a conspicuous position. There are many others but this selection will suffice for most gardens.

Herbaceous kinds are H. Ascyron, H. japonicum, H. perforatum, H. elegans, H. humifusum and H. linarifolium. H. perforatum, and possibly other kinds, are regarded as being poisonous to stock; therefore they should not be planted where they are accessible to cattle and sheep.

HYPHAENE (Hyphae'ne). African and Indian Fan Palms of the family Palmaceae. The name is derived from *hyphaino,* to entwine, and refers to the fibers of the fruits. These Palms are suitable for outdoor culture in the warmest parts of Florida. Among the kinds that may be in cultivation are H. crinita, H. natalensis, H. Schatan and H. thebaica, the Egyptian Doum Palm. For their cultivation see Palm.

HYPOCYRTA (Hypocyr'ta). Mostly small tropical shrubs but including one vinelike kind (H. Nummularia) that in its native habitat creeps on mossy tree trunks. All except H. Nummularia, which is wild in Mexico and Central America, are natives of South America. Hypocyrta belongs in the Gesneria family, Gesneriaceae. Its name is derived from *hypo,* under, and *kyrtos,* curved or pouched, referring to the swollen corolla tube.

These plants require the same cultivation as Columnea, which see. Kinds include H. glabra, flowers scarlet and orange; H. Nummularia, flowers red with a violet-tinged neck beneath the yellow petals; H. pulchra, flowers scarlet and orange; H. strigulosa, flowers orange-red; and H. Teuscheri, leaves olive-green with grey veins, flowers orange-red, bracts red.

HYPOESTES (Hypoest'es). South African and tropical tender shrubs and herbaceous perennials, few of which are in cultivation. The most commonly grown kind is H. sanguinolenta, to which the fanciful names of Freckleface and Polka Dot Plant have been applied. Hypoestes belongs to the Acanthus family, the Acanthaceae. The name is derived from *hypo,* under, and *estia,* a house, and refers to the fact that the calyx is covered by the bracts.

H. sanguinolenta is a native of Madagascar. It grows 1-2 ft. high, is herbaceous (nonwoody) and a most beautiful foliage plant. Its leaves are green, freely sprinkled with red or pink dots; its lilac flowers are not very decorative H. aristata, 3-4 ft. high has green leaves and showy spires of rosy lavender flowers.

For Greenhouse or Terrarium. This plant thrives in a humid, shaded greenhouse or terrarium where the minimum temperature is 55-60 degrees. The soil in which it is grown should be porous and contain an abundance of peat moss, leaf mold or other decayed organic matter. Old plants may be pruned into shape and repotted in spring but the best results are usually had by maintaining a stock of young plants by frequent propagation and discarding old ones when they become straggly. The plants may be pinched occasionally to induce branching. At all times the soil should be maintained in a moist condition. Specimens that have filled their pots with healthy roots will derive a benefit from weekly or semiweekly applications of dilute liquid fertilizer.

Propagation is very easily accomplished by means of cuttings inserted at any time in a bed of sand, sand and peat moss or vermiculite. Seeds also provide a ready means of increasing this plant. They should be sown in spring or early summer in a porous soil in a temperature of about 70 degrees.

HYPOLEPIS (Hypo'lepis; Hypole'pis). Mostly tropical Ferns which have long, creeping rhizomes and are allied to Cheilanthes. The name is derived from *hypo,* under, and *lepis,* a scale, from the marginal covering of the sporangia. They belong to the Polypody family, Polypodiaceae.

Ferns for a Greenhouse. As the fronds of these Ferns are soft and delicate they must be shaded from sunshine during the summer months and grown in a warm, moist atmosphere. They thrive better on a shaded and moist rockery in the greenhouse than when grown in pots. H. repens and H. tenuifolia are suitable for a hothouse having a minimum temperature of 60 degrees: the others are suited by a winter temperature of 50 degrees.

March is a good month for potting, using a compost of equal parts fibrous loam, peat and leaf mold, with some coarse grit and a few pieces of sandstone. The loam and peat should be of a fibrous or lumpy nature among which the creeping rhizomes can ramble. The pots or pans should be well drained.

Propagation is by division of the rhizomes in early spring, and by spores sown on sterilized soil in a moist and warm greenhouse in January or February.

Hypolepis millefolium, a New Zealand Fern of spreading growth, 9-18 in. high, bears fronds 12 in. or more long and half as wide. H. repens is a hothouse Fern from tropical America and the West Indies; the fronds are sometimes as much as 3-4 ft. long and 1-1½ ft. wide at the bottom. H. tenuifolia is an elegant Fern found in Malaya, Polynesia and Australia: the fronds grow 4-5 ft. long in a hothouse.

HYPOXIS—*Star Grass* (Hypox'is). Tender and hardy low-growing herbaceous perennial plants with grasslike leaves. They belong to the family Amaryllidaceae. The name is from *hypo,* beneath, and *oxys,* sharp, and refers to the base of the capsule. More than fifty species have been enumerated, but few are worth growing. They are natives of tropical Asia, tropical and South Africa, tropical and North America and Australia.

For a Frostproof Greenhouse. The most attractive kinds in cultivation are natives of South Africa and are suitable for a frostproof, sunny greenhouse, or for planting in light, sandy soil in full sun in mild districts. Hypoxis is readily increased by offsets in early spring and thrives in sandy loam and peat or leaf mold.

Hypoxis hirsuta, a native of North America, is a hairy plant, 6 in. high, with linear-lanceolate leaves, which bears yellow flowers in June and July. It is hardy in the North. H. hemerocallidea, 12-18 in., has long, hairy leaves and golden-yellow flowers in June. H. latifolia, with leaves varying in length from 6 in. to 2 ft., bears yellow flowers about midsummer. H. stellata, 9 in., has white or bluish flowers in May and June.

HYSSOP. See Hyssopus officinalis.

HYSSOPUS OFFICINALIS—*Hyssop* (Hysso'pus; Hyss'opus). A bushy herb that can scarcely be called a shrub, although the stems do not die down in winter and the leaves remain evergreen. It is a native of Europe and temperate Asia and is hardy. It is grown for its purplish-blue flowers, which are borne during summer. It is suitable for planting in herb gardens, its leaves and shoots having stimulant, carminative and pectoral properties; hence its use in rural medicines in cases of coughs and chest complaints. It can be increased by cuttings inserted in a cold frame in spring or by seeds. Ordinary garden soil suits it. Hyssopus belongs to the Mint family, Labiatae, and the name is said to have been used in ancient Greece. There are white and pink-flowered varieties.

HYSTRIX PATULA—*Bottle Brush Grass* (Hys'trix). An ornamental perennial grass of tufted habit producing simple spikes furnished with alternate clusters of flowers. The dried spikes are used in floral arrangements and it is sometimes grown in borders. It thrives in ordinary soil and is increased by division and by seeds. It is a native of North America. The name is derived from the Greek, *hystrix,* a porcupine, and refers to the long awns.

IBERIS—*Candytuft* (Ibe'ris). Hardy annual, biennial and perennial plants belonging to the Mustard family, Cruciferae. The name Iberis is derived from Iberia, the former name of Spain; several kinds grow wild in that country, and most are natives of southern Europe and western Asia. Several of the Iberis are valuable rock garden plants, being hardy, showy, and very easily grown in ordinary, well-drained soil, in an open, sunny position.

Sowing Seeds and Taking Cuttings. The annual and biennial kinds can be raised with the greatest ease from seed sown out of doors in spring. The perennial sorts root readily from cuttings inserted in a frame in June; they may also be pulled to pieces and replanted in September. Perennial Candytufts can also be easily raised from seeds sown in a cold frame or outdoor bed in spring or early summer, but improved garden varieties, such as Snowflake and Little Gem, do not come true to type from seeds.

The Gibraltar Candytuft. Iberis gibraltarica, the Gibraltar Candytuft, is a particularly showy plant, easily raised from seeds; the flowers, opening white, fade to pink. The plant is somewhat straggling in habit, but for hot, dry positions it is valuable. It is excellent in the wall garden; it grows 6-9 in. high and is evergreen but less hardy than I. sempervirens. Iberis saxatilis is a dwarf evergreen plant, with narrow leaves and corymbs of white flowers. It blooms in spring.

Evergreen Candytuft. Iberis sempervirens, the Evergreen Candytuft, is a magnificent perennial, of low, spreading habit, subshrubby at the base, forming wide cushions of lustrous green foliage, which are attractive in the rock garden even when out of flower. In spring the plant produces, at the tip of every shoot, a corymb of snow-white flowers in splendid profusion. Several named varieties of Iberis sempervirens are in commerce, the most valuable of which are Snowflake and Little Gem. Little Gem is neat and compact and is useful for small rock gardens. The variety Snowflake is one of the most showy and handsome white-flowered plants that we have for the rock garden, giving rounded domes of snow-white flowers in astonishing profusion.

This fine plant is also most useful as an edging in the front of the herbaceous border, and is invaluable in the wall garden. Few plants are more easily grown than this Iberis; almost any well-drained soil suits it, and although it is best in full sun, it does well also in partial shade.

The evergreen Candytuft, Iberis sempervirens, forms a compact mound smothered with pure white flowers in May.

The annual Candytuft, Iberis umbellata, is one of the showiest and most easily grown of all hardy annuals.

Honey-scented Annual. Iberis affinis is a charming dwarf annual species, 6 in. or so high, which bears honey-scented flowers, white or pale lilac. Although hardly suitable for the rock garden proper, it is very pretty when grown among the stones of a rock garden paved path, where it fills the air with its delicious fragrance.

Annual Candytuft. Iberis umbellata is the well-known annual Candytuft, which is represented by many fine named varieties, white, pink, crimson, purple, mauve, etc. It is one of the showiest and most easily-grown of all hardy annuals, and has moreover the advantage of doing exceptionally well in city gardens. It should be sown in early spring where it is to flower in summer; the seedlings should be thinned to 9-12 in. apart, to allow the plants to reach their full development and produce a profusion of flowers. This Candytuft is more suitable for the flower border than the rock garden, and it is really good as a cut flower. Iberis amara (coronaria) is another white-flowered annual which has produced the large-flowered Rocket Candytufts like Giant Snowflake, Spiral White, and hyacinthiflora.

Greenhouse Culture. The annual Candytufts are excellent plants for growing in cool greenhouses to provide flowers in winter and spring. They need full sunshine, a night temperature of 45-50 degrees, with a 5-10 degree rise in the daytime permitted, and a light, fertile, well-drained soil. They may be grown in benches for the production of cut flowers or in pots for other decorative purposes.

Seeds should be sown from September to February. The earlier-sown ones come into flower early in the New Year; later-sown ones provide a succession. In benches the plants should be set 4-6 in. apart; in pots one to a 4-in. or three to a 5-in. pot usually proves satisfactory.

Iberis sempervirens also makes a very satisfactory pot plant for early spring bloom. For best results the plants, 1- or 2-year-old specimens, should be carefully dug in the fall, potted in pots just large enough to hold the root balls without undue crowding, and be plunged to the rims of their pots in a bed of ashes or sand in a cold frame or outdoors. They may be brought into a greenhouse, in which conditions similar to those detailed above as suitable for annual Candytufts are maintained, from January to March, and will bloom within a few weeks.

Both the annual and perennial Candytufts may be grown in a cool, sunny sunroom by following the procedures recommended for greenhouse cultivation.

IBOZA RIPARIA (Ibo′za). A greenhouse perennial flowering plant from South Africa, which belongs to the Mint family, Labiatae. It has a semiwoody stem and forms a branching bush up to 4 ft. in height. The nettle-like leaves are notched at the margins, and the small cream-white flowers are produced in long, upright, branching spikes in winter. It is easy to grow and very decorative. The name Iboza is derived from the native name for this plant.

Good for a Cool Greenhouse. This plant requires a minimum winter temperature of 45 degrees and a compost of equal parts of loam, leaf mold and decayed manure with coarse sand freely added. Repotting is done in March. The shoots are first shortened to within 3 in. of their bases, and syringed frequently to make them break into growth. They are then repotted in pots two sizes larger. The plants are knocked out of the old pots, the crocks and loose soil removed with a pointed stick. The new pots are well drained with crocks, which are covered with a thin layer of rough siftings from the compost to prevent the soil from blocking up the drainage. An inch or two of compost is then placed in the pots and this is made firm with a potting stick.

The plants are lowered into the pots and the

compost is filled in around the roots and made firm.

After potting, they are shaded from sun until roots have entered the new soil, when they are fully exposed to the light. From June to October they may be placed on a bed of ashes outdoors to ripen the shoots for flower production. When the pots become full of roots, weak liquid fertilizer is given twice a week until the flowers expand. During the summer months and up to the time of flowering the soil must be kept moist; when the flowers have faded, the soil is only moistened when it becomes dry, up to the time of pruning and repotting.

When to Take Cuttings. Young shoots, 3 in. in length, are taken off the plants in March or April, the leaves from the lower half of the stem are removed and a cut is made just below the bottom joint. They are then inserted in a propagating case. The case is kept closed, to maintain a moist atmosphere, which prevents the leaves from wilting. Every morning it should be opened for a few minutes and the glass ought to be wiped on the underside to prevent the condensed moisture from falling on the cuttings and causing decay to set in.

Details of Management. When rooted, the plants are given more and more air each day and, after a week, are placed on the open greenhouse benches to harden the foliage. They are then potted singly in 3-in. pots, or, if extra large plants are required, three cuttings are potted together in a 5-in. pot. When well-rooted in these, they are repotted in larger pots and eventually hardened off. Bushy plants are obtained by pinching out the tips of the main shoots when the plants are established in 3-in. pots, and by stopping the subsequent side branches. No more stopping is required the first season.

The only kind is I. riparia, white, 3 ft., winter-flowering. It is sometimes known as Moschosma riparium.

ICELAND POPPY. See Papaver nudicaule.

ICE PLANT. See Mesembryanthemum crystallinum.

IDAHO, GARDENING IN. See Regional Gardening.

IDESIA POLYCARPA (Ide'sia). An attractive deciduous tree, found wild in southern Japan and in central and western China. It may exceed a height of 40 ft. The Chinese type is hardy as far north as Boston, Massachusetts, but plants raised from seeds of the Japanese type are not hardy north of Philadelphia.

The dark green, heart-shaped leaves are about 5 in. long and 5 in. wide, carried on long stalks. The yellowish-green flowers appear from the ends of the shoots in clusters in June and are followed by small fruits resembling bunches of grapes. The fruits are red when ripe. Some trees produce all female flowers, others all male, and yet others, both. The all-male-flowered trees do not, of course, fruit and the all-female-flowered ones only do so when a male tree is nearby.

Idesia polycarpa requires a sunny position in light, well-drained loamy soil, and propagation is by seeds sown in loamy soil in a cold frame in spring. It belongs to the family Flacourtiaceae and was named in honor of a Dutchman, E. J. Ides, an eighteenth century traveler in China.

ILEX: THE HOLLY

Ornamental Evergreen and Leaf-losing Fruiting Trees and Shrubs

(I'lex). The Ilex group is made up of evergreen and leaf-losing (deciduous) trees and shrubs, many of them of considerable decorative value both by reason of their foliage and fruits. (See also Berried Trees and Shrubs). Some are also decorative when in flower; although the flowers are small, they are usually white or cream-colored and very fragrant. Some Hollies have very spiny leaves, but even in the most spiny kinds there is a difference between the leaves of the lower branches and those of the higher ones; the leaves on the higher parts of trees bear fewer spines than those on the lower parts and leaves near the tops of trees may be almost spineless.

Why Some Holly Trees Do Not Bear Berries. Some Holly trees bear an abundant crop of berries, others bear none; the reason is that, normally, some trees bear all male flowers and others all female flowers; it is only when trees of both sexes are growing together that really good crops of fruit or berries are borne by most kinds of Hollies. Even then good fruit seasons do not occur every year, and a year of abundant berries may be followed by a year in which there are few or none.

The Hollies are very widely distributed in Europe, Asia, North and South America, the Canary Islands, Madeira, etc., and a very considerable number grow well in the United States. One kind, Ilex Aquifolium, the English Holly, a native of Europe and Asia, during centuries of cultivation has produced a large number of varieties, chiefly from "sports" which differ from the type in shape, color, the number of spines on the leaves, or in stature.

Holly belongs to the family Aquifoliaceae. Ilex is the Latin name used by Virgil for the Evergreen Oak, Quercus Ilex.

Seeds Take from One to Three Years to Germinate. The species or wild types should be raised from seeds whenever possible. Seeds take a long while to germinate, sometimes 2-3 years; therefore, if seedlings are not seen within a few months of sowing, it does not follow that they will not appear. As soon as the berries are collected they should be mixed with moist sand and kept in a cold frame or cool cellar for 12 months; they must be turned occasionally to ensure that they do not become dry. In the second spring after the seeds were collected, the mixture ought to be turned several times to make sure that the seeds are separated from each other; they should then be sown, sand and seeds together, and covered with sandy or gritty soil. An alternate method is to sow directly in a cold frame as early in spring as possible and before the freshly gathered berries have had time to dry.

When to Sow Holly Seeds. Holly seeds should be sown in spring, those of the common kinds in beds, the rare kinds in pots or boxes. Seedlings will probably appear in about 12 months and continue to come up during at least another year. If the seeds were not stored in moist sand at a low temperature before sowing, another year may elapse before the seedlings appear. Varieties, and the rarer species, are increased by cuttings, or by grafting or budding on stocks established in pots.

When to Take Cuttings. Cuttings of short shoots, about 4 in. long, with a slight heel of old wood attached, should be taken September–October and inserted in sand in a propagating case in a greenhouse. Rooting can be hastened by using one of the root-inducing hormones on the cuttings before they are inserted.

When to Plant Holly Trees. Hollies thrive in a great variety of soils, those of a loamy character giving good results, while fine plants are also seen on peaty soils. Some kinds are intolerant of root disturbance and evergreen kinds should be moved with good balls of soil. They succeed much better when moved in September, or just as new growth starts in spring, than at other times. The roots should not on any account be allowed to dry between lifting and planting, and after root disturbance it is a good plan to cut the branches back a reasonable extent in order to reduce the strain on injured roots.

After transplanting, evergreen Hollies may lose their leaves, but that need cause no uneasiness; it is Nature's way of restoring the balance between branches and roots. If, however, the leaves shrivel and remain on the branches, the roots are not beginning to function as they should, and the plants are going wrong. In such cases the branches should be cut well back, and the plants sprayed with water two or three times a day, and shaded from bright sun. Newly planted bushes or trees should not be allowed to suffer for want of water at the roots during the first two years after planting; as a precaution the ground above the roots should be top-dressed with compost, leaves, manure, or other suitable material.

Most failures with newly planted Holly trees are due to the roots having been allowed to become dry, or to planting at the wrong time of the year. Especially should transplanting during the winter months be avoided. If large Holly bushes are moved in winter they are very likely to fail.

Pruning Ornamental Hollies. Except when

The evergreen Hollies may be grown to form excellent hedges. This is the native American Ilex opaca.

The original specimen of the hybrid English Holly, Ilex altaclarensis variety James G. Esson, growing at The New York Botanical Garden.

The red-fruited variety of the English Holly, Ilex Aquifolium.

planted as hedges Hollies should not be sheared. It is much better to shorten branches here and there if a tree is unbalanced, than to shear it. At the same time branches should not be allowed to spread widely at the base; lower branches should be cut back to their source so that the lowest remaining branches are clear of the ground. When typical green-leaved branches appear on variegated-leaved Hollies, they must be cut out, otherwise they may outgrow the variegated parts. Severe pruning should be done in early spring, other pruning in summer or in the process of cutting branches for Christmas decorations. The shearing of Holly hedges should be done just before new growth begins in spring.

When Hollies show signs of deterioration they can be assisted by cutting back and dressing the ground above the roots with fertilized soil or well-rotted manure.

The English Holly. Ilex Aquifolium, the common Holly of woods and hedgerows in the British Isles and other parts of Europe, may grow 60-80 ft. high, with a trunk 12-15 in. in diameter in its native habitat, but is usually smaller. It is particularly useful for gardens but is less hardy than the American I. opaca. In the Pacific Northwest it thrives, and is hardy in sheltered places in southern New York. It succeeds in sun or partial shade. Its bright red berries are cheerful at the dullest time of the year. It is grown commercially in the Pacific Northwest and berry-laden branches command a good market at Christmas.

Some of the garden varieties called English Hollies are not pure derivatives of I. Aquifolium but are hybrids between that species and I.

Holly cuttings rooting in a shaded cold frame.

Perado, a native of the Canary Islands and the Azores, and I. platyphylla, which is a native of the Canary Islands. Such hybrids are correctly considered to be varieties of I. altaclarensis, the latter being a group name that includes all hybrids of the above-mentioned parentage. The name I. altaclarensis is sometimes restricted to one particular staminate (male) variety of the hybrid complex, but this is not the best usage. In the account that follows, the term English Holly includes both varieties of I. Aquifolium and of the hybrid I. altaclarensis.

Handsome Green-leaved English Hollies. The English Holly occurs in many distinct varieties. Among the best of those that have green foliage are the varieties next described. Camelliaefolia is a beautiful female Holly with glossy, dark green leaves that are much larger than those

Most Hollies produce male and female flowers on separate plants. In these cases only female trees bear berries and then only if a male tree is growing in their vicinity. Here are shown male flowers of English Holly.

An original tree of the Eldridge Holly growing at Great Neck, New York. Before the onset of winter the entire tree was enclosed in a wooden framework surrounded by burlap as a protection against damage by winter sun and winds.

of the common kind and bear very few spines on the leaf margins. In donningtonensis, Smithiana and Whittingtonensis, the leaves are narrower than those of common Holly, and bear fewer spines. In ferox (Hedgehog Holly), and various forms of ferox, spines do not occur on the leaf margins alone but on the face of the leaf as well. Angustifolia, ciliata, heterophylla, myrtifolia and pyramidalis have smaller leaves than the typical kind and often develop as low bushes. Varieties with leaves of abnormal shape are crassifolia, crispa, monstrosa, latispina and recurva. There are also some that bear few, if any, spines, such as integrifolia, laurifolia and scotica. The variety fructo-luteo resembles the common English Holly except for the fact that its fruits are yellow.

Kinds with exceptionally large leaves include the variety Hodginsii, which is very similar to and possibly identical with variety Shepherdii, and variety nigrescens, which has its few-spined leaves close together. The variety Van Tol, which has flat leaves with few spines and dark red berries, is one of two or three nearly spineless varieties sometimes called Dutch Hollies.

Variety James G. Esson, noteworthy for its fine glossy foliage and handsome red berries, was originally developed near New York City; it has proved to be one of the finest and best of the English Hollies. Other good English Hollies that have been developed in America are Brownell's Special, a large-fruited, heavy-fruiting variety with glossy foliage; Escort, which is a staminate (male) variety with dark, glossy green foliage; Firecracker, a tree of bushy, spreading growth which has orange-red berries; and Rederly, a closely branched tree that ripens its bright red fruits earlier than most others; the variety known as Eldredge Holly is of fine appearance and has a profusion of red berries.

Hollies with Variegated Leaves. Many variegated forms of the English Holly have been given distinct names. Good ones are aurea regina (Golden Queen), aurea maculata, aurea latifolia, aurea angustifolia, flavescens (Moonlight Holly), Golden King, Madame Briot, and Watereriana; in each of these the golden variegation is prominent, particularly on the outer parts of the leaves. In the variety aureo picta latifolia (Golden Milkmaid Holly) the golden color is in the middle of the leaves and the margins are green.

Good silver-leaved varieties are handsworthensis, Silvary, argentea marginata, argentea elegantissima, argentea regina (Silver Queen), and argentea mediopicta (Silver Milkmaid Holly); in the last named the variegation is in the middle of the leaf.

Weeping Hollies. Varieties with pendulous branches are pendula, with green leaves; argentea marginata pendula (Perry's Weeping), with silver-variegated leaves; and aurea-pendula, with gold-variegated leaves.

Native American Evergreen Hollies. The principal species of native American evergreen Holly is Ilex opaca, a native of the eastern United States from Massachusetts to Florida. It is not so handsome as the English Holly but it is hardier. In sheltered places it may be grown in a great many parts of the Northeast. Numerous varieties showing improvements in habit of growth, appearance of foliage, and fruiting qualities, have been selected and propagated. Among the best

The native American Holly, Ilex opaca, is a fine decorative tree that bears red berries.

of these are Arden, Bountiful, Cardinal, Christmas Spray, Merry Christmas, Old Faithful and Old Heavyberry. Canary is a form with bright yellow berries. Croonenberg is a fine compact variety that bears heavy crops of red berries.

I. vomitoria (Yaupon) grows from Virginia to Florida. It is a popular evergreen shrub or small tree in southern gardens, often seen in hedge and sheared specimen form. The small red fruits are borne in clusters. I. glabra (Inkberry or Winterberry) is native from Massachusetts to Florida in moist acid soil. It makes a dense clump, has plain leaves and black fruits. It is a useful evergreen for foundation plantings.

Evergreen Asiatic Hollies. Ilex cornuta (Chinese Holly) is an evergreen kind that is hardy in the Philadelphia area, and somewhat further north in sheltered spots. At its best it is a small tree, 20 feet or so tall. The thick, glossy leaves

The original plant of Ilex opaca variety Croonenberg, growing at Greenbrier Nurseries, Norfolk, Virginia.

A splendid specimen of Ilex cornuta variety Burfordii growing in Virginia.

are of unusual shape, typically quadrangular with 3 long strong spines at the apex and 2 at the base. Seedlings show great variation. I. cornuta Burfordii is a popular form with larger, smoother leaves, and a heavier crop of red berries. It is hardy as far north as Long Island, New York. I. Pernyi has small, spiny leaves and is usually seen as a shrub of distinctive appearance. I. Pernyi Veitchii is a form with larger leaves and showier in fruit. I. pedunculosa may grow to 30 ft. tall, is columnar in habit, similar to a pear tree. It has smooth leaves and the red berries hang on long stems. It is hardy in favored parts of New England; in that climate it develops as a shrub. I. Aquipernyi is listed as a hybrid between I. Aquifolium and I. Pernyi and

The Japanese Holly, Ilex crenata variety convexa, is a dependable evergreen shrub.

Most miniature of Hollies is Ilex crenata variety nummularia. It grows only a few inches high.

grows into a small tree of neat appearance; it is considered to be hardier than either parent.

Ilex crenata (Japanese Holly) is a variable and valuable shrub of compact habit and smooth leaves, very like Boxwood. It is hardy in favored parts of New England. Notable forms are convexa, of broad spreading habit; Helleri, very dwarf and spreading; microphylla, erect with small, very dark leaves; and nummularia, a miniature form, well suited for rock garden planting. In addition, there are a number of newer varieties that have been developed in America. Of these American-produced varieties of I. crenata the following are especially worthy: Green Island, a compact kind with small, dark green leaves; Kingsville, a low variety with rather narrow, dark green leaves; Kingsville Green Cushion, a low, spreading kind with glossy, dark green leaves.

Yet another good Japanese evergreen Holly is I. latifolia. This kind is hardy as far north as southern Maryland. It has large leaves and is of elegant appearance. It occurs as a native in parts of China as well as Japan. From China also comes

The annual Balsam, Impatiens Balsamina, blooms freely in summer gardens.

The Asiatic Holly, Ilex latifolia, is a handsome evergreen for planting in southern gardens.

Impatiens Balfouri is a rare Balsam that has lavender and pink flowers.

I. Fargesii, a kind with long, narrow, spineless leaves that is hardy at least as far north as New York City. I. integra, a native of Japan, is hardy as far north as Washington, D. C. It forms a large shrub of compact growth and has dark green, spineless leaves.

Deciduous Hollies. Leaf-losing Hollies are especially attractive in fall and early winter. Fruiting plants of the native American I. verticillata, Black Alder or Winterberry, and of I. laevigata, Smooth Winterberry, are very showy for some time after the leaves drop. These are natives of swampy places in the eastern United States. I. geniculata and I. serrata, natives of Japan, are showy in fruit in early fall. They are hardy in favored parts of New England.

ILLICIUM—*Aniseed Tree* (Illic′ium). Evergreen shrubs, or small trees, with aromatic leaves and flowers suitable for outdoor cultivation in the far South. They belong to the Magnolia family, Magnoliaceae. The name is from the Latin *illicio,* to entice or allure, and refers to the fragrance of the shrubs. About twenty kinds are known; they are chiefly natives of China and Japan, though two are natives of the southern United States.

For Peat Soil. The Illiciums will not succeed in lime soils. They thrive in sandy loam with plenty of leaf mold or peat added. The plants should be grown in pots until large enough to be planted permanently in spring.

Propagation is by layering the lower branches in autumn, by cuttings, and by seeds. Cuttings are inserted in summer in a propagating case in a greenhouse or frame; the latter must be kept close until the cuttings are rooted.

The Chief Kinds. Illicium anisatum (I. religiosum) is an evergreen shrub or small tree, with narrow oval leaves, which bears pale yellow flowers, 1 in. across, from March to May. It is a native of Japan. I. floridanum, from the southern United States, is an evergreen shrub, 8 or 9 ft. high, with lance-shaped, leathery leaves, 3 or 4 in. long, and maroon-crimson flowers from April to June. Illicium verum, an evergreen bush, 6-8 ft. in height, a native of south China, has lance-shaped leaves and bears globose, red flowers in autumn. It yields the Chinese or Star Anise, or Aniseed, used for flavoring.

ILLINOIS, GARDENING IN. See Regional Gardening.

IMANTOPHYLLUM, an obsolete name for Clivia, which see.

IMMORTELLE. A term sometimes applied to all Everlasting Flowers, which see; most commonly to Xeranthemum annuum.

IMPATIENS — *Balsam* (Impat′iens). Hardy and tender annual and perennial herbs from Asia, South Africa and North America. The name is derived from *impatiens,* impatient, and refers to the elasticity of the valves of the seed pods, which discharge the seeds when ripe. Impatiens belongs to the family Balsaminaceae. They are sometimes known as Touch-me-nots.

Tender kinds suitable for a greenhouse or window garden and for planting outdoors in summer are easily propagated by seeds sown in a

The Patience Plant, Impatiens Sultani, comes in a variety of colors and is suitable for growing in a warm greenhouse and as a house plant.

pot of sandy soil in a temperature of 55 degrees in March and by cuttings taken at any time of the year and planted in sand or vermiculite in a warm propagating bed. The best potting compost for these plants consists of two parts fibrous loam, one part leaf mold or peat moss with the liberal addition of coarse sand. They should be repotted as becomes necessary from February to October. Pots 5 in. and 6 in. in diameter are large enough for most decorative purposes. The plants may, however, be grown on for a number of years when large specimens are desired and will then need larger pots. During winter a minimum temperature of 55 degrees should be maintained.

Tender Kinds to Grow. A very attractive kind is Impatiens Sultanii, the Zanzibar Balsam, Patience Plant, or Sultana, a plant with fleshy stems and branches 1-2 ft. high. The flowers vary from rose-red to white through pink, rose, salmon and rose-purple. This plant flowers more or less continuously throughout the year. I. Sultanii variety variegata has gray-green leaves irregularly bordered with white, and carmine red flowers.

Impatiens Holstii, from East Africa, resembles the Zanzibar Balsam in habit of growth, and has red flowers. Since the introduction of this Balsam early in the present century, numerous hybrids have been raised between it and the Zanzibar Balsam which display a wide range of pleasing colors, and these are the kinds mostly grown today. Impatiens Sultanii, I. Holstii, and the hybrids are useful summer-flowering plants for beds and borders in lightly shaded places and are excellent warm greenhouse and window garden plants.

The largest flowered of the cultivated Balsams is Impatiens Oliveri from East Africa: the plants will flower when 18-20 in. high in 6-in. pots. If moved into larger pots as required and fed with weak liquid fertilizers, this Balsam will reach a height of 6-8 ft. in a large pot or tub. The pale lilac flowers are 2½ in. across. This plant succeeds in a cool greenhouse and may be planted out of doors in summer.

A very attractive Balsam for the warm greenhouse is Impatiens Hawkeri, 2 ft. high, with red stems, and large carmine flowers with white eye. It is a native of the South Sea Islands. I. Marinae has handsomely variegated white and green foliage............................?????
I. Petersiana, from western tropical Africa, has bronzy-tinted stems and leaves and carmine-red flowers; I. platypetala, from Java, is a Balsam with succulent stems and rose-colored flowers. I. platypetala variety aurantiaca has orange-yellow blooms each with a crimson eye.

The Annual Balsam. Impatiens Balsamina is the common annual Balsam, a plant equally as suited for growing in pots in a cool greenhouse as for planting for summer display outdoors.

Seeds are sown in a greenhouse, temperature 55 degrees, in March or April, or directly outdoors after the weather is warm and settled. The important points in the management of the annual Balsams are to encourage free and fast growth and to provide a rich, light soil containing leaf mold, decayed manure or compost.

The seedling plants are grown singly in small pots and from these are either planted directly outdoors or, if they are to be flowered in pots, are transferred to 5-in. and 6-in. pots, or three plants may be placed in a 7-in. or 8-in. pot. The plants grow from 18-24 in. in height. The best flowers are obtained when the plants are kept to a single stem, all side shoots being pinched out.

Two strains of annual double-flowered Balsam are listed by seedsmen. These are known as Rose-flowered and Camellia-flowered, so named in reference to the shape of the flowers. The colors include scarlet, red and salmon-pink, rose, cerise, violet, mauve, purple and white.

Impatiens Balfouri, a Himalayan kind, may be grown in the same ways as I. Balsamina.

Hardy Balsams. Impatiens biflora (Jewelweed) is found as a wild plant over a wide area in eastern North America. Growing 3-4 ft. high, it has ovate, coarsely toothed leaves and yellow flowers with red spots. It has limited use for the wild garden or a partly shaded border. Self-sown seedlings may become a nuisance unless they are reduced in number. I. pallida is closely related to I. biflora but is larger and has paler yellow flowers spotted with red. It too is native of eastern North America and is called Jewelweed. Another annual Balsam which is useful for naturalizing and which spreads by self-sown seedlings, is the Himalayan Impatiens Roylei, a plant 4-8 ft. high, with purple to white flowers.